Wilfrid Philip Ward

Witnesses to the Unseen

And Other Essays

Wilfrid Philip Ward

Witnesses to the Unseen
And Other Essays

ISBN/EAN: 9783744660549

Printed in Europe, USA, Canada, Australia, Japan

Cover: Foto ©Thomas Meinert / pixelio.de

More available books at **www.hansebooks.com**

WITNESSES TO THE UNSEEN

AND OTHER ESSAYS

BY

WILFRID WARD

AUTHOR OF 'WILLIAM GEORGE WARD AND THE OXFORD MOVEMENT'
AND 'WILLIAM GEORGE WARD AND THE CATHOLIC REVIVAL'

London
MACMILLAN AND CO.
AND NEW YORK
1893

TO

Lord Emly

THIS VOLUME IS DEDICATED

WITH AFFECTIONATE RESPECT

BY

THE AUTHOR

PREFATORY NOTE

The Essays in this volume, with the exception of the Introduction, have all appeared in the leading Reviews, and I have to thank the Editors of the *Nineteenth Century*, the *Contemporary Review*, and the *National Review* for their kindness in allowing me to reprint them. Considerable additions have, however, been made to some of the Essays, as they originally stood. Their scope and connection with each other are explained in the Introduction.

It may be worth while to add that the first Essay, which gives the book its title, was in part suggested by a conversation with the late Lord Tennyson. This fact, and his subsequent approval of the Essay itself, so far as it deals with the spirit of his own work, have, of course, a direct bearing on the worth of some of the views put forth in the Essay.

CONTENTS

INTRODUCTION

The essays in this volume, written at intervals in the course of the past twelve years, have a real connection with one another which it will be well to explain. They are, for the most part, suggestions towards the solution of a problem which is not fully stated in them,—a problem more or less familiar to us all, but which I must here endeavour to set forth in the light in which it is viewed in the following pages.

The problem is concerned chiefly with the answer to a very practical question, which had best be stated in all simplicity. It is this: What is and what ought to be the influence of the public opinion of our time, as represented by its intellectual leaders,—of what Germans call the Zeitgeist—in determining our own convictions? The answer is that it is and ought to be large, but that it is far larger than it ought to be.

Let us first consider something of what it is.

When a man of sensitive and receptive mind begins to be alive to the problems of the hour, and to associate with his contemporaries, he accepts, often enough without question, the conclusions which are placed before him in the name of "exact thought," or as the discoveries of an age of scientific progress. At different epochs opinions on such different subjects as Free Trade, Darwinism, the results of modern Old Testament criticism, have been accepted by many as a faith, long before they had weighed accurately the reasons alleged in their behalf, or even before they had any full or exact knowledge as to the conclusions to which their faith committed them. The word of the Zeitgeist, as in earlier days the word of the Church, has been the essence of the faith. As a man may be a good Catholic before he has acquired detailed theological knowledge, provided only he trusts the authority of the Church, so the devotees of the Zeitgeist have believed in its word before they knew in detail what it said.

And the Zeitgeist affects us all in another way. Mr. Lecky has pointed out that arguments which quite fail to appeal to one age seem absolutely convincing to the succeeding age. The assumption that this change follows an absolute law of intellectual progress does not appear to be borne out by the facts of the case, as I shall endeavour to show; but it is undoubtedly a testimony to the subtle and impalpable means whereby the Zeitgeist influences us; to the numerous minute preconceptions and axioms which have passed into the mind of the age, and which affect us all imperceptibly, sometimes beyond our power of analysing the why and wherefore. To one age metaphysical argument appeals powerfully. Another age, weary of the unsolved questions metaphysic has left, and of the unpractical and unreal problems which have been mooted in its name, refuses to be affected by any metaphysical argument at all. One age is sensitive to complete and coherent logical polemic, and is severe in its criticism of any logical flaw in the form of an argument. Another is alive to the narrowness of the field which logic covers, and to the comparative force of massive, though unsymmetrical proofs. It is affected rather by wide and suggestive views, and refuses perhaps in the end to regard the most urgent logical dilemmas as having a claim on its decision. To one age, as Mr. Lecky himself points out, the manifold phenomena of the universe suggest most obviously the direct action of supernatural agencies; while an age which has realised the extent of the underlying uniformities of natural law may be unaffected by the strongest evidence for a miraculous occurrence. It is obvious how far-reaching is the effect of such opposite tempers of mind on our estimate of arguments, and ultimately on our opinions on many subjects.

And both these forms of the influence of the Zeitgeist have especially a great effect on the attitude adopted in respect of the supreme problems of religious faith. Is there a God? Is the soul immortal? Is the Christian revelation credible? These questions are answered in the affirmative by public opinion in an age of faith; and the imagination of the man who is sensitive to the Zeitgeist avoids, at such a time, the initial suggestion of doubt, which comes from the uncertainty and divergency of all around him in an age of hesitation. And for the more thoughtful inquirer it is inevitable that the further consideration of such questions, as they have been treated by theologians and apologists, will be affected by the intellectual preconceptions of his time. If he has imbibed from his surroundings a distrust of metaphysics, a whole chapter in Natural Theology loses its effect on him. If he regards miracles as impossible, the invocation of their testimony will discredit rather than support the claims of Christianity. If the age in which he lives distrusts mere logic, as invoked to decide such far-reaching issues, Paley's evidences will provoke rather than help him. On the other hand, he may find at such a time in the unspoken and unanalysed suggestions of his own moral nature and experience, a value which was unknown to an age which postulated logical form as essential, and dwelt in an atmosphere of abstract philosophy.

These are some of the ways in which the Zeitgeist in point of fact may and does affect us, in our way of regarding problems of the hour, and in our religious convictions.

Now for the second question: How far ought it to affect us?

To one who believes in a law of unalloyed progress in human thought, reflection on the very great influence which the temper of the time has on his convictions will not be unwelcome. Such a one has, indeed, consciously given his faith to the Zeitgeist, and the more he feels himself to have caught its spirit, the more satisfied he is. He welcomes its "pious opinions," as well as its "definitions of faith," the latter forming the largest aggregate of attainable certainties, the former of attainable probabilities.

The view advocated in the following Essays is a different one from this. Setting aside for the moment the consideration that the law of progress may not work for an indefinite time, that declension may ultimately follow ascension, I endeavour to point out that the guidance of the Zeitgeist, even in an age of progress, is not necessarily trustworthy. Allowing even that the age is on the whole progressing towards further knowledge, the cultivated public opinion of the hour does not represent its fresh knowledge unalloyed. Public opinion tends to extremes. A given age tends to exaggerate the significance of its own discoveries, and to fill in their details prematurely and inaccurately. And it tends to carry too far its criticisms and revisions of the thoughts proper to an earlier time. The age which found such excessive intellectual satisfaction in the Thomistic adaptation of the Aristotelian metaphysic, which fed on the categories, whose deepest passions were aroused by the contest between Realism and Nominalism, was succeeded by an age which quite failed to do justice to the value of the *Summa contra gentiles*,—which would not even read it. The reaction from the mediæval readiness to believe in the miraculous led to an extreme of incredulity on the subject, which ultimately found voice in the celebrated argument of Hume. The suspicion of logical controversy which characterises our own time goes hand in hand with a tendency to excessive indefiniteness of thought, and revives in a very different spirit the attempt of the "Moderates" of the Oxford Movement to "steer between the Scylla and Charybdis of Aye and No." When Free Trade was one of the cries of the Zeitgeist in our own country, it took an extreme form which we are now learning to discount. Darwinism and the Tübingen criticism, when they were most dogmatically and definitely pressed upon general belief, were still more noteworthy instances of the exaggerated form in which the new truths, to which progress may lead, are held by the public opinion of the hour.

This consideration becomes one of gravest importance when it is applied to the painfully practical question of faith in God and in Immortality. In this, as in other matters, we are, as we have seen, deeply affected by the Zeitgeist. And it becomes a matter of greatest moment to estimate accurately the value of that influence.

It is perhaps a hopeful sign of the present age, so far as our own land is concerned, that the Zeitgeist itself in some degree recognises its own want of accuracy and finality. It is more inquiring and less confident than many of its predecessors. True so far to the great instrument of its typical achievements—the inductive method—it continues to note cautiously and accurately the phenomena of history, and refrains from a final decision which might be premature. Keenly alive as it is to the importance of the comparative method—of comparing the opinions belonging to one place and time with those of another—it begins to see that each age has had something to learn from other ages, and that we, in our turn, may have something to learn from our forebears. Reviewing the various ages of faith and doubt, it sees elements in each which were supposed to be stamped out once for all by its successor, reappearing again under different forms. The doubts of Sextus Empiricus were faced by St. Thomas Aquinas; but the triumph of the visible Church, which possessed the whole mind of thirteenth century Christendom, made them appear to him powerless where the Church was known. Yet they reappear point by point in the philosophy which took its origin in the "methodic doubt" of the Catholic Descartes.[1] And on the other hand, the faith of St. Thomas himself, so vivid in face of the paralysing considerations which he fully recognises, was a testimony to something in human nature which neither the Academics nor Empiricus had analysed or destroyed. The "grain of mustard seed" had escaped the destructive critics, and had shown what was the ultimate form and power, under circumstances favouring its development, of what in the germ stage had escaped them from its minuteness.

The present age, then, while characteristically an age of hesitation on these great questions, notes the nature of the law of progress as exhibited in the past, and has a lurking suspicion that it has not seen the end of supernatural belief or even of Christian faith. It is warier than its predecessors

[1] Cf. p. 3.

—warier than the Academics or Empiricus or even than the Humes and Gibbons of a time which had a longer sequence of alternatives between ages and civilisations of doubt and of faith to impress it. Nothing escapes its questioning; and though the fanaticism of Atheism is little indulged in, an infinity of grades of Agnosticism, including under its influence persons whom the *census* would distribute through many creeds, is even predominant. But this Agnosticism itself, if we examine it in the full breadth of its extent, not in its professed leaders, or even in its professed maintainers, but throughout the many shades by which it colours contemporary thought, has in it a hopeful, as well as a destructive, element. It notes the failure of the old corporate faith; it points to the causes of its failure; it analyses the old Natural Theology and finds it inconclusive; it scrutinises and dilutes the Christian evidences with the aid of the new discoveries in comparative religion; it contemplates, often sadly, the calm and scientific examination of the biblical documents, so long saved by our reverence, and by the modesty of past ages, from exposure, and from the dissecting knife; it asks, if sometimes with irritation, more often with reluctant sadness, how the faith of the people, already stricken, can ultimately survive the destruction of so much which had for centuries been inseparably bound up with Christianity—of much which had been deemed essential to the very belief in God and another world. And yet, with all this, there is a lurking suspicion that the end of the matter is not reached.

The vitality of religious belief and its many revivals are remembered. The victory of Christian faith after the scepticism of the later Roman republic and over the individualism which had seemed so triumphant in the Rome of Augustus is not forgotten. The sentiment—"after all when criticism has gone its furthest, what a history remains in that of Israel, what a character in that of Christ, how unlike all else in the story of the human race," gains ground. The dogmatism of materialism is already rejected. Idealism and transcendentalism—shadowy, it is true, and of manifold hue—are being reinstated. The statement "nothing can be known" becomes daily more and more "beyond this 'bourne of Time and Place' is the Unknowable,—or at least the Unknown." Professed tokens of the supernatural are not regarded in Hume's temper. Even the attention devoted by our contemporaries to thought-transference and hypnotism, and to the various subjects of "psychical research," shows a keen interest in the borderland of spirit, at variance with last century materialism and scepticism. The evidence for the miracles at Lourdes is regarded with a very different *animus* from that which Hume would have exhibited towards the holy thorn of Port Royal. Our own age feels, if any age has ever felt, "that there are more things in heaven and earth than are dreamt of in our philosophy."

All this betrays, I say, a half-consciousness of something beyond its own acquirements, which was wanting in such an age of scepticism as that of

Gibbon and Voltaire. And it may be worth while to inquire whither the consciousness may lead and what it suggests.

In the first place it suggests, as I have implied, a dim realisation, which it may be possible to press home, that the characteristic tenets of any age need balancing and correcting by the knowledge acquired in other ages. And correlatively it suggests that an individual will do well not to throw himself unreservedly and without question into the currents of thought specially characteristic of his time, but to keep his head; to learn from the discoveries and advances of the time, but to avoid its excesses. Public opinion tends, I have said, to extremes. It moves at one time towards credulity, at another towards scepticism or panic. We now see that the wave of triumphant confidence which accompanied the wonderful spread of Christianity in mediæval times did bring with it a tendency to excessive credulity. Over and above that ready belief in the miraculous which prevailed in days when the wide extent of natural law was little understood, there came, with the victory of the Christian Church, a general anticipation and ready acceptance of wonderful legends which illustrated or gave token of the Divine presence within her. No marvel was hard to believe while such a marvel was standing fresh and living before the eyes of the people. The generous love which the new-found gospel inspired felt criticism of the heavenly by the earthly to be unworthy and ungrateful. That beliefs were beyond reason, made them all the more credible if they came in company with the triumph on earth of Him whose "Kingdom was not of this world."

So felt the poet of our own time—

O had I lived in that great day,
  How had its glory new
Filled earth and heaven, and caught away
  My ravished spirit too.
No thoughts that to the world belong
  Had stood against the wave
Of love which set so deep and strong
  From Christ's still open grave.

It was an age, then, in which popular belief accepted miracles and legends uncritically. The individual who wished to be a philosopher in an age of faith, who strove to keep his head, and to avoid the characteristic error of the time, as well as imbibe its true genius—its ethical ideals and spiritual discoveries—had need to apply canons of criticism proper to another age. We now see that the Natural Theology of that time needs supplementing; that it appealed in part to a temper and to pre-existing beliefs peculiar to the then state of society. The opinions current among the unquestioning as to the accuracy of the historical narrative in the Bible were excessive. Legends which the criticism of the Maurists and the Bollandists has since expunged from Church history were accepted without question. Physical science had not yet given to miraculous explanations any *primâ facie* improbability; and if they were not improbable, Faith made them, in such cases, normal and even probable. These and a mass of other things were swept in in the wake of the tremendous advance of Christian faith, and of the victory of the Christian Church which, as Cardinal Newman has said, made revelation appear as visible a reality as the sun in the heavens.

And similarly one living in an age of destructive criticism has to beware of the extremes of public opinion on the other side. The great Christian miracle carried in incidental credulity in its wake. All legends which claimed to illustrate it seemed to be tinged with the halo of its glory. We must beware now lest having removed these fragments from a light which was not their own, we conclude not merely that this light was not theirs by rights, but that the halo which has surrounded Christian revelation itself is only the reflection of our own disordered imaginations; lest the legends having walked in, under false pretences, with Christianity, Christianity, with equal injustice, be expelled with the legends. The step from one conclusion to the other is very great, but it is often lightly made. *Ubi tres medici ibi duo athei.* The habit of dwelling on the *minutiæ* of physical sequences, so characteristic of an age of scientific discovery, biasses the mind unduly against the supernatural. Much that fills the unscientific with wonder raises no wonder in the man of science, who is familiar with its causes. And yet the rustic to whom all the phenomena of life are a miracle, is not more extreme or irrational than the doctor who sees no wonder in the mechanism because he knows its details; who looks for no "why" beyond nature because he finds the "how" in nature itself. The reasoning, again, of him who views each event as the immediate interposition of Providence is not more at fault than that of the man who denies to his God a power of modifying natural forces which he allows to every man who throws a stone or lights a fire. Thus, while a man living in an age of faith had good reason to apply a habit of criticism which he would find little general, one who lives in an age of criticism will do well to give his attention very closely to many of the phenomena of an age of faith as a corrective. The characteristic discoveries of his own time he will imbibe without any determined effort. The modifying truths proper to another time he must needs apply himself to with industry; and they can only be apprehended by an emancipation, at least momentary, from habits of thought and sympathies which have become very habitual and very close to him.

This duty, which common sense enforces, is becoming, I have said, dimly recognised in our own time, even by public opinion itself. But in the nature of the case public opinion cannot sufficiently inculcate a task so individual in its character. Public opinion has got so far as dimly to realise that there may be more to be seen by an age which comes after us than we see at present; and that possibly this "more" may include some kind of revival of belief in the supernatural. But this, though removed from an agnosticism which is as final and as dogmatic as atheism, still remains a state of opinion of which uncertainty is the prevailing characteristic. Nor has it got so far as to recognise that, in view of all the circumstances, any reasonable certainty in relation to the supreme problems of religious faith is attainable at the present time. But it respects faith as a phenomenon; it feels that it has not altogether mastered its springs; it is perhaps not altogether without hope of some new twilight after darkness, though it has despaired of a return of the sunlight.

Taking advantage, then, of this tendency of the age, in virtue of its own Zeitgeist, to suspect the completeness and entire accuracy of its own conclusions, I endeavour, in the following Essays, to specify some particulars as to the existing and as to the lawful relations between the individual and the opinion of his times.

In the first Essay—*Witnesses to the Unseen*—the characteristic of the present age as an age of intellectual hesitation, and of uncertainty in reference to supernatural beliefs, is emphasised. For those who have recognised that the Zeitgeist is almost always an inaccurate guide, and who are nevertheless alive to the folly of a position of intellectual isolation and total independence,—of the average mind pursuing its own course without reference to the insight and convictions of the wide and powerful natures and minds around it,—the question arises: How are they best to gain the truths which the age is exhibiting without lapsing into its defects or excesses? And the answer suggested is that those master-minds which have been keenly sensitive to the force of the destructive criticism of the time, and have preserved nevertheless a vivid faith in the supernatural, have a *primâ facie* claim as trustworthy guides. Reversing Mr. Morley's boast that Christianity will be destroyed by being explained, the Essay suggests that a phenomenon which is beyond the explanation of an age of criticism, a faith which can coexist with a keen appreciation of the force of that criticism, has in it an unexplained element which justifies its vitality. While the typically critical minds do not appear to realise the power and reality of faith, there are on the other hand men whose vision of the supernatural is keen, and who nevertheless realise to the full the significance and force of the negative and critical attitude. This second class thus exhibits a *primâ facie* claim to a wider and truer vision of the phenomena as a whole. The Essay thus urges the validity of De Maistre's saying, "Truth can understand error, but error cannot understand truth." Pascal's was typically such a mind; but he lived in a time when its significance appeared less than it does at present.

But, besides the influence of such minds as intellectual guides, a further and more prominent purpose of the Essay is to illustrate their power as an antidote to the unreasoning panic with which an age of doubt is calculated to inspire the multitude. It is suggested that these men, who see and express the reasons for doubt with force and weight, and yet retain the higher vision of the supernatural, should be witnesses to its reality. Their work, in restoring confidence to public opinion, is compared to that of the Christian martyrs, who, in an age of slavery to pleasure and of paralysed moral impulses, bore witness, by courting pain and death itself, to the unseen force which supported them. Such individual witnesses wrought by degrees, under Providence, the new confidence in the powers and worth of human nature which became manifest in the corporate faith of the Christians. And the question is asked whether the witnesses to faith who endure fully the trials proper to an age of doubt, may not be the pioneers to renewed confidence, as the witnesses to the power of supernatural virtue, who sought the pain and death which seemed intolerable to an age of sensuality and moral paralysis, ultimately restored confidence and gave strength which without their example would have appeared impossible. Kant, Cardinal Newman, and Tennyson, are named as in different ways and degrees evincing the peculiar intellectual and moral temper necessary to such a work, and laying down the lines on which it should be carried on.

In *New Wine in Old Bottles*, the composite elements whereof the public opinion of a given time is made up are further considered. The process whereby the legacy of untrue beliefs, bequeathed by an age of credulity, may be discarded by individuals without their lapsing into the extreme of discarding also the characteristic truths of such an age, is discussed: and the patient and tentative testing which is required before the truths of a former age can be safely disentangled from its falsehoods, is considered and illustrated;—the revision of the old explanations of Scriptural inspiration necessitated by the doctrine of evolution and modern biblical criticism being especially instanced.

In the *Wish to Believe*, one common axiom of an age of doubt is discussed—the axiom that the desire for belief in the supernatural is, normally, a distraction, biassing the mind in its view of the evidence attainable in favour of such belief. The view indicated in the Essay is that this axiom partakes of the one-sided character so common in the maxims of an age. The Zeitgeist is inclined to dismiss the *Wish to Believe*—regarded as a factor in religious inquiry—indiscriminately and as an element characteristic of a credulous age. I endeavour, on the other hand, to discriminate between the "wish to believe" which is the foe to due impartiality, and the "wish to believe" which is the necessary antidote to apathy. And while admitting that the phrase "passion for knowledge" more truly expresses the essence and aim of this second wish, I try to illustrate the fact that such a passion necessarily becomes, in its concrete activity, the wish to find true a religion which appears to offer wide spiritual knowledge. And this passion for knowledge is not only, as Pascal has so urgently insisted, absolutely demanded by right reason, but is essential to a due appreciation of the strength of the Christian position. As the passion for knowledge made Newton wish to be able to assure himself, and in the end actually led him to assure himself, that the law of gravitation was certainly true—and thus to gain finally the key to so much which was else chaotic—so in many minds the wish to confirm their belief in Christianity arises from their passion for that religious knowledge which gives the key to man's life and destiny. The apparent paradox in this analogy—as an analogy between discovery and the mere estimate of existing and long-discovered evidences—seems to disappear if we accept the view, set forth elsewhere in the Essay, as to the necessarily personal nature of the inquiry into Christianity by each individual; the full apprehension of its proofs being such as in great measure to depend on individual experience and personal realisation.

The view of Cardinal Newman's teaching and genius indicated in *Witnesses to the Unseen* is incidentally elaborated and illustrated in the fifth Essay, entitled *Philalethes*. This Essay likewise calls attention to a really unusual instance of controversial unfairness in one of the Cardinal's critics, and analyses some of the Cardinal's views as to the assumptions implied in the attitude of various schools of thought towards the Christian miracles.

The two remaining Essays—the second and the fourth—are concerned, one with further illustrations of the work and character of Cardinal Newman, and the other with the consideration of an instance of the vagaries into which the religious sense does, in point of fact, lead able men who have accepted the negative position which is the extreme logical development of the Zeitgeist. It does not profess to be a review of Positivism, but is an attempt to test what the result would be if our countrymen took some of the Positivist teachers seriously and endeavoured to carry their popular teaching into practical life. The tone of this Essay is necessarily less serious than that of the others; but I trust that my readers may feel, as I did, that such a tone was the inevitable result of the Essay to which it was a reply.[1]

[1] Cardinal Newman wrote to me of the tone suitable to such a criticism of popular Positivism :—"It required to be done with both good humour and humour as you have done it. You have been especially happy in your use of Mr. Pickwick, but this is only one specimen of what is so excellent in your article." I may be allowed, also, to recall with gratitude the Cardinal's approval of the line of argument in the *Wish to Believe*, in a letter which led to the intercourse with him which was my privilege during the last years of his life. "When an old man feels," he wrote, "as I do after reading your Essay, great pleasure in the work of another, he may speak of its author and to its author with a freedom not warranted by personal intimacy. I do really think your Essay a *very* successful one, and I have more to say of it than I have room or leisure to say it in."

WITNESSES TO THE UNSEEN

Mr. Pater remarked not long ago that we have all lost our faith. This remark, however little we may consider it true, is felt by most thinking men to *represent* a truth. And the truth it represents was more exactly expressed to the present writer by a veteran and very acute observer of our times, in commenting on the change which the last fifty years have brought about in public opinion. "When I was young," he said, "a man who advocated agnosticism or negation in matters of religion had to veil his full meaning, and to assume an apologetic tone; now precisely the same holds of the man who defends religious certainty. Cultivated public opinion was then in favour at all events of theism as unquestionable; now it is equally pronounced against all religious certainty *as* certainty." Cardinal Newman saw the turn of the tide in this direction thirty-five years ago, and expressed the incoming phase with characteristic point and force. He stated it thus:—

> It is absurd for men in our present state to teach anything positively about the next world, that there is a heaven or a hell, or a last judgment, or that the soul is immortal, or that there is

a God. It is not that you have not a right to your own opinion, as you have a right to place implicit trust in your physician, or in your banker; but undeniably such persuasions are not knowledge, they are not scientific.[1]

This, I say, is the true account of the new phase of public opinion to which Mr. Pater has referred. No religious truth is admitted as acknowledged beyond question; and those who hold to dogmatic Christianity, or even to definite Theism—and they are not a few in spite of Mr. Pater's statement to the contrary—are deprived of the support to the imagination which an age of faith afforded. Further, as the effect of public opinion cannot be neutral, as absence of confidence means presence of doubt, the conditions of our time render faith especially liable to trial in a sensitive and receptive mind. What is widely questioned seems thereby to be questionable. That support which individuals have a right to look for from healthy public opinion, in a healthy society, is taken away; and each one is thrown on his own resources, to a degree which actually lessens the proofs available for religious belief. Corporate action, mutual confirmation and support, are a usual and natural condition of trust and knowledge, in religion as in other things; and doubt in the air renders them to a great extent impossible. A panic will cause a run on a bank, which in ordinary circumstances would be felt to be, and would actually be, safe enough. The fever of doubt makes each man want greater tangible security than is needful or attainable in the ordinary course of life. Each client wants to count

[1] See *Idea of a University*, p. 387.

his gold; each believer wants to realise all his reasons—to have them in his hand and before his eyes. The tacit compact of mutual trust and forbearance is broken; and disorganisation and ruin are the consequence.

There was another time, often compared both by believers and doubters to the present,—the time when the old Roman virtue and religion, noble in part as things then were, had given way to dissoluteness of life and scepticism of intellect. Open the pages of Sextus Empiricus, and you find a startling anticipation of the state of things which Mr. Pater observes among us. We are accustomed to think of the subjectivity of our own time as peculiar; as the outcome in the popular mind of the movement inaugurated by Descartes; as the extension of the principle of self-scrutiny, and of the critical examination of our faculty of knowing, its limitations and its analysis. The relativity of knowledge, again, is regarded as an outcome of this inquiry—indicated by Kant among others, and impressed on the English mind by Herbert Spencer. Locke's incisive criticism on the arbitrary assumptions of dogmatic schoolmen is an inheritance of which we are proud. That the syllogism is a *petitio principii*, and that deductive reasoning is therefore sterile, is a view which we gain from J. S. Mill. The existence of evil is held by many to be a fact which modern thought has for the first time realised in its bearing on Theism. Yet the third century of the Christian era was acquainted in detail with each of these questions, and applied them to a root and branch destruction of religious faith, from traditional Paganism, to the purer and higher Theism of the Stoics.[1] And over and above the definite points of attack there was then, as now, the thought—vague but supremely paralysing to one whose introspection is sensitive and real,—How can anything be certain in these difficult matters, when the wisest men disagree?[2]

It was from a civilisation which was haunted by these ideas that Christianity emerged; and that wonderful transformation from helpless doubt and paralysed moral impulses to deep and unwavering trust, and a fixed ideal of action, clearly realised and hopefully followed, has been the marvel of succeeding ages, and the witness to the divinity of the Christian religion; until, perhaps, by sheer force of repetition the story has lost its natural vividness. It is difficult to feel that to be unique and extraordinary which has been familiar to us from childhood.

What was it that transformed passive spectators of the drama of life into energetic actors? What turned the stream from delicate intellectual criticism, and refined sensuality, and absorption in the art of living and the interest of life, and the placid and self-indulgent routine of the Roman villa, the baths and banquets, the splendid equipages and lazy pride, to

[1] The τρόποι τῆς σκέψεως of the later sceptics of the Empire include each of the points here specified. Cf. Sextus Empiricus, *Adversus Mathematicos*, ix. 207.

[2] Œnesidemus gives as his tenth "reason for doubt" the "opposition prevailing among human opinions as to justice and injustice, good and evil, religion and law," and "the opposition between philosophers in their opinions." Cf. Stockl's *History of Philosophy*, Finlay's translation, p. 155.

the narrow, intense, exclusive, resolute, austere, self-effacing, and resistless torrent of Christian faith and enthusiasm? The story has, as I have said, often been told; and to Christians its bare outline speaks of forces which unaided human nature could never approach to supplying. But this is not what I wish for the moment to insist upon.

The question here asked is *how*—in the order of providence—a public opinion, characterised by intellectual scepticism, and individualism, and moral paralysis, was changed; and what lesson the past may teach to the present? I do not ask if the change proves the truth of Christianity; I only ask how it came about. How did individualism in religious opinion pass into a corporate enthusiasm in which doubt was as abnormal as undoubting faith had been in the earlier conditions? St. Thomas Aquinas in the thirteenth century saw, as clearly as Empiricus in the third, the difficulties attending on proof by the individual mind of even the first truths of natural religion. He points out as clearly as the pagan sceptic that men with a reputation for wisdom often teach contrary things on the very first truths of religion. He speaks of this as, in many cases, an insuperable obstacle to the knowledge by this or that person of the truths in question through the unaided light of reason.[1] Yet the teaching of the corporate Church remains to him a living fact, and he states the

[1] "Remaneret igitur humanum genus, si sola rationis via ad Deum cognoscendum pateret, in maximis ignorantiæ tenebris; cum Dei cognitio, quæ homines maxime perfectos et bonos facit, non nisi quibusdam paucis, et his post temporis longitudinem proveniret."—*Contra Gentiles*, I. c. 4.

difficulty which to Empiricus in his isolation was overwhelming, with the greatest force and without the smallest dismay. How came the change from the public opinion which unnerved Empiricus to that which strengthened and supported Thomas?

The "constancy of the martyrs" is a phrase which has for so many centuries been a commonplace in theological and evidential text-books, that it requires some effort to bring it from the land of *formulæ* to that of realities. And perhaps for some readers it will be necessary to say at starting that I have no intention of entering on the questions disputed by sceptical historians from Gibbon to Mr. Lecky.[1] Such controversies do not affect the main theme of my present essay. There is no question that it was chiefly the witness borne by intense conviction, tested often by

[1] I have carefully confined my remarks to two points in connection with the complicated history of thought at this period, on either of which an historian like Mr. Lecky is as explicit as any orthodox Christian writer. The first is the destruction of the old corporate faith among the Romans of the first three centuries of the Christian era, and the prevalence either of scepticism or of individualism in religion. "The path was cleared," writes Mr. Lecky, "by a long course of destructive criticism. The religions and philosophies of mankind were struggling for the mastery in that great metropolis where all were amply represented." The second point is that the intense conviction of the early Christians, witnessed in devoted lives and martyrdom, was the most potent instrument in the spread of Christianity. On this point Mr. Lecky is equally explicit. "Noble lives," he writes, "crowned by heroic deaths, were the best arguments of the infant Church. . . . Justin Martyr tells us that it was the brave deaths of the Christians that converted him." I have not followed him into the more disputable question as to the other transforming elements to be noted then or later on. The persecutions were the turning-point in the first formation of a corporate Christian public opinion. Mr. Lecky holds that in pagan Rome the Christians had secured a moral power which made their total extinction the only alternative to their final victory. "The question of their destiny was a simple one," he writes; "they must either be crushed or they must reign. The failure of the persecution of Domitian conducted them inevitably to the throne."—See Lecky, *History of European Morals*, vol. i. pp. 410, 418, 441.

torture and death, to the power of Christianity, which from the first, fanned the flame, and changed the spark of individual certainty to the blaze of corporate faith. "Noble lives," writes Mr. Lecky, "crowned by heroic deaths, were the best arguments of the infant Church." The intensity of the belief of individuals has received undying testimony in the fact that the word which only meant "witness" has become inseparably associated with the suffering by which witness was willingly borne. Whether we hold with Matthew Arnold only that Christ "lived while we believed," or prefer the alternative that truth may continue truth though the human mind is changeable and unfaithful, it is an admitted element in that great transformation that faith kindled faith. The "witnesses" or "martyrs" whose vision of the next world was such as to be undimmed by the immediate prospect of suffering and death, or by the atmosphere of doubt around them, helped to expel that atmosphere, and to restore confidence in the possibilities of human nature for virtue, and in the ground for faith and hope. The depth of the faith prevailed over the breadth of the doubt; the intensity of moral purpose over the extent of indolence and sensuality: and on an infinitely greater scale, and in a sphere where directly supernatural forces intermingled with the natural, was evidenced the power of individual heroism by which a great general or a great citizen will stem a panic among followers or fellows, restore confidence, expel by very shame unworthy thoughts or designs, bring forth by his word and example unsuspected traits of heroism in ordinary men, set the good forces accumulating and fructifying by mutual interaction, and kill the bad; until the death of the one and the unchecked growth of the other issue in a complete transformation of the character of state or army.

Individual "martyrs" or "witnesses" for the faith, then, wrought a great transformation in that earlier age of agnosticism; and it is to individual witnesses that we must look now, if there is to be the hope of a change, though the nature of the danger and of the remedy is in some respects markedly different. Similar as were the intellectual perplexities raised by the philosophers of those days, it will scarcely be doubted by a student of the period that the force determining public opinion was far more deeply moral then, and is more deeply intellectual at present. Intellectual scepticism played on the surface of widespread moral anarchy in the days of the Empire; moral disorganisation is only threatening to crown in our own day the ever-widening doubt as to the validity of all religious faith. And the character of the witness who is to help us must differ as the character of the danger differs.

Servility to pleasure and abject shrinking from pain are, I suppose, the mainspring of any movement of utter moral degeneracy; and how they translated themselves into action in the days of the Empire we may read, or avoid reading, in the pages of Petronius. The witness which was needed for this special danger was that of the hero and saint, to whom pleasure and pain are alike despicable. The intellectual scepticism readily fell once the moral basis on which it rested was destroyed. But when the proportions are reversed the character of the witness in some degree changes. The witness, in an age of sensuality, to the possibility of a noble morality, and to the worth of the soul and its connection with the unseen world of reality, was one who saw pleasure and despised it, who saw pain and embraced it, if to avoid the one and to endure the other were the conditions of that higher life which was his one inspiring aim. The witness to faith amid difficulties primarily intellectual, is he who sees and feels those difficulties vividly, and yet sees clearly beyond them the highest truth which to others they render obscure. It is the endurance of torture which testifies to the martyr's heroism and love; it is the keen sense of the reality and force of intellectual difficulties which alone can give the intellectual witness for the faith real power in the present day. The suffering element—in the one case suffering of sense, in the other of mind—is requisite for bearing effective witness, whether in the moral order or the intellectual.

There is, indeed, no comparison between the two in the category of Christian greatness. The intellectual witness is inferior to the martyr of old, as thought is morally inferior to action. But thinking aright is often a necessary condition to acting aright; and so the intellectual witness may be equally indispensable. Again the moral witness—the hero or saint—has ever been needed in time of trial, and is needed still. The intellectual is comparatively a requirement special to the time that is coming upon us. The seductions of the life of pleasure in frail human nature constantly call, in some measure, for those heroic witnesses to the Unseen World to whom what appears so attractive in the twilight, is seen in its true unsightliness by the all-revealing light of faith, and spurned as of no account. The intellectual witness supplies a need less universal in time and place, but absolutely necessary here and now. The crowd gaze at the one witness the Roman crowd oppressed and enslaved by sensuality, and without hope of anything better or more real: and the question passes from breast to breast, "What gives him this confidence which makes pleasure and pain, which are all in all to us, of no account to him? The agony he endures we can see; the force which supports him is unseen. Yet to him the former is nothing, the latter everything. He feels the agony; he writhes under it; it kills him. Can what is unreal prevail over what is so real and so terrible?" And in like manner—though in so different a field the numbers who are anxious in mind; who have shared in the general reaction from the old peaceful confidence; who have realised difficult questions; who have been thrown back on their unnatural isolation and have felt unequal to answering them; whose bewilderment has looked on doubt as the only reasonable state in the circumstances, regard the intellectual Witness to the Unseen in a similar spirit: "The criticism of Feuerbach, or of Strauss, or of Huxley, or of Matthew Arnold, or of Renan cannot be fatal, for *he* feels it and states it with greater force than I can, and yet is unabashed. If he did not see the difficulties his faith would not help me: I should esteem it mere prejudice. But one who sees better than I do the agnostic view of life, and sees the certainty of religious truth in spite of it, and beyond it, redresses the balance of sceptical public opinion. If he shows stronger sight where I *can* see, I will trust his perception of what to me is unseen." Such a witness as this, I say, is needed at present. Whether his strength is mainly intellectual or greatly moral does not radically affect his peculiar work. Thomas Aquinas would have been such a witness had he been among us; Bacon would have helped us in his measure. Men can preserve moral insight for some time after they have failed to turn it to the best account. And they may help others to see to good purpose what they themselves see and neglect. But they are still witnesses, as he may be who "preaches to others" and yet "himself becomes a castaway."

It is an interesting illustration both of the reality and of the comparative novelty of this requirement, that the great German thinker who in the early part of this century—before the agnostic movement had touched, generally, even educated minds—was regarded as sceptical in his influence, from his keen sense of the difficulties attending on the theory of religious knowledge, is now among thinking men felt to be a power distinctly on the side of faith in the high purpose of human life, and in the fundamental truths which explain that purpose. However much we may disagree with the details of Kant's scepticism, his marvellous critical *acumen* is felt to be a guarantee of the accuracy and firmness of his grasp of the truths of natural religion. Difficulties which were so little felt one hundred years ago that to mention them was to unsettle the average mind, are now so generally recognised that to face them, and yet to believe with undiminished confidence, has a reassuring effect. To a generation which was blind to the danger his frankness seemed falseness; to the present generation such candour is, for some minds, the indispensable condition of influence. Kant was the prophet of scepticism in an age of belief; he is a witness, in a sceptical age, to man's moral nature and its connection with the Unseen World.

The need for witnesses will bring its own supply. In the very outset of the movement we have not been without our "protomartyrs." Amid the sudden and rapid spread of doubt, and the almost abrupt abandonment of the old safeguard of reverent abstention from dispute on sacred subjects, there have been those who have felt to the full the force of the flood which has carried away weaker minds, and have yet stood firm. Professor Huxley has said that he could compile a primer on Infidelity from Cardinal Newman's works; and it is curious that he has failed to see the peculiar significance of this statement. Newman was, in the very outset of the agnostic movement—which he foresaw in marvellously close detail before it had shown its true character to the world at large—a "martyr" or "witness" in the sense I have indicated. He saw and felt every reason for doubt which the sceptic could allege; but he saw something beyond, which was to him as much higher and truer than the "muscæ volitantes" of a questioning and negative philosophy, as the vision of Christ was more potent to Stephen or Ignatius than the infuriated mob or the onslaught of the lion. The very intensity of his confidence that the constant failures and mistakes of our powers of analysis do not touch the truest springs of faith and trust made him ever fearless in facing and proclaiming those failures, which to a hesitating mind would have been so unwelcome and alarming, and to a truly sceptical mind so significant.

This characteristic of the late Cardinal has been understood by others if not by Mr. Huxley. Perhaps it has not been so generally recognised in the case of one—almost his contemporary—who, though differing from him widely in his history and falling far short of the conclusions which Newman knew to be essential to the preservation of religious truth, had, nevertheless, a similar gift in a high degree in respect of those first truths, the denial of which is the essence of agnosticism. Tennyson was, I believe, the first to coin the phrase "know-nothing creed" which represents the modern movement better than any other. The feeling of the average agnostic of the nineteenth century about God is exactly given in these lines:—

> He is only a cloud and a smoke who was once a pillar of fire,
> The guess of a worm in the dust and the shadow of its desire.

The earlier stages whereby this feeling has gradually obtained a hold on so many minds have been faithfully reproduced by the same poet. He has fulfilled the double condition I have laid down for the intellectual witness. He has felt the doubt; he has known the faith. The faith has ever been deeper; the difficulty has always been real. The mysteries of providence may suggest to him that man in his ignorance and superstition "built him fanes of fruitless prayer;" but there is deeper feeling and clearer indication of the poet's sympathy in the parting request of Arthur:—

> If thou shouldst never see my face again,
> Pray for my soul. More things are wrought by prayer
> Than this world dreams of. Wherefore, let thy voice
> Rise like a fountain for me night and day.
> For what are men better than sheep or goats
> That nourish a blind life within the brain,
> If, knowing God, they lift not hands of prayer
> Both for themselves and those who call them friend?
> For so the whole round earth is every way
> Bound by gold chains about the feet of God.

The long wail of doubt and difficulty against Nature and Providence which we find in *In Memoriam*, or in *Despair*, does not prevent the abiding conviction that a loyal will should be unabashed by them; and that there is an intellectual light, could we but see it, which would make all things plain. It is true that we read how man

> . . . trusted God was love indeed
> And love Creation's final law,
> Tho' Nature, red in tooth and claw
> With ravine, shriek'd against his creed.

But we are not allowed to forget that the temptation to listen to Nature's "shriek" may mean the absence of that "faith which comes of self-control," or that there is a higher and truer mental vision than our own,

> Seraphic intellect and force
> To seize and throw the doubts of man.

I have named three "witnesses"—Kant, Newman, and Tennyson—who are, each in his measure, typical. One flourished immediately after Hume had first, with power not since surpassed, marked out the lines of the agnostic position. The second ruled the stronghold of English thought just before the wave of doubt had broken on the popular mind. The third lived his most active mental life in the very midst of the dissolution of the spirit of belief, and has ever been regarded as specially sensitive to the intellectual conditions of his time. Kant wrote in a day when scepticism was for philosophers—before it had made its way to "the people." He was awakened from "his dogmatic slumbers" by Hume. He took in hand with far deeper metaphysical *acumen* and with German thoroughness the inquiry, which Locke had already attempted, into the nature and limits of our knowing faculty. He exhibited, in a degree not paralleled in the history of thought, the combination of a critical and even sceptical intellect, with moral enthusiasm and deep practical convictions; and this is, as I have said, an essential qualification for individual power on the side of belief at the present moment. We may hold that the complete separation of the two is unreal; and we may consider with Cardinal Newman that a true theory concerning human certainty must take account of the insight afforded by the practical reason. Nevertheless Kant's mode of treating the subject was—even from the limited point of view I am regarding—peculiarly instructive. The very completeness of his distinction between the two aspects brought into relief a neglected truth. If his entire separation of practical belief from speculative groundwork was unreal, it was a reaction from a yet more unreal fusion. The scholastic "irrefragable demonstrations," the "nimia subtilitas," and pretensions to exhaustive logical proof on all subjects which Leo the Thirteenth has recognised in some of the schoolmen amid all their ability, had made the theory of belief far too complete. It was felt not to correspond with actual facts. The vision "through a glass darkly"[1] was in some cases almost forgotten; and first principles were laid down with an absoluteness which corresponded neither to their accuracy nor to their power of self-justification. And amid the suspicion, which had been growing since the days of Descartes, that their axioms could not endure, there remained in many minds the impression that to tamper with them was to destroy the validity of religious belief. Criticism was identified with scepticism. Objections not fully answered must be allowed to destroy certainty. What was not fully analysed could not be accepted with confidence. Kant, then, in the course of a much

[1] Perhaps the most typical instance of the combination in the scholastic movement of extraordinary acuteness with an exaggerated estimate of the powers of the speculative intellect was Abelard. I need hardly say that the criticism in the text does not apply to such writers as St. Thomas or St. Bonaventura. I refer to that tendency which characterised scholasticism in so far as it disparaged the mystical side of religion and the reverent temper of the great patristic writers.

fuller and more technical work, struck out a conception of the greatest practical effect, in the separation of actual conclusion from theoretical analysis. He helped to form that tone of thought which regards the limits and defects of the speculative intellect not as a motive for practical scepticism, but as a reason for seeking elsewhere what reason apart from moral light—reason, that is, which is maimed and truncated—cannot supply. By carrying to the utmost limits conceivable his theoretical scepticism, while at the same time his own faith and enthusiasm were unshaken, he taught, with whatever exaggeration, a lesson most needed for the time which was coming—of firmness in obedience to the deepest practical convictions and highest insight, in spite of difficulties in detailed analysis which to the individual intellect may seem unanswerable.[1]

And in the limited but all-important field of practical religious conviction Cardinal Newman grasped this lesson and pressed it home on his own generation. No number of difficulties need amount to one doubt,—"difficulty and doubt are incommensurable,"—this was his version of the lesson which may be learnt from Kant's *Critique of Practical Reason*. And Tennyson, though his form of expression is not the same, enforces on the whole the same doctrine. He dwells on the wanderings of the human intellect, the thousand questions it can ask for one that it can answer, the difficulties of formal proof, the different

[1] I may refer for some very suggestive passages on the true significance of Kant's *Critique of Practical Reason* to Mr. W. S. Lilly's recent work, *The Great Enigma*, pp. 277 *seq.*

views we take in different moods of the same proof, the relativity of all knowledge if it is analysed, and yet the force with which beliefs, which such thoughts seem to destroy, justify themselves by their own intensity and light.

> Thou canst not prove that I, who speak with thee,
> Am not thyself in converse with thyself,
> For nothing worthy proving can be proven,
> Nor yet disproven,

he writes. And while the intellect, when moving in mere speculation, and as a spectator of the riddle of life, tends to lose itself, to become morbid and paralysed, and reach no conclusion, we are reminded with equal power of the light shed by a living practical faith, which brings us into the action of life, and gives knowledge and experience which cannot be translated into language intelligible to purely passive speculation, any more than the glow of the hunting field or the wild excitement of the field of battle can be known by those who have always lived an inactive life. To this extent faith is its own evidence, and establishes itself by a *solvitur ambulando.* The doubt is seen by him who has shaken it off to have been in great part the result of hesitation and inaction, due to the absence of perceptions which action alone can supply; and faith justifies itself to the mind which is aroused from undue passivity. Faith sees further and more truly, just as the confident rider sees clearly, and acts promptly, and takes the fence successfully, while the man who hesitates fails to see with precision, and fails in gaining the additional experience and perception which prompt action on that first rapid vision would have brought. The whole being moves together, and sight, action, experience, and knowledge are inseparably linked. Hopefulness, promptness, decision, affect mental perception as well as moral action. "Cling then to faith," the poet warns us:—

> She reels not in the storm of warring words,
> She brightens at the clash of "Yes" and "No,"
> She sees the Best that glimmers thro' the Worst,
> She feels the Sun is hid but for a night,
> She spies the summer thro' the winter bud,
> She tastes the fruit before the blossom falls,
> She hears the lark within the songless egg,
> She finds the fountain where they wail'd "Mirage"!

The question however arises, what account is to be given of this higher vision which Tennyson calls Faith? How do we explain the fact that it is unseen or passed over as a blind impulse by the sceptic? How can acute minds ignore what professes to be so real?

The answer which may be drawn in different degrees from all three writers to whom I have referred seems to be that the sceptic makes an unreal isolation of the speculative intellect, and refuses to view life as a whole—in its hope and its action as well as in the analysis of the passive impressions of the mind.[1] If a man were to sit still and sketch a landscape from one point of view, he might indeed be exact in his picture from that point, but he would gain compara-

[1] The scholastic distinction between *sensatio activa* and *sensatio passiva* brings out, in one limited field, the incompleteness of this procedure, and the necessity, in order to obtain real knowledge, of something beyond passive receptivity in the human consciousness.

tively little knowledge of the country. He could not know all that was to be known of it without using his faculty of locomotion. He could not tell by mere sight the nature of the soil; nor, by looking from a distance, the botanical interest of the plants which enter into his sketch as vague patches of colour. Again the flying birds, which he sets down as dots, have each a nature and a history ascertainable by activity and inquiry. To know what is to be known he must use all his faculties; whereas he sits down and uses one set only, with painful exactness, perhaps, and greatest industry, with greater technical accuracy than many a man will show whose common sense makes him bestir himself and gain a truer practical knowledge of the country and its features. And this seems to be the answer suggested by these writers. The sceptic is using but one set of faculties and assuming the proportions due perhaps to his special point of view to be real. The tall hill in the distance measures a less angle than the horse in the foreground. Change your standpoint and this apparent untruth is instantly corrected; sit still and measure reality by the picture and you go quite wrong. So too the sceptical mind falls into the very snare of relativity against which it protests, and viewing our capacities for knowledge as identical with our capacities for speculation, refrains from the activity and movement which are the natural corrective to relativity and one-sidedness. It views religious evidence as purely metaphysical, or as purely historical, instead of measuring it in the actual working of life, in action as well as in theory; as a belief in the living soul and in its effects on that soul, as well as in its previous condition of a creed or set of formulæ; as an expression of the moral nature as well as the object of mental contemplation.

This general view, I say, would serve to explain the wanderings of the sceptic in spite of his acuteness. His method is wrong. Kant stated the three great questions to which philosophy addresses itself to be: "What can I know?" "What ought I to do?" "What may I hope?" and it is a special characteristic of the thinkers I have referred to that they see the intimate relations between the three. The sceptic separated them, and wrote as though knowledge could be completely dealt with apart from hope and action. The Christian philosopher of the middle ages often did the same, though from another point of view. When a thinker lived, as the schoolmen did, among those with whom the second and third questions had but one answer—the answer given by Christian ethics and the belief in immortality—the first question was apt to be treated, as a matter of technical philosophy, with the help of assumptions really based on Christian morality and Christian hopes. Now that the change of public opinion has led these assumptions to be questioned, it is recognised that either they must be abandoned and scepticism accepted, or "duty" and "hope" must be treated co-ordinately with "knowledge." The school of Hume chose the former alternative; the school which looks to the Kantian conception as expressed by Cardinal Newman adopts the latter. The truth of ascetics—that a life of neglected duty brings loss of faith—completes with them the truth of philosophy—that moral dispositions are required for the very recognition of certain first principles of religious knowledge

> Belief in God and in another world (wrote Kant) is so interwoven with my moral nature, that the former can no more vanish than the latter can ever be torn from me. The only point to be remarked here is that this act of faith of the intellect assumes the existence of moral dispositions. If we leave them aside and suppose a mind quite indifferent to moral laws, the inquiry started by reason becomes merely a subject for speculation . . . supported by strong arguments from analogy, but not by such as are competent to overcome persistent scepticism.[1]

And the other two writers are equally emphatic on the same subject. The effect of this on any theory of belief is obvious. If moral perception is increased by moral action; if religious knowledge (in the sense explained) in part depends on moral perception; if moral action is often prompted by a hope which falls short of certainty; then it is clear that the three elements—knowledge, hope, and duty—constantly interact, varying in degree and effect according to the faithfulness of each individual and his circumstances; and probation for those living amid the influences of modern thought does not keep the character it had in happier days of being mainly dependent only upon fidelity on the second point, "what ought I to do?" apart from the other two, but on alertness and persistency in rejecting no light on any one of the three.

[1] *Kritik der reinen Vernunft*, ed. Hartenstein, p. 547.

How subtly this is indicated in Tennyson's *Ancient Sage*, where the young man who goes to the Seer for advice—

> One that loved and honour'd him, and yet
> Was no disciple, richly garb'd, but worn
> From wasteful living,

is contrasted, in life, in hope, and in knowledge, with the ascetic prophet! The reader feels how the ever-changing hopes and aspirations of the inconstant pleasure-seeker, his purposeless life, his nerveless acquiescence in the inclination of the moment, go hand in hand with an acute and passive sensitiveness to each fragmentary view of the world which scepticism suggests, and an inability to concentrate the mind or to form a deeper or more complete estimate. This restlessness and changeableness lead him to feel that

> Man to-day is fancy's fool,
> As man hath ever been.

There is in thought, as in life, the kind of surface-perception which is increased by inaction and dissipation. The sensualist is morbidly sensitive to pain. The sceptical mind is morbidly alive to those side-lights of human existence and of the world's drama whose connection with its central purpose is not seen. In majestic contrast stands forth the sage himself, ascetic in life, concentrated in hope, profound in thought, firm in faith; too full of his life-work to think much of pleasure; with an inward light which is undimmed by the darkness of the world around. To the youth faith is but an idle gleam amid the earthy life which has become so real to him:

> Idle gleams will come and go,
> But still the clouds remain.

With the sage the gleam is allowed to gain entrance, and to be steadily seen:

> Idle gleams to thee are light to me.

And the seer's final answer to the youth's scepticism is not a treatise on philosophy, but the rebuke of vice, and the statement of plain duty as the condition of higher vision; the true solution consisting rather in making him see more, than in establishing in detail the fallacy of his sceptical complaints. It is the sense of proportion, and the fulness of vision which are wanting; and these cannot be acquired without that knitting together of a nature unstrung by dissipation which persevering moral action alone can effect.

> Let be thy wail and help thy fellow men,
> And make thy gold thy vassal, not thy king,
> And fling free alms into the beggar's bowl,
> And send the day into the darken'd heart,
> Nor list for guerdon in the voice of men.
> A dying echo from a falling wall;
>
> . . . .
>
> Nor roll thy viands on a luscious tongue,
> Nor drown thyself with flies in honied wine;
> Nor be thou rageful, like a handled bee,
> And lose thy life by usage of thy sting;
>
> . . . . .
>
> And more—think well! Do-well will follow thought,
> And in the fatal sequence of this world
> An evil thought may soil thy children's blood;
> But curb the beast would cast thee in the mire,
> And leave the hot swamp of voluptuousness,

A cloud between the Nameless and thyself,
And lay thine uphill shoulder to the wheel,
And climb the Mount of Blessing, whence, if thou
Look higher, then—perchance—thou mayest—beyond
A hundred ever-rising mountain lines,
And past the range of Night and Shadow—see
The high-heaven dawn of more than mortal day
Strike on the Mount of Vision!
So, farewell.

While the writers I have named are agreed in these general characteristics, that they are sensitively alive to the sceptical appearance of certain aspects of the world, if man's moral nature be overlooked or deadened, they differ in some degree in the proportion assigned to particular manifestations of that nature. With Kant—in the passage I have cited and elsewhere—the "sense of law" is foremost. For Tennyson the depths, revealed in the power of the human heart to love, occupy a large space. While Newman—combining in his nature the philosopher and the poet—finds at once the sense of law and of deepest personal love, in conscience; and appeals to both as testifying to a personal lawgiver and a God of love.

Let us compare for a moment—to select a small portion from a large subject—the sense expressed by Newman and Tennyson alike of the mystery of the world—the apparent purposelessness of all that is greatest and noblest; the moral greatness of what the universe treats as insignificant, the moral insignificance of what nature allows to triumph; and the thought and belief which calms each in his perplexity.

Is all that we see and know indefinitely great, and

part of a vast plan of whose meaning our moral nature gives us a glimpse which we are to understand more fully hereafter? the poet seems to ask. Or is that glimpse a cheat revealing only an *ignis-fatuus*, and is death the end of all, and life the measure of its worth? Is the agony of human sorrow, the exaltation of human tenderness, the self-abandonment of the love which is stronger than death, a spark from something spiritual, divine and eternal? Or is it but the expression of self-preserving instincts in a living atom, an insignificant and infinitesimal component part of a planet whose proportion to the universe is inappreciable? Are the deeds of men to be regarded in their worth on the first view or on the last? Was Democritus right or Heraclitus? Is the sense of infinite *pathos* a mere combination of self-protecting feelings, and is a sneer the most truly intellectual attitude? Or do tears see to the depths and does laughter view only the surface? "A tragedy to those who feel, a comedy to those who think":—does heartless thought take in all the truth, or are feelings facts which it fails truly to reckon with?

Such is the fundamental train of thought which accompanies him as he surveys in the great poem of *Vastness* the contrasted views of this universe, great or insignificant according to the light in which it is regarded.

Many a hearth upon our dark globe sighs after many a vanish'd face,
Many a planet by many a sun may roll with the dust of a vanish'd race.
Raving politics, never at rest—as this poor earth's pale history runs,—

What is it all but a trouble of ants in the gleam of a million million of suns?

. . . . . .

Star of the morning, Hope in the sunrise; gloom of the evening, Life at a close;
Pleasure who flaunts on her wide down-way with her flying robe and her poison'd rose;

. . . . . .

National hatreds of whole generations, and pigmy spites of the village spire;
Vows that will last to the last death-ruckle, and vows that are snapt in a moment of fire;
He that has lived for the lust of the minute, and died in the doing it, flesh without mind;
He that has nail'd all flesh to the Cross, till Self died out in the love of his kind;
Spring and Summer and Autumn and Winter, and all these old revolutions of earth;
All new-old revolutions of Empire—change of the tide—what is all of it worth?
What the philosophies, all the sciences, poesy, varying voices of prayer?
All that is noblest, all that is basest, all that is filthy with all that is fair?
What is it all, if we all of us end but in being our own corpse-coffins at last,
Swallow'd in Vastness, lost in Silence, drown'd in the depths of a meaningless Past?
What but a murmur of gnats in the gloom, or a moment's anger of bees in their hive?—

And the wail is broken off, and one line assures us that peace and trust remain to the poet—trust in man's higher destiny and in the meaning of life. It is a line which is only understood by reading the whole of *In Memoriam*—

Peace, let it be! for I loved him, and love him for ever: the dead are not dead but alive.

With Cardinal Newman we have the same sense of an aimless and purposeless surface of things, though the scope he takes is more limited; but his solution goes more directly to conscience itself, which draws to it and purifies those deep human feelings, which Tennyson rightly derives from the highest source. He writes as follows :—

The world seems simply to give the lie to that great truth [the existence of God] of which my whole being is so full; and the effect upon me is, in consequence, as a matter of necessity, as confusing as if it denied that I am in existence myself. If I looked into a mirror and did not see my face I should have the sort of feeling which actually comes upon me, when I look into this living busy world and see no reflection of its Creator. This is to me one of those great difficulties of this absolute primary truth, to which I referred just now. Were it not for this voice, speaking so clearly in my conscience and my heart, I should be an atheist, or a pantheist, or a polytheist, when I look into the world. . . . The sight of the world is nothing else than the prophet's scroll, full of "lamentations and mourning and woe."

To consider the world in its length and breadth, its various history; the many races of man, their starts, their fortunes, their mutual alienation, their conflicts; and then their ways, habits, governments, forms of worship; their enterprises, their aimless courses, their random achievements and acquirements; the impotent conclusion of long-standing facts, the tokens so faint and broken of a superintending design, the blind evolution of what turn out to be great powers and truths, the progress of things, as if from unreasoning elements, not towards final causes; the greatness and littleness of man, his far-reaching aims, his short duration, the curtain hung over his futurity, the disappointments of life, the defeat of good, the success of evil, physical pain, mental anguish, the prevalence and intensity of sin, the pervading idolatries, the corruptions, the dreary, hopeless irreligion, that condition of the whole race so fearfully yet exactly described in the apostle's words, "Having no hope and without God in the world,"—all this is a vision to dizzy and appal; and inflicts upon the mind the sense of a profound mystery, which is absolutely beyond human solution.[1]

[1] *Apologia*, p. 241.

Such is the Cardinal's sense—not less acute than the poet's—of the darkness and chaos of a world in which moral light is an uncertainty, and spiritual faith an unreality. And that conscience which is the great witness to the truth which the world seems to deny is thus described by him, as including at once Kant's sense of law, and the revélation of that capacity for personal love of which Tennyson speaks in its human manifestation :—

Conscience always involves the recognition of a living object towards which it is directed. Inanimate things cannot stir our affections; these are correlative with persons. If, as is the case, we feel responsibility, are ashamed, are frightened, at transgressing the voice of conscience, this implies that there is One to whom we are responsible, before whom we are ashamed, whose claim upon us we fear. If, on doing wrong, we feel the same tearful, broken-hearted sorrow which overwhelms us on hurting a mother; if, on doing right, we enjoy the same sunny serenity of mind, the same soothing satisfactory delight which follows on our receiving praise from a father, we certainly have within us the image of some person, to whom our love and veneration look, in whose smile we find our happiness, for whom we yearn, towards whom we direct our pleadings, in whose anger we are troubled and waste away. These feelings in us are such as require for their exciting cause an intelligent being: we are not affectionate towards a stone, nor do we feel shame before a horse or a dog; we have no remorse or compunction on breaking mere human law; yet, so it is, conscience excites all these painful emotions, confusion, foreboding, self-condemnation; and, on the other hand, it sheds upon us a deep peace, a sense of security, a resignation and a hope, which there is no sensible, no earthly object to elicit. "The wicked flees when no one pursueth;" then why does he flee? whence his terror? Who is that he sees in solitude, in darkness, in the hidden chambers of his heart? If the cause of these emotions does not belong to this visible world, the object to which his perception is directed must be supernatural and divine.

With these specimens I must close. I have no wish to exaggerate the scope of the special work of which I have spoken. It cannot take the place of detailed critical inquiry into problems with which none of the three writers I have named have dealt. But here again a similar work is done, if not quite in the same way or by the same persons. The Christian critic in all departments may be a witness to the many as he is a guide to the few, if his temper be, in his own work, what I have described in connection with trains of thought primarily philosophical. Such writers as Professor Bickell of Innsbruck and Bishop Lightfoot,[1] by their width of mind and their loyalty to truth, combined with their deep and unquestioned learning, may be a source of confidence and light to the thousands whose knowledge of destructive Biblical criticism does not go beyond the popular sketch of its effects in *Robert Elsmere*; while they are gradually, each in his measure, working out for themselves, and for other thoughtful scholars, a *modus vivendi* between what is true in modern criticism and what is essential to Christian faith. Thoroughness and honesty in painful, laborious, and anxious work, unshrinking recognition of the difficulties of the case, are here again the prerequisites; but the persevering adherence to these

[1] This Essay was written during the life-time of the late Bishop of Durham, and I have retained the reference to him rather than substitute the name of any living critic, as no other name appeared to me quite so suitable to my theme.

conditions, which is appreciated by so few at the outset, has, by a divine law of equity, its own far-reaching reward. Often misunderstood and condemned at first even by good men, it justifies its claim in the long run to the true "martyr's" work. It is in its place an extension of the general law of painful labour as the condition of fruit; of sowing in tears that we may reap with joy. The unwieldy and unstable crowd who form public opinion are won at last to trust; and in this department, as in others, those who have combined full appreciation of the difficulties of each problem with unwavering faith, stand forth to the age as Witnesses to the Unseen.

THE CLOTHES OF RELIGION

A STUDENT of human character was once anxious to see over a lunatic asylum. The doctor who superintended it, being very busy, said that he would depute one of his patients to show him over it. "He is a very intelligent man," the doctor said, "though a monomaniac. He talks so sensibly on subjects unconnected with his *monomania* that you would never suspect any deficiency in his mental furniture. And, indeed, I think it possible that you will not discover where his mind *has* given way." The visitor found it to be just as the doctor had prophesied. His guide talked to him about all subjects connected with the asylum—and, indeed, about other subjects too,—with intelligence quite above the average. The phenomena of madness and the peculiarities of mad people formed a specially favourite topic; and his remarks upon them were most sensible, and betrayed not the slightest sign of his malady. The visitor found it hard, in spite of his previous information, to believe that one so sober in his way of talking and thinking —nay, so much above the average in common sense and intelligence,—was indeed mad, and half thought that the doctor must have made some mistake, or that his patient had recovered from any mental derangement he might once have had. However, as he was approaching the end of his inspection, he thought he would make one attempt to test the man's condition, and asked him if there were not such people as monomaniacs in the asylum. His guide promptly answered that there were many such, and forthwith commenced an interesting description of the various forms of monomania he had met with. Some, he said, fancied themselves to be made of glass, and rubbed their hands hard with towels in the morning, until they declared that the dust was gone, and that they were in their natural state of transparency; others thought that certain individuals were constantly plotting against their lives, and always slept with a loaded revolver at their side—the place of which was, however, supplied by a toy-gun furnished for them by the keeper. Others, again, thought themselves to be great personages in history—Cæsar, Napòleon Bonaparte, or the Duke of Wellington. "And the most curious part of it is," added the man, "that many of these are most intelligent and sensible if only you do not discuss their monomania with them. They talk about other subjects so sensibly that you would not suspect them to be mad at all." This was too much for the visitor. It seemed impossible that a man who was really a monomaniac could see this very peculiarity so distinctly in others, and yet be unconscious of it in himself. "There must be some mistake," he thought; "this cannot be the patient of whom the doctor spoke. He must be one of the officials connected with the place."

Just as he was preparing to leave, his guide pointed to a man who sat reading a book, in a room the door of which was open, near the entrance of the asylum. "We were talking," he said, "of monomania. There is a curious specimen of a monomaniac; —a very well-read, sensible, and intelligent man, until you get him on Greek history. Then you will find out his weakness. He is persuaded that he is Alexander the Great, and nothing will shake his conviction. Like the philosopher in Johnson's *Rasselas*, who thought he could control the winds and the weather, he acknowledges that he cannot prove to you that he is Alexander, but nevertheless he *knows* it. Why, he remembers the battle of Arbela, and poor Darius' flight. He will describe Diogenes to you minutely, and past conversations with him. He will give you an accurate picture of the appearance of Thais and Timotheus, and a graphic account of the scene of Dryden's Ode: he says he remembers the whole thing vividly." The visitor remarked that it was very curious. "You know he is *not* Alexander," said the guide, showing for the first time a somewhat wild expression in his eyes. The other took this as a joke. "I should think there was considerable doubt as to his identity," he replied. "Ah, but," said the guide, "I *know* he is not; I have good reason to know," and he looked very mysterious. "I will confide a secret to you," he continued; "I have not yet told you my name. I am Philip of Macedon, and until I came to this place I had never set eyes on that man. I remember my son Alexander well; he was much taller and fairer. I can't possibly be mistaken." The cat was out of the bag, and our friend went away much amused and even more surprised.

I have told this story—which I believe to be substantially true—at some length, because it is, I think, a very instructive parallel to something which aroused the attention of many of us a few years ago. I speak of the utterances of Mr. Herbert Spencer and Mr. Frederic Harrison in the *Nineteenth Century*, on the subject of Religion.[1] Readers of the essays to which I refer will recollect that Mr. Spencer, after explaining that the old idea of a Personal God, such as Christianity believes in, is plainly unscientific, and is merely a development of the primitive belief in Ghosts, and after maintaining that we have no capability of acquiring any knowledge as to the ultimate cause of existence, bequeathed us, with his parting breath, a few capital letters for a religion. He had destroyed for us, it is true, certain objects of worship and belief to which we fondly clung—Conscience, God, the Soul; but he did not "leave us orphans." He sent his spirit to comfort us with a new religion, whose deity is the Unknowable. The Christian God consisted of a Trinity, namely, Father, Son, and Holy Ghost. The Unknowable will not be behindhand in this respect. It, too, consists of a Trinity—Infinity, Eternity, and Energy. It is "absolutely certain," he wrote, that we are in "the presence

[1] "Religion: Retrospect and Prospect," by Herbert Spencer, which appeared in the *Nineteenth Century* for January 1884; and "The Ghost of Religion," by Frederic Harrison, which appeared in the following March.

of an Infinite and Eternal Energy, from which all things proceed." And this Unknowable energy is, he has explained, the true object of the sentiments of awe and worship—and a far more worthy object than the old-fashioned God whom it endeavours to replace.

Here, then, is the Religion which Mr. Spencer has left us; and Mr. Harrison, in some very pregnant sentences, and with the aid of some very happily conceived phrases, has shown that Mr. Spencer's bequest is really not a Religion at all, but only the Ghost of a Religion. He points out that "the attempt, so to speak, to put a little unction into the Unknowable," by describing it in terms "with so deep a theological ring as we hear in the phrase 'Infinite and Eternal Energy from which all things proceed,'" is really a "philosophical inaccuracy." He reduces Mr. Spencer's statement to its true logical limits, and divests it of the unction and enthusiasm which that writer had endeavoured to infuse into it, in the following passage:—

Fully accepting Mr. Spencer's logical canons, one does not see why it should be called an "absolute certainty." "Practical belief" satisfies me; and I doubt the legitimacy of substituting for it "absolute certainty." "Infinite" and "Eternal," also, can mean to Mr. Spencer nothing more than "to which we know no limits, no beginning or end," and, for my part, I prefer to say this. Again, "an Energy"—why *an* Energy? The Unknowable may certainly consist of more than one energy. To assert the presence of one uniform energy is to profess to know something very important about the Unknowable; that it is homogeneous and ever identical throughout the Universe. And, then, "from which all things proceed," is, perhaps, a rather equivocal reversion to the theologic type. In the Athanasian Creed the Third Person "proceeds" from the First and the Second. But this process has always been treated as a mystery; and it would be safer to avoid the phrases of mysticism. Let us keep the old words, for we all mean much the same thing; and I prefer to put it thus. All observation and meditation, Science and Philosophy, bring us "to the *practical belief* that man is ever in the presence of some *energy or energies*, of which he knows nothing, and to which, therefore, he would be wise to assign no limits, conditions, or functions." This is, doubtless, what Mr. Spencer himself means. For my part I prefer his old term the Unknowable, though I have always thought that it would be more philosophical not to assert of the Unknown that it is Unknowable. And indeed, I would rather not use the capital letter, but stick literally to our evidence, and say frankly the unknown.

This is, to my mind, quite unanswerable common sense. Mr. Spencer has no right—has, indeed, no logical power—to have his cake after he has eaten it. If we have no reason to believe in an all-powerful and all-holy Author of Nature, we can have no right to cherish the feeling of boundless awe and reverence which such a being alone could rightly claim. Still less right have we to squander such feelings upon the unknown energies which underlie the phenomena with which we are acquainted. What reason have we to suppose these energies to be worthy of reverence at all, except on a principle which, as Mr. Harrison tersely puts it, would hold "*ignotum omne pro divino*"? The fact seems to be that Mr. Spencer, belonging as he does to that race of religious animals called "man," and unable in consequence to do without an object of worship, having pursued his critical philosophy to the point at which absolute negation is reached in the domain of theology, finding nothing else within his reach is forced to worship *it;* and, to give it a little more dignity, he has to dress its skeleton-like form in capitals, and write it Absolute Negation. Here is his monomania. To suppose that by dressing up nothing he can make it something—and not merely something, but the object of those deepest feelings which, for good and for ill, have played a wider and more important part than any others in the history of our race—is surely little short of a monomania. To conceive that out of the statements "nothing can be known," and "a sort of a something exists which is beyond our knowledge," we can evolve the absolutely certain existence of an Unknowable object of worship, consisting of an Infinite and Eternal Energy whence all things proceed, is to introduce a new species of Evolution which Mr. Spencer himself could hardly sanction when in his right mind. The leap is very great, and as Darwin confesses, "*Natura non facit saltum.*"

Mr. Harrison seems to me, then, in this portion of his criticism, to reason with an accuracy and sobriety which are quite beyond praise. He brings Agnosticism back to its true position, and it resumes its character of negation. "So stated," he says, "the positive creed of Agnosticism still retains its negative character." And this cannot be religion. Religion "cannot be found in this No-man's-land and Know-nothing creed. Better bury religion at once than let its ghost walk uneasy in our dreams." His conclusion is stated in yet stronger terms in the following passages, which must be quoted, as I shall shortly have to refer to them in detail:—"How mere a phrase must any religion be of which neither belief, nor worship, nor conduct must be spoken!" "A mother wrung with agony for the loss of her child, or the wife crushed by the death of her children's father, or the helpless and the oppressed, the poor and the needy, men, women, children, in sorrow, doubt, and want, longing for something to comfort them and to guide them, something to believe in, to hope for, to love, and to worship, they come to our philosopher, and they say, 'Your men of science have routed our priests, and have silenced our old teachers. What religious faith do you give us in its place?' And the philosopher replies (his full heart bleeding for them), and he says, 'Think on the Unknowable.' And in the hour of pain, danger, or death, can any one think of the Unknowable, hope anything of the Unknowable, or find any consolation therein?" "The precise and yet inexhaustible language of mathematics enables us to express, in a common algebraic formula, the exact combination of the unknown raised to its highest power of infinity. That formula is (x^n) . . . . where two or three are gathered together to worship the Unknowable . . . . they may be heard to profess their unwearying belief in (x^n), even if no weak brother with ritualistic tendencies be heard to cry, 'O x^n, love us, help us, make us one with Thee!'"

So far, I repeat, Mr. Harrison has shown so just an appreciation of the consequences of the Agnostic position, so quick an eye in detecting and exposing

Mr. Spencer's mania for transforming scientific negation into an object of worship, by means of his own enthusiasm and capital letters, and so clear an insight into the deflection from just reason which this involves, that he figures as before all things a sober and cautious thinker. If the death-knell of the old Theology be indeed sounded, all reasonable religious worship must die with it. No enthusiasm and no rhetoric can persuade a sensible man that it is reasonable to worship that which he has no means of knowing to be worthy of worship. We must be content, if Theism be destroyed, to bid farewell to religion for good and all, and, in company with Mr. Huxley rather than Mr. Spencer, to look upon all speculations and thoughts connected with it as of no more practical concern to us than the politics of any supposed inhabitants of the moon.

At this point, however, as we give utterance with a sigh to this conclusion, we observe a strange look come over Mr. Harrison's face. "I am sure the Unknowable will not afford a rational religion," he says in effect. We readily assent, and allow the point to have been proved by him. "Ah! but I am quite certain it *cannot* be the real Religion," he continues, "because I know that the worship of Humanity is the real Religion." "I am Philip of Macedon, and I know that is not my son." We are startled beyond description. He continues—and we can listen to the explanation as given in his own words—"The religion of man in the vast cycles that are to come will be the reverence for Humanity as supported by

Nature." His hearers are inclined to interrupt him: "Prune down your capital letters, at all events. Let us examine your statements on their own merits —as they are in themselves and without the clothing of enthusiasm. You have been ruthlessly undressing the Infinite Eternal Energy; you have knocked all assumed dignity out of the Unknowable; you have laughed at it because it has managed to get itself spelt with a capital U;—in common fairness, then, do the same by your own gods. Let us see calmly, and by careful and sober analysis, what humanity supported by nature comes to, in itself, and without unction or capitals, and how far it will be able to serve us as a religion." But we must hear Mr. Harrison out. "The final religion of enlightened man," he continues, "is the systematised and scientific form of the spontaneous religion of natural man. Both rest on the same elements—belief in the Power which controls his life, and grateful reverence for the Power so acknowledged. The primitive man thought that Power to be the object of Nature as affecting man. The cultured man knows that Power to be Humanity itself, controlling and controlled by Nature according to natural law." This is certainly a marvellous collapse of the critical and cautious spirit by which the earlier portion of Mr. Harrison's paper was distinguished. How Humanity controlled by Nature can hear our prayers any better than x^n; how we can be grateful to it if it is an abstraction; how it can deserve gratitude if it is the net result of human and natural forces on an unhappy world;

how it can comfort us in sickness, or give us hope on the bed of death any better than the Unknowable—these difficulties, which naturally arise, Mr. Harrison does not explain. Consistency and sobriety of reasoning vanish directly he touches on his monomania, and enthusiasm and capitals are the order of the day. In company with Mr. Spencer, he has relentlessly pursued the path of negation, until they have arrived at the common conclusion that all that is known is phenomenal nature in its operation on mankind. Here, then, is the exhaustive division of all things—Phenomenal Nature and the Unknown. But at this point comes before us the truth of the saying, "*Naturam expellas furcâ tamen usque recurret.*" All that need of something to reverence which George Eliot lays down as a primary demand of our nature, the satisfaction of which is essential to happiness, comes in full force upon both. It matters not that their reason has decided that nothing exists to satisfy the need. A starving man has been known to endeavour to appease his hunger by eating a pair of boots, in default of any more attractive species of food; and in like manner the Positivist and the Agnostic, finding in reach only Nature and the Unknown, make a desperate effort to satisfy their religious cravings with these very unpromising objects. The Positivist takes Nature, the Agnostic the Unknown; and by a mental process, which can only be characterised as monomania, they contrive to enjoy a sort of religious Barmecide's feast.

The truth seems to be that these philosophers

having conspired together to kill all real religion—the very essence of which is a really existing personal God, known to exist, and accessible to the prayers of His creatures—and having, as they suppose, accomplished their work of destruction and put religion to death, have proceeded to divide its clothes between them. By the clothes of religion I mean those ideas and corresponding emotions with which our minds have surrounded the objects of our religious faith, and which were their natural and due adornment, and the phrases which had become associated with religious feelings and belief. The saying of the Psalmist, which was applied to other slayers of their God, may be used of these also—"*Diviserunt sibi vestimenta mea et super vestem meam miserunt sortem.*" "They have parted my garments among them, and on my vesture they have cast lots."

The Ideas of Infinity, Eternity, and Power, which have hitherto clothed the Deity, fell to Mr. Spencer's share, together with the correlative emotion of awe. Mr. Harrison came in for a larger quantity—though perhaps less indispensable, and more allied to the perfection of dress which Christianity introduced than to the simple clothes of Natural Religion, necessary for decency and dignity. Brotherly love, the improvement, moral, mental, and material, of our fellow men, Self-Sacrifice for the general good, Devotion to an Ideal—here are some of the "clothes of religion" which Mr. Harrison and the Positivists have appropriated. And having appropriated them, both these philosophers try to persuade themselves and the world that, after all, the clothes are the important part of religion, and that if they dress up something else in the same clothes, its worship will do just as well as the old Faith. Mr. Spencer dresses up the Unknowable with Infinity, Eternity, and Energy: Mr. Harrison dresses up Humanity with Brotherly Love and the worship of an Ideal. But the clothes won't fit. The world may be duped for a time, and imagine that where the garments are there the reality must be; but this cannot last. It is not the cowl that makes the monk, and it is not the clothes that make religion. The misfit is too apparent to remain long unnoticed; and then, again, the clothes cannot even cover the whole substance of the new creed. Mahomet and Hume, two of the saints in the Positivist Calendar, are patent excrescences; and the clothes of Christianity can by no stretching be made to cover them at all. Red Riding-Hood thought for a time that the wolf which had put on her grandmother's clothes was her grandmother in reality; but the long rough arms, the big eyes, and the large teeth, which the clothes could not hide, helped to betray its real nature. The clothes of Religion will never fit either the Unknowable or Humanity. The misfit will arouse suspicion; and if suspicion makes us look closely we shall see the teeth and rough arms. But it is not until each has been stripped of its clothes that it will be visible in its full deformity—or, rather, to drop for a moment our latest comparison, in its full meagreness and unsubstantiality. Mr.

Harrison has stripped the Unknowable. Let us now endeavour to strip his own Deity—"Humanity, as controlling and controlled by nature according to natural law."

But before proceeding further, let me endeavour to explain more in detail my meaning in calling the religious language and conceptions which the Agnostic and Positivist have preserved "clothes of religion." The very essence of Religion is belief and trust. All the emotions which the great Object of true religion arouses, whether as God creating or as God Incarnate, have their whole *raison d'être* in our absolute belief and trust. They are called forth by facts and realities, and their beauty, depth, and essential character depend on this. They differ from mere sentiment just as a man's love for his wife differs from the sentiment he may have for a heroine of romance. No love is too ardent for God, *because* He is all-good and all-loving; no awe too deep, *because* He is all-wise and all-powerful; no trust too absolute, *because* He never deserts them that put their trust in Him. So too as to the sentiments proper to Christianity. The Martyrs did not die for a feeling or an idea as such; they died because they *believed* Christ to be God, and that He bid them go through all torments rather than deny Him. They believed Him to exist, and that death would unite them to Him whom they loved, for whom they suffered, whose smile was their joy, whose every word and action was their rule of life, and union with whom was the only perfect end of their being. "If Christ is not risen," said the

Apostle, "then is your faith vain." The root of their devotion was belief in a real fact. Convince the would-be martyr that Christ is no longer in existence, is not approving his action, and will not welcome him after he has passed through the gates of death, and his love and devotion evaporate. The essence of the deepest feelings consists in their being aroused by a reality; and if that be taken away, the feelings themselves lose all meaning and dignity. The clothes of a handsome man are intended to set off the essential dignity of his appearance. Put them on a scarecrow, and be they never so rich and well-made, their dignity is gone. *Their* dignity was part of *his* dignity. And so too religious sentiments depend for their dignity on religious belief—on belief in really existing Objects to which they may be worthily applied.

I say, then, that all these phrases, ideas, and emotions which are associated with religion are its fitting clothes, but that the essence of religion, the central figure which they adorn, is trust in real objects worthy of these things; and further, that while these clothes are suitable to a belief in God and the supernatural—while they are the normal accompaniment and fitting ornament of supernatural belief—they are nothing less than grotesque when they array the Unknowable or the Positivist deity Humanity. Awe for the Infinite Godhead is fitting, is dignified, is rational. Awe for a sort of a something of which we can know nothing is grotesque. But this Mr. Harrison himself has sufficiently shown. It remains now to consider his own deification of Humanity, and to see how badly the clothes of religion fit it, and then to perform in its regard that kind office which he himself performed for the Unknowable—to take the clothes off and see how it looks without them.

Our task presents, at first sight, some difficulties. The grand simplicity of the Unknowable, with His three robes of Infinity, Eternity, and Energy, made it easy work to unvest Him. And once He was unvested the whole of His religion was exposed. Awe for the Unknowable is the beginning and end of the Agnostic religion. But with Positivism the case is otherwise; and when we glance at Comte's Catechism and at Mr. Harrison's Addresses, and see the terms Supreme Being, Immortality, Last Judgment, Choir Invisible, Sacraments, look at the formidable calendar of over five hundred Saints, examine its elaborate ritual and numerous precepts of devotion, we are inclined at first to think that if these be clothes, and we are to find the real figure beneath, the process of undressing will be long and tedious. But this is not so. Mr. Maccabe, the ventriloquist, was for many years in the habit of giving entertainments involving a rapid and complete change of dress, and I have seen clothes prepared for his, or similar performances, which in spite of their apparent number were so arranged that the loosening of one or two strings, whereby they are secretly fastened, is sufficient to make them all come off easily enough. And so, too, the exposition of one or two root principles in the Positivist religion will very readily lay the whole fabric bare in spite of its apparent complexity.

And now, to begin at the beginning, the Power which we are gratefully to reverence as controlling our destiny is Humanity. And what is Humanity? Comte's latest expression for it was, "the continuous sum-total of convergent beings" the whole human race taken together. It includes all that are to exist in the future, and in consequence Humanity, or "The Great Being," as Comte styled it, is as yet incomplete. Certainly, at first sight, when we are told to have "grateful reverence" for the whole human race as acting upon us in connection with Natural Law[1] and controlling our life, many of us will demur. "You should trust in Providence," said a clergyman once to a poor man who was in distress. "Ah! sir," replied the man, "that Providence, he have always treated me badly. Last year he killed my wife, the year before he burnt down my house. and the year before that he drove two of my children mad, and now he's sending the bailiffs to take what little I have left me. He bean't a kind 'un to me. But there's One above as'll punish him some day, and as'll make it right to me and give me back what I've lost." The man had taken Providence as being tantamount exactly to the Positivist Deity. He regarded it

[1] "The devout submission of the heart and will to conform our life to the laws which govern the world is religion." So said Mr. Harrison in his New Year's Address for 1884, and the "Providence" for which we are to have "grateful reverence" is "Humanity as controlling and controlled by" these laws.

as exactly, to use Mr. Harrison's phrase, the Power controlling his life,—as natural forces and the mass of mankind in their capacity of controlling his destiny. And if you had told him that there was *not* One above to reverse the unpleasant machinations of this earthly Providence, I should have doubts of his inclination to give much grateful reverence to the ruling Powers which would remain.

But both M. Comte and Mr. Harrison eagerly explain the inaccuracy of this conception of Humanity, the "Great Being." It excludes all "the worthless and the evil, whose worthlessness and evil die away in the tide of progress and good." These are Mr. Harrison's words, and Comte speaks to the same effect. I am afraid that this explanation would not have much effect with the poor man of whom we have spoken. He would probably insist, his mind being unable to rise to so large a conception as the "tide of progress and good," that the Power controlling *his* life at all events includes an evil and unhappy influence, and would ask how he is to feel grateful towards a Power which makes him unhappy, however happy it may make his companions or his successors, and however much it may minister to their progress? Perhaps this is a narrow-minded view. Every religion must have its mysteries; and this problem is probably one of the mysteries of Positivism, for whose solution it is unbecoming to be impatient. Let us, however, go a little further into particulars as to the elements whereof Humanity—the Supreme Being—is composed.

Seven years must intervene after the death of each individual,—so the Positivist Catechism explains,—before the Last Judgment of posterity decides whether or no he is to be "incorporated in the Supreme Being" and honoured with a commemorative bust. Only *worthy specimens* of humanity are a part of this Great Being. It is called generally Humanity, because the evil members do not count,—because evil is absorbed in good. We are only to worship the good,—those who have exercised a beneficial influence on the race, and who enjoy (the Catechism tells us) an Immortality consisting in fame, and in the operation upon their successors of the energies they originally set in motion. Progress is the great end; and these men are deified as having contributed towards it. The chief constituent elements of the Supreme Being who have lived in the past, the principal worthies of Humanity who have gone from among us, are commemorated by days set apart in their honour in the Positivist calendar. Mahomet, St. Bernard, Phidias, St. Thomas Aquinas, Hume, Galileo, Newton;—here are names taken at random, but showing the wide embrace of Positivism, and the heterogeneous character of the progress it commends. So then, Humanity, or the Great Being, if submitted to a process of disrobing parallel to that which reduces the Unknowable, Infinite, and Eternal Energy to certain unknown energies or energy to which it would be wise in our ignorance to assign no limits, becomes merely—those members of our race who did in the past or will in the future exercise an influence in favour of its progress. And religion consists in an acknowledgment of these beings, and "grateful reverence" for their good offices,—in worship of them as constituting, in conjunction with the forces of Nature, the "Power which controls our life." I am quite sure that none of us have ever denied their existence; and I think that most of us have a profound reverence for such men as Newton and Phidias as types of genius, and gratitude for their services. So then we have, it seems, been Positivists without knowing it. But I am afraid this happy conclusion will not serve us very long. There will be men of a matter-of-fact turn of mind, who will insist that all this explanation is much ado about nothing; that to roll together these worthy persons and call them Humanity, and to call the worship of them, in their effect on us, Religion, is not a process of Religious teaching at all, but only a bad joke. They will insist that the name "Religion" does not make the *thing*. Mr. Harrison, after unclothing the Unknowable, proceeded to examine its essence, and to test its claims to the title "Religion." We have, in our turn, done a good deal of undressing. Let us now make sure whether we have reached anything which can make good its claims to the same title. We have to see how far the so-called religion of Humanity will guide life, support in affliction, give hope in death. These are functions which Mr. Harrison expressly recognises as belonging to all religion worthy of the name. It was by these tests that the Unknowable was tried and condemned. Let us, then, see how in actual practice Positivism fulfils them.

Let us suppose what Reid calls "a plain man" of average common sense, who, in a world where belief in God is overthrown, is anxious to take every advantage of the assistance Positivism can offer him. Progress is the great end and aim, as his Catechism tells him; and all who contribute to this end are, as we have seen, incorporated in the Supreme Being after death. The Calendar contains 558 names of the typical heroes of the past who have achieved this distinction, and in whose footsteps Positivism bids him tread. He reads Mr. Harrison's address of last New Year's Eve, and learns from it that the Positivist Saints are in no way limited as to the line which their sanctity takes. "Let us put aside all kinds of limitations," he said; "let us honour the great and holy spirits of every religion worthy the name. Let us remember the saints of poetry and the saints of art, science, politics, and industry." "Let us turn to the great spirits whose images surround us in this hall—Moses, Homer, Archimedes, Newton, Caesar, St. Paul, Charlemagne, Dante, Shakespeare, Guttenberg, etc. . . . A kindly word, a clear thought, or a brave result does not die with the body that was associated with it. Shakespeare, Raphael, Dante, St. Paul, Homer, and Moses enable us to think, live, and enjoy better hour by hour." This is truly a vast and varied field for worship. And as Mr. Harrison proceeded to explain that not only all these 558 Saints, but all their acts, and all the acts of all others who have lived in the past—except the worthless, whose acts are, he considers, swallowed up in the general progress towards good—contribute to the sum of Humanity, we can hardly be surprised at the climax of his remarks. He said that "words failed him to give an adequate idea" of the vastness of this thought. "The dull monotony of prose did no sort of justice to their feelings; . . . on the present occasion even poetry could not adequately express their feelings, and they must resort to music, because the very indefiniteness of that art could clothe an almost infinite idea." Infinite, one is inclined to add, much as a square inch of ground may be considered infinite if it is measured by the infinite number of infinitesimals of which it is composed. Mr. Harrison's language reminds me of that of a Parisian shopwoman, who once charged the present writer a very high price for a note-book, and said in self-defence, by way of showing the infinite value of the book, "*Mais, Monsieur, c'est un livre extraordinaire. Vous pouvez écrire là-dedans tout ce que vous voulez.*" This was an almost "infinite" idea.

But to return to our "plain man." His purpose being practical, he endeavours to gain from the contemplation of these heroes some guidance as to how he is to obtain the same good success as they did, and to walk in their footsteps. He looks to their example as a guide for conduct, as that of men who have accomplished the aim which Positivism holds up for each of us. And here he is at once puzzled. The Progress aimed at and achieved by the Saints seems to be not only heterogeneous, but even opposed. Which contributed really to human progress—Augustine, whose one aim was to extend the influence of Christianity, or Vespasian, who tried to exterminate it? Which should he imitate, the chaste St. Bernard or the unchaste Mahomet? All these names are in the Calendar, and the whole 558 form a most imposing array, well fitted to arouse the "glow"[1] which, as it may be remembered, Mr. Harrison commends: but as models of conduct they at once puzzle the straightforward inquirer, as embodying directly opposite ideals.

Still, the Positivist teacher insists that each was a "holy spirit," according to his lights and in his own way, and the student will perhaps let this pass, and proceed to fix upon one or two as embodying the type of excellence which most appeals to him, dismissing the "infinite idea" as well fitted for "glow," but little suited for action. His primary object being moral conduct, as that is what was associated with the bygone religion, and the motive for which is now lacking, he fixes, perhaps, on St. Bernard or St. Paul. And here, again, rises a fresh difficulty. Directly his meditation on St. Bernard becomes vivid he comes to realise the fact that the Saint's consistent rectitude and self-devotion leaned for support on a *faith* which supplied both a trust in present assistance and a belief in an aim to be achieved. "How am I," he asks, "to have the

[1] "Those who were assembled in that hall had met with the view of understanding better, and of adding some breadth and depth and glow to the old sentiment and practice," with regard to the grateful remembrance and commemoration of the heroes of the past.—See the *Times'* report of Mr. Harrison's Address on New Year's Eve, 1884.

strength and consistency of St. Bernard when the whole source whence he derived them is gone? The sight of the goal—of the future life—and the consciousness of God's presence and assistance nerved his arm. How can I fight as he fought without them?" But the Positivist priest, nothing daunted, will tell us of the *new* faith and the new aim which supply the place of the old; and will forthwith explain that Humanity supplies the faith and Human Progress the aim. But here I am afraid that Positivism will begin to unclothe itself very rapidly so far as its effect on moral conduct goes. We are very near the strings I have spoken of, which so quickly unloose its manifold robes. And the issue will be most clearly shown by a practical instance, not of exalted virtue but of ordinary right conduct. That a man should refrain from beating his wife because he believes in a God whose claims on him are paramount, and who will reward him or punish him according as he refrains or does not refrain, is reasonable and natural. But that love for the human race should make him refrain when love for his wife was an insufficient motive is hardly to be expected. "Keep yourself up for my sake," said Mr. Winkle to Mr. Pickwick, who was in the water. The author remarks that he was probably yet more effectively moved to do so for his own sake. And to tell a man to be good to his wife for the sake of the human race has in it a considerable element of similar bathos. It is exactly parallel to the well-known method of catching a bird. No doubt if you can put salt on his tail you can catch him. And so, too, if you can get a man to love the human race with a surpassing love, no doubt he will treat his wife well. But the first step in putting the salt on is to catch the bird; and the first step towards loving the human race is to have tenderness for those who are nearest.

The conclusion, then, to which I fancy the "plain man," whose questions are perversely practical, will come on this subject, after a short cross-examination of his teacher, is something of the following kind. The progress of the human race is, as Comte's own Calendar implies, the progress of very various kinds of activity. There must be scientific progress, artistic progress, moral progress. Newton, Raphael, and Thomas a Kempis are all parts of the Supreme Being. And those who have contributed to each of these departments have had faith and hope in the aim they worked for. Science and art will no doubt continue to have their devotees as heretofore—no thanks to Positivism, for they are devotees not in virtue of the general thought of progress, but in consequence of their genius and enthusiasm in relation to a special object. But where is the *moral* regenerator of mankind in the past or the consistent pursuer of virtue who has worked without faith in supernatural guidance and sanctions? I have somewhere heard a saying—I forget to whom it is ascribed—"In astronomy I should be sorry to hold a different opinion from Newton, and in religion I would not differ from the Saints." This seems to point to that indissoluble connection between moral progress and spiritual faith of which I speak. And if, in meditating on the heroes of morality, we find that their action has been invariably inspired by a faith—that their strength came from a belief in supernatural guidance, that what conscious genius has ever been to the great painter, that consciousness of the inspiration of a higher Power has been to the moral reformer and to the saint—where is our hope that, if all such faith be parted with, that progress of which such faith was the very life can be continued? Positivism, then, seems to leave the motives, hopes, and beliefs which have hitherto inspired men to work for the progress of the race in secular sciences and arts just where it found them, consisting, not in the general worship of human progress, but in devotion to some particular department of study; while it fails to give any faith parallel to that which has hitherto been found indispensable to moral progress. And this is surely to fail in exhibiting even that small amount of religiousness which it professes to exhibit. It gathers together all the sentiments and beliefs which are associated with the various types of activity, and gives them the name of "religion"; but upon examination we find that the one type of activity which *ought* to be associated with religion is left without its belief and motive. High moral greatness must remain in such a scheme a mere idea, having no motive force left whereby it may realise itself in action.

So much, then, for the practical effect of this system on conduct. And what of the consolation it gives in affliction? of the hope in death? It seems a mockery to speak of it. And how is it that Mr. Harrison has failed to see the obvious *tu quoque* which his criticism on the Unknowable must provoke in this connection? When the mother of whom he speaks, wrung with anguish for her loss, asks for consolation, does it seem greater irony to say to her, "Think on the Unknowable," than to say, "Think on Humanity or Human Progress?" It is hard to say whether it would be a more grotesque or a more pathetic spectacle to see a humble, simple-minded woman betake herself to Mr. Harrison in such straits, and attempt to gain consolation from the thoughts he holds out. It would probably be, in the words of the proverb, a comedy to him that thinks, but a tragedy to her, for which she would feel. "Your son is not dead," the Positivist says, "he has joined the choir invisible. He lives even more in the energies he has set in motion and the works he has done, than while he was yet here." But the woman, having a hopelessly concrete mind, asks for further explanation, and tries to get beyond the phrase—the clothes—"choir invisible." She asks *how* he lives—what are the works—where are the energies? "He lives in all of you whom he influenced. He lives in the results of his labours. That bench which he made, that useful table,[1] keep him more with you than ever. Cherish them. He lives in them though you see him

[1] Mr. Harrison is very express in his statement that those who enjoy immortality in the Positivist sense are by no means exclusively distinguished people. "We are apt," he said in the Address last referred to, "to associate the memory of the men of the past with the great men alone. But all men of the past had a common life with us, and were in us, and round us, and with us—all but the worthless and evil," etc.

not." This is really no exaggeration of Mr. Harrison's statement. The saints of industry live in their works, he says. "We live by one another, we live again in one another, and, therefore, as much after death as before it, and often, indeed, much more after death than before it."[1] It is breaking a butterfly on the wheel to insist upon the poor woman's failure to gain consolation from such thoughts. Or take again the thought of Human Progress, which is supposed to be so soul-inspiring. What does it come to if, with the persistence of grief, she asks for a concrete instance? I suppose she must be told to think of the electric telegraph or of the steam plough.

What, in short, has Positivism to offer to those in distress? Only illusions and dreams. I do not mean in every case untrue dreams. An historical play may represent true facts, but they are not a part of the spectator's life, or of the reality with which he is or ever will be in contact. And similarly for Positivism to soothe anguish by bidding you think on facts relative to human progress is to bid you forget what are facts to you in what are dreams to you. Christianity bids you dwell on a hope and a reality connected with your own life—tells you that God is with you and will comfort you, and will make it good to you in the future if you are faithful to Him in time of trial. Positivism bids you not mind your trial, because somebody else has been good or successful—bids Mrs. Jones not cry at her son's death, because Mrs. Smith has just added another baby to the human race; and

[1] See Mr. Harrison's Address for New Year's Eve already referred to.

if Mrs. Jones be patient enough and hopeful enough to pursue her questioning yet further, and ask why it should give her consolation and hope that another or many others are happy, she will be told that she is only a part of the Great Being, and that evil and woe, of which her loss is a part, are swallowed up in the tide of progress and do not matter. She should rejoice in the progress of the Great Being, and remember that it is the only concrete Reality, and that she is in fact only a component part of it. At this point she will, I think, with a sigh desist from further questioning. Rasselas, Prince of Abyssinia, having searched long and vainly for one who should give him practical guidance as to how he might find happiness in this life, came at last upon a philosopher who with much confidence insisted that the road was plain. It consisted in living according to nature—in acting upon one simple and intelligible maxim, "that deviation from nature is deviation from happiness." "'Sir,' said the Prince, with great modesty, 'as I like the rest of mankind am desirous of felicity, my closest attention has been fixed on your discourse; I doubt not the truth of a position which a man so learned has so confidently advanced. Let me only know what it is to live according to nature.' 'When I find young men so humble and so docile,' said the philosopher, 'I can deny them no information which my studies have enabled me to afford. To live according to nature is to act always with due regard to the fitness arising from the relations and qualities of causes and effects; to concur with the great and unchangeable scheme of universal felicity; to co-operate with the general disposition and tendency of the present system of things.' The prince soon found that this was one of those sages whom he should understand less as he heard him longer. He therefore bowed and was silent; and the philosopher, supposing him satisfied, . . . rose up and departed with the air of a man that had co-operated with the present system."

To sum up, then, the contrast between Positivism and Religion under Mr. Harrison's three heads—belief, worship, conduct. Religion offers belief in a really existing Superior Power, in whom it is reasonable to trust, who will, in return for our trust and fidelity, guide us in life and bring us through the darkness of this world into light and happiness. Positivism bids us keep the feeling of trust without the reason for trust; bids us trust in forces which we know to be untrustworthy, so far as our own future is concerned, and which many of the deepest thinkers consider to promise no ultimate benefit for our race. That is to say, Positivism bids us keep the feeling after its motive is gone—keep the clothes after the substance is destroyed. And, to help our minds to sustain the illusion which this implies, it uses phrases which, as originally expressing realities, readily call up the feelings and ideas which those realities claimed as their due. Thus it speaks of a Supreme Being, a Power controlling our life, of Immortality, and even of Sacraments.

So much for belief. Next as to worship. The religious prayer and meditation consisted in communing with real persons, unseen but trusted, and in making vivid by force of imagination what was believed to be real,—just as one who is haunted by a nightmare may make an effort to throw off his unhappy illusions, and bring his mind to dwell on the comparative happiness of his real life, real and known to be real, though less vividly felt at the moment than the dream he knows to be false. Positivist worship is here again the clothes without the essence. The essence of the religious prayer and meditation is that the imaginative effort and aspiration are felt to be a process of reaching out towards realities, and it is precisely this that Positivism drops out of its worship. The effort of imagination, the aspiration, the communing with other minds in spirit, are preserved, but the objects are all unreal. The religious meditation aims at the fullest sense of reality; the Positivist attains to perfection only in the illusions of the mad-house. Religion says to him who is in trial, "Your trial is but a dream compared with the happy reality which exists for God's servants." Positivism says, "Your trial may be sad, but don't think of it; live in dreamland." It is the remedy of one who takes to drink that he may forget the trials of life: and let him who thinks that constant dram-drinking, and its consequent illusions, can give substantial comfort and make an unhappy life happy, rest content with the Positivist Clothes of Religion, and declare that they are as good as the reality they profess to replace.[1]

[1] It will, I hope, be understood that I am speaking of the effects of religion in this life—of its practical working on earth. The "need for religion,"

And, finally, the effects of any general acceptance of Positivism on moral conduct and moral progress would be the natural consequence of the nature of its belief and worship. A man may indulge in the pleasures of day-dreaming, but none save a madman will act on a dream as though it were truth. The goal of physical progress is in sight, and the motive for scientific labours is untouched by Positivism. But the goal both of moral conduct for the individual and of moral progress for the race is in the world of spirits; and if that world be only a dream no motive is left for the self-denial involved in the pursuit of virtue. The moral hero must become, as soon as human nature has completely adjusted itself to this new creed, an ideal conception belonging to the past —noble to think on as the hero of chivalry is, with his armour, his battle-axe, and his lance in rest; but not to be imitated, because he is not adapted to the intellectual conditions of the age. A man who went to the Franco-German war, accoutred after the fashion of Richard Cœur-de-Lion, would find his costume and weapons of little use against Krupp guns or mitrailleuse. And a man who, inspired by St. Bernard's moral greatness, attempted to imitate it, without religious faith himself, and in a world without faith, would soon find that all motive for consistent action of this nature was dissolved. He would find the type old-fashioned and quite unable to resist the onslaught

which Positivism professes to supply, is a need here. Of the life hereafter it is obviously irrelevant to speak, except so far as the hope for it is an important element in the working of religion *here*. And it has been alluded to so far and no further in the text.

of a belief which destroys the essential and central motive for moral heroism. Here then, again, in the domain of conduct, we have the conception left and the reality gone. We can still admire the beauty of self-devotion, but, as a practical reality, it is impossible. Once more the clothes without the substance. Clothes in every case. Phrases, emotions, ideas are kept; the essence of religion is gone. Surely if it is to be war to the knife between the philosophers and the old religion—if, indeed, they think they have killed it, it would be more becoming in them to bury it clothes and all, and give forth a sigh over its grave, as Schopenhauer did, than to keep its clothes as perquisites wherewith to array their own children. The former is, at all events, the ordinary procedure of civilised warfare; the latter is rather suggestive of the hangman.

But I have already dwelt too long upon the claim of the Positivist scheme to the title of "Religion." It only needs that we should look closely at its features, and remain for a short time in its company, that we may find out how grotesquely unlike it is to all that mankind has hitherto meant by the term, and how completely it must fail of all practical helpfulness. The danger is that it may pass without close observation, and may sustain its claim by means of the clothing it has borrowed. If we hold intercourse with it, and listen to its voice, we become speedily convinced that it is not the voice of religion. Readers of Æsop's fables will remember that a certain animal once tried to pass himself off as a lion by putting on the lion's skin; but his voice betrayed him. I do not mean to imply that the voice of Positivism is the voice of the ass, but it certainly is not that of the lion. All that remains now is to point, as shortly as may be, the moral to be drawn from what has preceded.

The two essays of which I have spoken are perfectly agreed as to one thing—that the central features of the old Theology are effete; that a Providence ruling the destiny of the world, who watches over us and hears our prayers, who will guide us if we are faithful to Him, who is all-good, all-wise, and all-powerful, is a bygone conception. Mr. Harrison says of Mr. Spencer's paper: "It is the last word of the Agnostic philosophy in its controversy with Theology. That word is decisive . . . as a summary of philosophical conclusions on the Theological problem it seems to me frankly unanswerable." They seem likewise to be agreed that mankind cannot do without some religion. The problem, then, which each discusses in his own way is—what is to be the religion of the future? We have, in company with one philosopher, laughed at the so-called religion of the Unknowable; and we have endeavoured to show that if that be laughable, *à fortiori* so is the religion of Humanity. What, then, is the net result of our inquiry? Surely this: that the philosophers who would destroy Theism and Christianity can *not* give us a religion in their place; and that the destruction of Theism is the destruction of Religion. "Which is the harder question," asked a great Christian thinker of our day, "whether the world can do without a

F

religion, or whether we can find a substitute for Christianity?" Our philosophers answer the former question in the negative, and attempt to answer the latter in the affirmative—we have seen with what indifferent success. And if they fail whose ability is unquestioned, and to whose interest it is to do all in their power to succeed, we may confess the attempt to be hopeless. It is well, then, for those who occupy their minds with the speculation on these subjects which is now so rife, and who are unsettled in their religious convictions, to face frankly and honestly the central issue of the whole controversy. Modern philosophy may profess to prove that we can have no knowledge of God or of Immortality; but let us not deceive ourselves as to the result of such proof. It can give us no ideal vision and no practical hope to replace those it would destroy. It professes to offer us the tree of knowledge; but if we accept it, we must give up all hope of the tree of life. It says to us, as the serpent did of old, "Ye shall be as gods." But this is false. We have seen that it is untrue. Its hopes are delusive, its religion a lifeless skeleton. This does not prove it to be false; but it makes a sensible man less content to accept it finally as true. The inquirer who clearly sees this is led to look back at its initial assumption—that the faith and the hope of the believer in God *are* unreasonable. And that is all we wish. Let the glamour of "advanced thought" and the dream of "the progress of humanity" lose their brightness and fade away; let men soberly and earnestly strive to ascertain whether they cannot find in their own hearts and minds, in their own experience and observation of mankind and of the world, sufficient reason to preserve them from the hopeless pessimism, which is so ill-disguised by the clothes of the old Religion, and their path will be illumined. Their minds will be enlightened, and faith will return to them. What natural reason and earnestness for knowledge commence, God's grace will complete. *Facienti quod in se est Deus suam non denegat gratiam.* This was the hope which the old scholastics held out for the heathen who had not found God; and it is surely no less applicable to those who, in our day, have lost Him in the mazes of philosophical speculation. It is hard to hear a "still small voice" in the din of controversy: and it is hard to distinguish the sun of truth through a cloud of words. But he who is determined, in all earnestness and patience, to hear the voice if it is to be heard, and to see the sun if it is really to be seen, will, sooner or later, succeed in his endeavour. *Whether* it will be soon or late no man can say; but the time will come when, during a momentary lull in human disputing, the Divine voice will come distinctly and unmistakably on the ear of the attentive listener; when the clouds will disperse and reveal the sun in his glory.

NEW WINE IN OLD BOTTLES

We hear a good deal in the present day of the love of truth which animates the explorers of physical or historical science; and those who do not unreservedly sympathise with them are said to be indifferent to truth—or even to be its enemies. It is perhaps worth while to remind ourselves that truths may be lost as well as gained; that there are old truths to preserve as well as new truths to learn; that scientific discovery is concerned only with new truth; that though all truth is intrinsically consistent, it may not always appear so in the course of its attainment; and that at a given stage a too exclusive concentration on steps towards new truth may obscure for the individual mind its perception of truths already possessed. The truest discoveries may come upon an individual, or even upon a nation, accompanied by all the peculiarities of a new fashion; and it is of the essence of the new fashion to neglect and undervalue the old; to develop a pet tendency out of due proportion; to pass over as of no account that which is out of harmony with itself; to absorb the attention of its votaries for the moment as though it were all-sufficient; to discourage and expel by its sneer that which is unlike itself. These are the characteristics of all fashions, intellectual or social, artistic or religious. The question, then, may be asked whether qualified sympathy with a particular scientific movement may not sometimes be due to suspicion of its form as a fashion, its surroundings and exaggerations, rather than to any want of love for the truth to which it is leading; to an attachment to old truth rather than indifference to new—nay, to love of truth itself measured by the quantity and importance of the knowledge preserved rather than by its novelty alone.

That great intellectual movements have in the past had the characteristic of exaggerating for the moment their own importance, and expelling and discrediting much that was really valuable, needs no proof. The littérateurs of the Renaissance despised the Bible. The deep and subtle intellects of the medieval scholastics were in so little repute at the time of the Reformation, that the popular nickname for the remnant who read the works of Duns Scotus furnished for our own day the word "dunce."[1] Or, to take an instance of scientific discovery proper, Bacon's doctrine of induction, in insisting on the value of observation, so undervalued the deductive method of the older logic, which was required for its fruitful exercise, that while he bequeathed to us the

[1] See Trench, *Study of Words;* 19th edition, p. 144.

greatest instrument of discovery we possess, his system as he expounded it was almost useless.[1]

Fashions reign intolerant and imperious; but fashions die and truth lives. Though obscured or lost for a season it prevails in the end. Time prunes the excrescences of novelty. Lovers of Horace do not now despise the literary features of the Bible. No one in our own day denies the subtlety of the scholastic intellect; no one hopes for discovery without deduction from hypothesis. But, learning from past experience, those who love old truths and wish to preserve them *in their own generation* will do well to wait till discoveries are mellow, and have lost the dangerous characteristics of new fashion, and can rest peacefully in company with all that is true in our inheritance from the past, before they finally estimate their bearing on the universe of knowledge. There are old truths whose knowledge is of vital importance to each individual; and he cannot afford to lose them, even though his grandson should eventually regain them. Let him then be chary of allowing the raw exaggerations which accompany new discoveries to mutilate or destroy his inheritance. Let the two be kept apart until the new is ripe for assimilation with the old. "No man seweth a piece of raw cloth to an old garment, otherwise the new piecing taketh away from the old, and there is made a greater rent: and no man putteth new wine into old bottles; otherwise the wine will burst the bottles, and both

[1] This is brought out in a very interesting manner by Jevons (*Logic*, p. 255). See also Dean Church's *Bacon*, p. 244.

the wine will be spilled and the bottles will be lost."[1]

These remarks are suggested by recent attempts, to which public attention has been drawn, to find a *modus vivendi* between Christian faith and advancing science. We have in the first place the scheme of Mrs. Humphry Ward, as set forth in the manifesto to which Dr. Martineau's subscription has given a weight which it could not otherwise have had.[2] The tone and spirit, however, of the manifesto are the tone and spirit of *Robert Elsmere* and not of Dr. Martineau. The peculiar vividness with which Dr. Martineau realises the bearing and importance of the dogmas to which he adheres—definite Theism, the life of prayer, personal immortality—and which makes him far more in sympathy ethically with Mr. Hutton, or the late Mr. F. D. Maurice, than with any school of negative criticism, is entirely absent from the manifesto, which brings us rather into the vague and enervating atmosphere of *Robert Elsmere* than the bracing oxygen of *A Study of Religion.* Read in the light of its origin and with *Robert Elsmere* as its commentary, it is so complete and melancholy an illustration of my theme, that its discussion need not detain me long. "Hope in God and love of man," this is the meagre remnant of the old truth which Mrs. Ward's scheme, as explained in her preface to the manifesto, aims at preserving and fostering. The study of biblical criticism and of comparative religion is to be one

[1] St. Mark ii. 21.
[2] See *Pall Mall Gazette*, March 10, 1890.

main instrument for increasing the spiritual stature of the neo-Christians, and we know from *Robert Elsmere* the manner in which this is conceived;—the latest theories in criticism accepted bodily, not as steps, as hypotheses with more or less of plausibility, to be examined and re-examined, to be tested as to their unconscious and unproved assumptions, and the views of human nature and of the supernatural which these presuppose; but to be swallowed wholesale, and judged to be final by a mysterious "historical sense" which is without appeal. The natural exaggerations of a discoverer, the tendency of novelty, of which I have spoken, to assume for the time the undue preponderance of a fashion, the tentative character of the proofs themselves, are entirely ignored. If the Tübingen school were in fashion, its conclusions would be interwoven as integral parts of the new gospel. The general acceptance of any suggestion of an able critic as a proved fact, has eviscerated natural religion itself. Theism has become a manifestation of a divine "something" in good men; immortality has ceased to be a certain hope. If Reuss and his friends share the fate of Baur and Volkmar, the articles of belief must undergo a corresponding change. Were the scheme to last, its gospel would have to be considerably remodelled every ten years at least, and a *formula* for retractation should in common prudence be provided in the new liturgy.

But more than this, the inspiring ideal of Christ's character, which is to be the animating principle of its philanthropic work, may well cease to inspire when criticism has been allowed to rove freely, with no better rudder or compass than the scheme furnishes. M. Renan will not be excluded from the programme, and to many minds his conclusions will be far from satisfying. The "frightful accesses of enthusiasm" which he describes, the acquiescence in pious frauds which he postulates in his account of the central figure of the Gospels, may temper the enthusiasm of some, and will hopelessly bewilder more. The figure which is supposed to be one of ideal perfection may in the end appear to combine the very unstimulating mass of contradictions which it conveyed to Bishop Alexander of Derry :—

> Divinely gentle yet a sombre giant,
> Divinely perfect yet imperfect man,
> Divinely calm yet recklessly defiant,
> Divinely true yet half a charlatan.

Enough has been said. In such a plan there is no *modus vivendi*, no recognition of the independent claims and basis of old truth. New methods, new exaggerations, new fashions have been swallowed with a wholesale timidity, and in defiance of all the lessons which history teaches as to the advancing tide of truth, with the constant incidental errors, which, like the back-draw of each wave in a flowing tide, are its normal accompaniment. We may sympathise with the kindness and philanthropy in the practical aim of such a plan, but of stable intellectual basis it has none. The new wine has been poured bodily into the old bottles, and the bottles have burst forthwith. The scheme preserves only a few of their fragments.

But a much more serious and important attempt at the *modus vivendi* to which I have referred is contained in the collection of Essays entitled *Lux Mundi*, issued a few years ago by some influential members of the High Church party.

To many the special interest of the volume will arise from the mode and motive of its composition. It is not the work of a number of men airing pet theories on the relations between science and religion: but it arose, as we gather from the work itself, from the practical experience of a few able and thoughtful tutors and clergymen in the University of Oxford, as to the necessity of reconciling apparent contradictions between current Christianity and current biblical criticism and other scientific movements, for the sake of their own faith and peace of mind, and that of their friends. It is this actuality of the problem it attempts to solve, and the accompanying sense which many readers will have that that problem is a very real one for themselves, which raises the discussion from the rank of mere abstract speculation, and gives it an interest for the general reader as well as the professed theologian. The two deep feelings which inspire the writers are a devotion to many elements in traditional Catholic Christianity and belief in its essence (as they conceive it) on the one hand, and on the other a sense of the discrepancy between modern research, physical and critical, and certain features in the current Anglican teaching. This discrepancy has doubtless been forced on the writers with peculiar vividness by the difficulties they have witnessed in the minds of young men, at an age when the logical powers are keen, and a sense of inconsistency the more urgent because the experience, which life brings, of the many puzzles and enigmas which the finite mind must patiently bear with to the end, is yet to come. On the other hand, men of the old school whose minds have been formed, and whose associations have been welded together, before the problems raised by the theory of evolution and modern biblical criticism became pressing, fail to realise the vividness with which these theories and their apparent consequences press on those who are in process of educating their intellectual nature and shaping and arranging their convictions. Such men see no difficulty because they see no reality (as it has been expressed) in a series of hypotheses or scientific proofs, which have come before them after their capacity for assimilating new ideas and principles as active and determining forces has, in the course of nature, become dulled.

Thus Archdeacon Denison has characterised this book—a book, be it observed, prompted apparently by the motive of saving the faith of many who are in danger of losing it—as "the most grievous specimen of defence of truth of all those I have had to contend against, and the most ruinous under all the circumstances of its production, a blow *ab intra* without parallel." And other divines of influence are known to entertain similar feelings.

It is not to my purpose to discuss the problems

raised by *Lux Mundi*: the work of writers of so much weight and ability would call for fuller treatment than my limits allow. But, looking at the opposite attitudes of Mr. Gore and Archdeacon Denison in the light of the opening remarks of this essay, an important question suggests itself. If Mr. Gore finds that those who seek his sympathy or guidance are hard-pressed by the apparent inconsistency between the outlook suggested by science at the moment and the religion they have been taught, is he not bound to make some such attempt as *Lux Mundi* to solve the problem, if only to help men to hold by their faith? On the other hand, if what I said at starting is true,—that scientific advance, in the rawness, inaccuracy, and imperfection of its different stages, is far more exacting in its demands for sacrifice of traditional interpretations than truth requires,—may not Archdeacon Denison be right in discouraging a *modus vivendi*? Does not *Lux Mundi* tend to the rashness of pouring new wine into old bottles? Still the retort will be that young men cannot be influenced by advice which appears to ignore the march of science, and will not listen to conservatives who tend to think that the distinctive glory of their age is an idle boast.

The fact is that the problem is a double one: truth is to be guarded, and individual consciences are to be protected; and the matter cannot be dealt with satisfactorily unless this is recognised. The young man cannot practically, in the present day, be simply told not to believe in scientific progress. Such a course would put his faith in opposition to his common sense. On the other hand, the ever-growing, ever-changing forms of scientific opinion may not be in such a state that the Church can commit herself to them, or should condescend to revise and guard her statements to suit what may be a temporary phase of opinion. Such a thought suggests an explanation of the mode of action often pursued in the Catholic Church in these matters, though her application of the same principle is, as we shall see, naturally somewhat different in different ages.

The question formed a theme of interesting discussion at the International Scientific Congress of Catholics at Paris, which I attended in company with the late Father Perry, S.J., in 1888, and which held its second session in 1891. And I the rather choose that Congress as furnishing a sort of text to my remarks, as it partook of the actuality and practicalness which, as I have said, lends such interest to *Lux Mundi*. It was no authoritative meeting in its form, but an assembly which included many very distinguished and eminent Catholics, who met to discuss scientific and critical questions, and who made use of the opportunity for comparing notes as to how practically an individual could and should stand with reference to the modern speculations to which I have referred.

Let me, as indicating a line of thought which I found to be a common one among the congressists, make a citation from the introductory address of the organiser of the Congress, Monseigneur d'Hulst, rector of the Catholic University of Paris.

Il a toujours existé, il existera toujours des dissentiments parmi nous sur les points que l'autorité de l'Église n'a pas tranchés. Les occasions de rencontre sont nombreuses entre la science et la foi. Si la foi est immobile, la science ne l'est pas. C'est la gloire de la parole divine d'être toujours semblable à elle-même. C'est l'honneur de la pensée humaine de n'être jamais contente d'elle-même et de reculer sans cesse les bornes toujours étroites de ses connaissances. Mais entre deux termes contigus, dont l'un est en repos, l'autre en mouvement, il est inévitable que les points de contact se déplacent. Si le déplacement se faisait toujours au nom d'une certitude absolue, l'accord serait facile entre croyants ; car autant ils sont convaincus qu'une proposition révélée n'a rien à craindre des constatations scientifiques, autant ils sont prêts à affirmer qu'une proposition démontrée n'encourra jamais le démenti autorisé des juges de la croyance. Ces deux axiomes représentent les deux faces d'une même vérité enseignée en termes exprès par le Concile du Vatican et par toute une série d'actes pontificaux, et qu'on peut résumer en cette formule : *le dogme catholique ne saurait être pris en défaut par les faits.* Mais le problème est moins simple que cela dans la pratique.

La science, en effet, arrive rarement d'un bond à la certitude. Elle procède par l'hypothèse, s'essaie aux vérifications expérimentales et s'achemine à travers des probabilités grandissantes vers le terme désiré de l'évidence discursive. Encore si cette marche était régulière et constante ! Mais non. Il y a des tâtonnements et de fausses manœuvres ; il y a des chevauchées hors de la route : *magni passus, sed extra viam ;* il y a des hypothèses qui jouissent longtemps d'une certaine faveur et que de nouvelles recherches obligent d'abandonner. Tant que dure leur crédit provisoire, bon nombre d'esprits trop prompts à conclure les confondent avec les dires absolus de la science, et pendant ce temps-là on se demande comment les mettre d'accord avec l'enseignement chrétien.

Les uns disent : "Le désaccord est manifeste, c'est l'hypothèse qui a tort." Les autres répondent : "L'hypothèse est bien appuyée, c'est vous qui interprétez mal la croyance. Ce que vous prenez pour l'enseignement catholique n'est qu'une façon d'entendre cet enseignement, façon bien naturelle tant qu'on n'avait pas de raisons d'en chercher une autre, mais qu'il faut abandonner à la demande de l'expérience." Sans doute, si l'autorité suprême intervient pour fixer le sens indécis du dogme, le dissentiment fait place à l'unanimité. Mais il est rare que cette autorité se mêle ainsi aux virements de bord de la science. Gardienne prudente de la parole sacrée, protectrice bienveillante de l'activité humaine, elle attend d'ordinaire, se contentant de surveiller le mouvement et de condamner les excès de part et d'autre. Pendant ce temps-là, deux tendances se manifestent parmi les catholiques : celle des hardis, qui sont parfois téméraires ; celles des timides, qui sont parfois arriérés. Et là encore la situation se complique et les reproches se croisent. Les hardis prétendent que ce sont eux qui sont prudents, parce qu'ils réservent l'avenir et épargnent aux théologiens la nécessité de s'infliger plus tard à eux-mêmes un désaveu. Les timides répondent que ce sont eux qui méritent la louange décernée aux braves, parce qu'ils témoignent moins d'appréhensions devant les attaques de la science, plus de confiance dans la victoire finale de la conception traditionnelle.

Encore une fois, Messieurs, ces divergences sont inévitables, et vouloir les prévenir serait interdire aux croyants de penser. Aussi bien, le danger n'est pas dans ces discussions loyales et fraternelles, un peu vives parfois, mais toujours placées sous la double garantie du respect réciproque et d'une commune docilité envers l'Église. Le péril commencerait le jour où l'on prétendrait engager l'Église elle-même dans l'expression d'opinions particulières.

Et ce péril croîtrait si cette imprudence était le fait non plus d'un écrivain ou d'un groupe, mais d'une assemblée nombreuse et accréditée par le mérite individuel de ses membres, par l'éclat de leurs travaux et de leurs services ; si une telle assemblée usurpait sans autorité le rôle d'un concile.

This passage brings into special relief the help which the constitution of the Catholic Church may give in dealing with the double aspect of the problem to which I have already referred. Where there is no clear distinction between the individual teachers and the final living authority of the Church, the immediate skirmishes called for by each fresh scientific hypothesis, which has for a time a hold on public opinion, seem to commit the whole faith of a Christian to the counter movement which is made on the spur of the moment. An undergraduate comes to his tutor full of Baur's theory as to the dates of the Gospels in the days when Baur reigned supreme, or looking on Darwin's account of the origin of the moral sense as finally proved, and his adviser tells him that though not in keeping with traditional Anglicanism both may be accepted. In many cases Baur's theory, as discrediting all approach to contemporary evidence of Apostolic Christianity, has, as we know, been found to weaken or destroy all belief in the received Christian history; to commend the "myth" hypothesis; and even to lead to Agnosticism. And the evolution theory of conscience has often had a parallel result. Years pass on: the exaggerations of the Tübingen school become discredited, and Wallace brings his great authority to destroy on purely scientific grounds the urgency of the young man's original difficulty as to the moral faculties of mankind. The tutor sees that a little patience would have saved his pupil. Or suppose he has taken the opposite course, which Archdeacon Denison would perhaps prefer, and has said "You cannot accept

Baur or Darwin," the young man, overcome by the tide of popular opinion and the tyranny of the Zeitgeist, refuses to retain belief in a religion so antiquated, so unable to keep pace with the times. Years pass; irreligious habits are formed, and by the time that scientific teachers have modified their decision he is incurably a godless man of the world.

I do not deny that want of tact on the part of a Catholic teacher might issue in a similar result. But I want to point out the vital importance of the third alternative which obviously suggests itself in the case of a Catholic. He may simply be told, as Monseigneur d'Hulst reminded his hearers, that the Church has not contemplated what is new, and has not pronounced on it; and he may be reminded that neither has science pronounced fully and finally. The lesson appropriate to the situation is that of prudence and patience. There stand the corresponding principles, of scientific progress and development of Christian doctrines; and the limits of their application, so far as the trials *hic et nunc* to individual faith go, have to be decided to the best of the Catholic tutor's or adviser's ability. The double guidance attainable from the Church's general principles and decisions, and from their application to a new case, is parallel to the double action of preacher and confessor. The preacher preaches in general terms the principles of Christian morality and duty. The confessor listens to his penitent's account of his special case; judges as best he can as to his circumstances and disposition, and decides which of the principles, universally true in themselves, apply to the particular instance. Further knowledge may modify his decision in the confessional; nothing can change the principles of morality he preaches from the pulpit. One is a statement of absolute and abstract truth; the other is concrete and relative. It is a system for dealing with each case as it arises, with the half-knowledge of facts and circumstances, which is possible at the moment, liable to reconsideration, capable of addition, capable even of absolute contradiction in presence of new discoveries as to antecedents, surroundings, and character; yet all the while it is the application of the same eternal principles of right and wrong.

So the individual teacher looks at the analogies in Church history and at the general principles laid down by theologians, and to their treatment of similar cases, and decides to the best of his power what is tenable by a Catholic with respect to a new scientific hypothesis; but he does not and cannot commit the Church to the conclusion he draws except so far as he may say he thinks it is the true conclusion. He understands to the best of his power the real bearing of the hypothesis on dogma; endeavours to distinguish the traditional interpretation of a Christian belief from its essence, and decides as he can for the individual conscience he is helping. But his knowledge and his applications of it are liable to error. His acquaintance with theological precedents may be one-sided and incomplete. His apprehension of the scientific hypothesis may be so wrong as to make him miss its true bearing. And a change in his opinion and counsel as science advances, or as his knowledge is corrected, is quite as consistent with the Church's truthfulness as the confessor's change is with the changeless moral law.

But this is not all. While individual Catholics often have what may be called a certain provisional power of reconsideration[1] where the Church has not decided authoritatively, we may also see in the Church a power of assimilation and of ultimate consolidation of her teaching in its relations to assured scientific advance, or well-examined and tenable hypotheses. While her caution protects her against those whims of the Zeitgeist which prematurely claim the title of discoveries, the activity of her life enables her *in the end* to find a *modus vivendi* with what is really valuable in intellectual movements, or really true in scientific achievement. This is a special prerogative of a living authoritative tribunal which, from the nature of the case, cannot be clearly asserted by any ruling power whose nature is documentary. And the Church has, on occasion, exhibited this principle of progressive assimilation in a marked manner.

It is perhaps instructive to note the illustration the principle in question receives from cases which often seem at first sight instances of unmixed narrow-

[1] St. Thomas expresses this power, so far as the interpretation of Scripture texts is concerned, as follows: "Since the divine Scripture may be expounded in many ways, it is not right to attach oneself so strictly to any one opinion as still to maintain it after sure reason has proved the statement supposed to be contained in Scripture false; lest on this account Scripture be derided by infidels and the way to faith closed against them." This passage is cited in the very interesting article on Creation in the Catholic Dictionary as bearing on the interpretation of the account of Creation in *Genesis*.

ness and bigotry on the part of ecclesiastical authority. In days when the temper of the age, as shown in all religious parties, was less sympathetic and tolerant than at present, when every school of religious thought asserted its claims by more or less stringent persecution of its opponents, the slowness of the Church to commit herself prematurely to any novel form of thought which seemed at first sight at variance with traditional teaching, naturally led to intolerance on the part of the teachers or officers of the Church. There was in this as in other matters less of individualism than at present; and a new opinion to which the Church refused to commit herself was often not tolerated in private persons, as a matter of discipline. There was probably less need for toleration for the sake of individual consciences, as scientific discovery had not yet got so firm a foothold as to be in many cases a living source of difficulty; and the greater simplicity of thought in these matters made especially true Cardinal Newman's saying, "Novelty is often error to those who are unprepared for it from the refraction with which it enters into their conceptions." The immediate danger to conscience and faith may generally have come rather from the admission of startling novelty, than from over-severe repression of individual opinion. We can, perhaps, see in this fact the reason why, though some might suffer unfairly from such a policy, ecclesiastical authority tended to be more chary then than now of allowing—apart from infallible decisions, and as a matter of practical guidance—new opinions, not absolutely proved, and which at first sight shook dogmatic beliefs, whose traditional interpretation had from the temper of the age become for many indistinguishable from their essence. That very duty of protecting the Christian's conscience which, as I have said, is the motive of the immediate action of the Christian teacher as distinguished from the final decision of the Church herself, would, in many cases at all events, lead to an opposite policy in circumstances so different. The over-subtle mind of the present day, readily grasping the real weight of evidence for a new scientific discovery, more readily than formerly distinguishing between the essence and the traditional interpretation of dogmatic belief, has more to fear from the temporary denial of what may prove true, and less to fear from the readjustment of explanations of dogma: whereas the bulk of medieval Catholics would feel less the weight of scientific proof, and more the shock of novelty in expression. Just as the simple Silas Marner believed in God's justice and in its unfailing expression in the decision by lot, and to find the lots unfair was for him to find that there was no just God; so, when thought was ruder and education rarer, there was greater danger of identifying a religious truth with its popular forms of expression. To invalidate the latter was to shake belief in the former. Perhaps then of the two alternatives our teachers would now be more ready to allow provisional freedom, as a concession to a puzzled intellect, where the will seems to have no disposition to indocility, while formerly independent thought, as arguing disobedience in spirit and having less *primâ facie* claim to genuineness and simplicity, would be checked; the double change of circumstances bringing the further excuse for a change of policy, that the novelty, which is now more quickly interwoven with a modified expression of dogma, would formerly have seemed inevitably to contradict it. But doubtless an individual in advance of his generation was liable in days of old to suffer from a rule of action suited to the many. The condemnation of Galileo may be considered to be an instance of this by those who think that he himself was hardly used by ecclesiastical authority. The primary duty of protecting religious belief in the mass of Christian souls may have called for a check on the propagation of an imperfectly ascertained discovery for which the minds of the faithful were unprepared, and which seemed to impugn the authority of Holy Scripture. This is the view of the matter indicated by Cardinal Newman in his preface to the last edition of the *Via Media.*

Be this as it may, a marked instance of the earlier method of procedure—of the condemnation on grounds of prudence of a system which was ultimately assimilated with Catholic teaching—was the case of the peripatetic philosophy. Though, of course, unconnected with discovery properly so called, it assumed in the twelfth century, as Schlegel has pointed out, very much the position of "advanced thought" at the present day. When it came over to the West, from the hands of the Arabian revivalists, whom the era of Haroun al Raschid had first begotten, it was looked upon as the daring, enterprising philosophy which appealed to the highly cultured intellect. Portions of the Stagirite's logical works had gained a footing a few years earlier, and his dialectical method had attracted some of the most brilliant minds of the Western Church. The new philosophy was the "rationalism" of the day. The most celebrated of the early advocates of the Aristotelian dialectic was the famous Abelard, who applied it to theology in the Western as John Damascene had already done in the Eastern Church. It is not to my purpose to dwell fully on its history. We all remember the historic conflict between St. Bernard the Abbot of Clairvaux and Abelard. St. Bernard saw that the scholastic method as it stood exalted reason at the expense of faith. That mystical and mysterious side of religion which must ever remain only seen in part—through a glass darkly—was exposed to the pretence of full analysis, and to a shallow confidence in the all-sufficiency of syllogistic deductions. The tendency which he saw was that expressed by another saint, who beheld in a vision a theologian attempting with his measuring tape to ascertain the height of the gates of heaven. "Posuit in cœlo os suum," said St. Bernard of Abelard indignantly, "et scrutavit alta Dei." They met for a public disputation, but Abelard's courage, it is said, failed him; and he refused to defend his own doctrines. Abelard, the prince of Western scholastics, was condemned in Rome. Nor did this sense of the dangers of the new method quickly pass away. Seventy years later Aristotle's metaphysical works were burnt by order of a council at Paris, and a papal legate, by direction of Innocent the Third, forbade their use to the faithful.

Here we have an extreme case of the first side of the principle to which I am referring. The rationalistic spirit was the danger of the times. It was the danger from which the conscience and faith of the multitude were to be protected; and ecclesiastical teachers, in the rough and summary manner which was customary at that time, put their hand down upon the cause of the evil and checked it. Whatever was good or bad, true or false, in Aristotle, here was a practical danger. The province of faith was being ignored, and a secular and rationalistic spirit propagated. As the summariness of a court-martial provides less accurately than a civil trial for just treatment of the individual, and yet is called for by the danger to larger interests, so St. Bernard and Pope Innocent, leaving nice distinctions for a less critical juncture, checked the new philosophy with prompt energy.

All the more remarkable, in remembrance of this, is the fact of which Catholics have been specially reminded of late years by Leo the Thirteenth. It would have been a strange vision alike to St. Bernard and to Abelard could they have seen the Encyclical "Æterni Patris" in which a few years back the present pope traced the lineal descent of the philosophy of St. Thomas Aquinas from Leo, Gregory, and Augustine; and could they have turned to the volumes in which it was contained, and found the Aristotelian dialectic and Metaphysics adopted into its very essence.

And yet this fact is but the other term of the Church's double attitude, which shows itself in a jealousy of hasty and dangerous submission to novel doctrines—which is, nevertheless, compatible with her assimilation in the end of however much they contain which is true or intellectually valuable. In the reign of Innocent the Third a system fraught with the associations of the paganism of Aristotle and the pantheism of Averroes, the Arabian commentator, which had not yet found place for faith, and advocated the autonomy of the reason, was claiming acceptance in the name of the intellect of the day. This intemperate claim had simply to be met by a decisive check. In St. Thomas's time all was changed. Years had passed, and the details of Aristotelianism had been discussed and weighed in the academic circles of the *Schola Theologorum*. Albert the Great and Alexander of Hales had adopted such of its principles as were consistent with Christianity, and interwoven them with the ethics of the Fathers, texts of Holy Scripture, and the decisions of Church authority. In this new garb and surrounded with these new associations and safeguards, the condemned *Metaphysics* lost their terrible character. The dialectical method was held in check by the faith and sanctity of St. Thomas, and the insistence on the mystical side of religion which we find in his great scholastic contemporary, St. Bonaventura. The danger of exalting reason and destroying faith had passed away under these altered circumstances. Time had been allowed; and the contemptuous sneer of the hasty rationalist of the twelfth century, that Catholic faith was irreconcilable with the best products of the human reason and the great thoughts of the philosophy of Grecian antiquity, was falsified. The saying "Roma patiens quia æterna" received a fresh illustration, which succeeding ages, so unsparing in their criticism of the temporary conflicts between secular science and religion, would do well to note.

Now to point, as briefly as may be, the moral with which I set out. The principle of double treatment which the Church has variously applied at different times seems to have peculiar importance in view of the circumstances of our day; and the constitution of the Church undoubtedly offers certain facilities for its application. Outside the Church a decision for the immediate guidance of Christians tends to become final. A book with the weight attaching to *Lux Mundi*, from the ability and position of its writers, is as near an approach to an *ex cathedra* decision as to what are within the limits of Anglican orthodoxy as the case admits. On such a subject there is no effective court to revise its declarations. The case of *Essays and Reviews* has shown (if it needed showing) that, so far as the State Church is concerned, the utmost freedom in dogmatic matters is compatible with retaining official status as a member of the Church of England. For those, on the other hand, who consider that the only true Anglicans are those who retain the traditional dogmas which they deem the Anglican Church's inheritance, disowning, as they generally do, the Privy Council and Crown as a final court of appeal, and accepting in practice no living authority as dogmatically supreme, the opinion of a weighty section of their number as to what is compatible with their position, is in a sense final. There will always be a certain number to follow suit, and there is no machinery to check either the increase of adherents to such views, or their further development in the direction of free thought. Thus we find a Review of position describing this book as the Manifesto of the High Church party.[1]

On the other hand, a Catholic book on similar lines would be necessarily tentative, and would be liable to many hierarchical grades of revision and reconsideration. It might be condemned as dangerous or inopportune, yet much of it might be ultimately adopted as true. It might be (as in a recent case in France) approved by an ecclesiastical superior, and then censured by a more authoritative tribunal. And yet such a double fact need not prevent much of the substance of a book from being finally declared consistent with Catholic doctrine. Or, on the other hand, in view of the harm done by too much public discussion, or of the intrinsic unimportance of the work, it may be left unnoticed; and yet the points it raises may receive in due time and place more or less authoritative treatment, limiting the degree to which it can safely be accepted. A work of this kind, if expressly dealt with, is weighed by an authority which considers in its different functions what it is wise to say, what is possible, what is probable, what is calculated to

[1] See *Academy*, March 8, 1890.

produce a false impression, what, though creating a true impression in itself, will jar with some article of belief which has not yet been fully explained, as well as what is in itself absolutely true or absolutely false. And this last, in religion as in science, is a matter on which infinite caution and slowness are natural and necessary. Fénelon's *Maximes des Saints* was condemned as objectively containing false doctrine, but the pope refused to censure the author's own meaning (*in sensu ab auctore intento*), which he subsequently set forth, though his enemies pressed for such a condemnation. The famous congregation *de Auxiliis* allowed as tenable the extremely opposite doctrines of Thomism and Molinism, contenting itself with condemning only such conclusions on either side as struck at the morality of the active Catholic life. A common form of reply in Rome, when a decision is asked for as to the lawfulness in a "penitent" of some habitual course of conduct, is "that he is not to be disquieted" (*non esse inquietandum*), a purely personal precept involving the refusal to decide on the principle. The authority does not attempt to enunciate there and then a general principle which is to apply to all possible cases, and yet desires in the interests of the individual to give him the practical rule which his case demands.

Many steps, then, are possible towards supplying materials (so to speak) for the Church's ultimate decision and guiding individuals provisionally, which yet do not commit the Church finally and fully one way or another. And this likewise leaves time for another important factor in the progress of universal truth—the further development and analysis and proof of scientific hypotheses themselves. Thus when finally the truth emerges with scientific certainty, a double office has been performed—minds have been familiarised with an hypothesis, and prepared for its reconciliation with Christian teaching should it prove true, and at the same time positive assent on the part of the Church herself has been withheld to what may after all prove to some extent false. It is hardly worth while to recall the application of such a principle to the innumerable varieties, advocated on purely scientific grounds, which our own day has witnessed in Darwinism — the numerous and partially conflicting theories of physiological selection, sexual selection, development and atrophy by use and disuse, and the very different limits assigned to the operation of natural selection itself by Wallace and Darwin; facts which, however, do not affect the belief most of us have that Darwin discovered a *causa vera*, whose exact operation and limitations it will take many generations to determine. But Darwinism is a signal instance in both departments of what has just been said. Not only do we see the very considerable modifications which it is gradually undergoing at the hands of men of science, but within the Church its tenability, and the degree and form in which it is tenable, and the precedents and means for its reconciliation with Scripture, have within the last twenty years been discussed to an extent amounting almost to a literature.

I will observe, finally, that the *modus agendi* I have described—though doubtless many will consider that the immovable limits set to its operation in the Church by past decisions of an infallible authority prevent its being adequate to the requirements of the case—seems, as a principle of action, to be only an extension of that philosophic temper of mind which, in their own departments, all great natural philosophers, the Darwins and the Newtons of history, have enjoined. It combines readiness to consider the working of every possible hypothesis with great slowness in ultimate decision on its limits or on its truth at all. We remember how Newton for sixteen years refused to consider the principle of gravitation established because of a very slight discrepancy between the time he calculated to be taken by the moon to fall through space and by a stone at the same height. "Most men," writes a competent authority,[1] "would have considered the approach to coincidence as a proof of his theory." Sixteen years later more accurate calculations as to the moon's distance removed the apparent discrepancy. And then he finally declared his hypothesis to be proved. Again, few of us have failed to contrast the slowness and accurate measurement by Darwin and Wallace of conclusions drawn with any certainty as to the details of evolution, with the sweeping generalisations of their second-rate followers. Darwin and Newton have at once the greatest instinctive confidence that they are on the road to truth, the greatest quickness in noting the

[1] Professor Jevons.

possible significance of phenomena, and the greatest slowness in finally stating what conclusions are ascertained beyond doubt.

In the absence of a living and final authority and of such a system as we have been considering, a religious body tends, as I have said, to become identified (without any internal principle of recovery) with the momentary conclusions of its members in view of contemporary controversy. Thus I see no inherent principle in the High Church party which would prevent its gradual development into a ritual system with dogma almost entirely eliminated; nor do I see any principle in the scheme of Mrs. Humphry Ward which would prevent such views as Renan's from suddenly finding themselves in the ascendant.

With this suggestion I bring my imperfect sketch to a close. My purpose has not been polemical, and my sympathy with the aim of the authors of *Lux Mundi*, so far as it is the outcome of the real *crux* of all thinking Christians, is very deep. But I think a principle is to some extent lost sight of in these controversies which has been exhibited by the Church even when its application may be open to criticism, and in times of corruption and tyranny. Two interests are, as I have said, at stake—individual faith and conscience, and abstract truth. A provisional concession to a school of criticism, which at the moment enjoys, perhaps, undue ascendency, may be needed for individual consciences, and yet it would be very unwise to commit the Church finally to such a concession: and conversely the general and public inculcation of new and startling views, wholesale, may be dangerous, even though they should ultimately prove to be in great measure true. The discoveries of science are among the acknowledged *criteria* used by the Church in the explanation of Scripture; but the time is probably far distant when we shall be able to appraise with confidence many of the tentative conclusions of Reuss and Wellhausen.[1]

[1] I may be allowed to refer the reader to the last chapter of the second edition of my work, *W. G. Ward and the Oxford Movement* (Macmillan), in which one or two of the lines of thought suggested in this essay are more fully developed.

SOME ASPECTS OF NEWMAN'S INFLUENCE

It probably struck many persons, at the time of Cardinal Newman's death, that the general feeling of enthusiasm displayed on the occasion was quite out of proportion to the extent to which he or his writings are known. The thought that a great man had passed away, a high example of unworldliness been taken from us, possessed many who felt and knew little more than this. It used to be said that the great Duke of Wellington's influence for good while he lived was immense, even on those who knew nothing of him except that a great example of English courage and English sense of duty was still among us. And in the sphere of spiritual life Newman had a similar influence.

The consequence has been, however, in the case of Cardinal Newman, that many who have written and spoken of him with genuine feeling—to whom the knowledge that the author of *Lead, kindly Light*, still lived and prayed at Birmingham was a real source of spiritual strength—have given a very imperfect account of the man himself. There have indeed been not a few beautiful sketches by personal friends and admirers. But he has also been described, both in print and in conversation, by epithets which have struck those who knew anything of his writings or of himself with a sense of their incompleteness and unsatisfactoriness. "Mystic," "giant controversialist," "learned theologian," "recluse"—such descriptions have seemed little nearer the mark than the discoveries of the few who have found fault, and have noted that he lacked imagination, and that his style was inferior to that of Mr. Stevenson.

And yet perhaps the failure to characterise him rightly arose, in some cases, from the difficulty of the task—from the complexity of his nature. "Prose-poet" gives a fair description of Carlyle; "A great thinker in verse" is a true account of Browning by an able critic; but a many-sided genius like Newman's refuses to be explained or even suggested in a few words. And when we ask ourselves *why* we are dissatisfied with the epithets in question, it is not easy in a moment to give the reasons. The descriptions contain some truth. There was in him something of the mystic. He was full of power in controversy. His mind had been absorbed in patristic theology. His life was one of seclusion. Yet these epithets, singly or collectively, quite fail to give any idea of him, or of the nature of his influence. We remember the story of the Buddhist who was asked to describe "Nirvana." "Was it annihilation?" "No," he answered impatiently. "Was it the beatific vision of the great Unknown?" "No," with equal impatience; and so on with further queries. "What was it then?" "How can you ask what is so plain? . . . Nirvana is . . . *Nirvana.*" And so in the present case. "Not a theologian, not a mystic, not a controversialist. Newman was *Newman.*"

However, as many have succeeded in bringing out *some* at least of those distinctive elements which are felt in their combination by the majority of his readers, it may be worth while for each, according to his lights, to put his mite in contribution. Let us look through the phrases I have cited and attempt to limit their "connotation" as applied to Newman.

"Mystic!" Yes; he had a keen hold on the unseen world, on the mysterious teachings of conscience, on the shadow of God's presence in the human heart, and of God's wrath on the world at large. But the typical mystic lives in the clouds. He is not in touch with things around him. He is little interested in the microscopic inspection of the play of life about him. And what is to be said of the Cardinal from this point of view? He loved to talk on current topics of the day. "He was interested," says J. A. Froude, speaking of his Oxford days, "in everything which was going on in science, in politics, in literature." He could throw himself into spheres of action far removed from his own. "What do you think," a friend asked, "of Gurwood's *Despatches of the Duke of Wellington?*" "Think?" he replied; "they make one burn to have been a soldier!" His senses were keenly alive to the small things of earth. How delicately he weighs in *Loss and Gain* the respective attractions of sights, scents, and sounds! Ascetic though he was, he chose the wines for his college cellar at Oriel. Vivid and real as was the world of religious mystery to him, he could give the closest attention to matters of secular detail. He could, in a moment, pass from the greatest matters to the smallest. Gregory the Great left his audience with ambassadors to teach the Roman choristers the notes of the "plain song"; and so, too, Newman would leave the atmosphere of religious thought and meditation and betake himself to his violin. He is still remembered by the villagers at Littlemore as teaching them hymn-tunes in their boyhood.[1] It was a recreation to him in later life to coach the Oratory boys for the *Pincerna*[2] or the *Aulularia*. He delighted in Miss Austen and Anthony Trollope. He enjoyed a good story from *Pickwick*. All this limits very much the application to him of the popular idea of a "mystic"; and yet all this is true of a man whose sense of religious mystery was surpassed by few.

"Giant controversialist!" Certainly the original edition of the *Apologia*, the *Letter* in answer to Pusey's *Eirenicon*, and the *Lectures on Anglican Difficulties* are masterpieces of religious controversy; and yet we can fancy the Cardinal smiling quietly if he heard himself spoken of as a "giant controversialist." "Tell me what books to read on such

[1] *Guardian*, Sept. 3, 1890, p. 1358.

[2] The *Pincerna* was Newman's expurgated version of the *Eunuchus*.

a subject," an old pupil asked him. "Why do you ask me?" was the answer; "I know nothing about books." How—we can see it in every page of his works—he hated the pedantry and parade of controversy! He would help inquirers, but he cared not to do the work of sledge-hammer argument. If it was done it was done for the sake of his friends and of anxious seekers after truth, and not for the sake of opponents whom he had no hope of convincing. He believed in the proverb, "He who is convinced against his will is of the same opinion still." He said fifty years ago that if views were clearly stated and candidly recognised, all controversy would be either superfluous or useless — superfluous to those who agreed in first principles, useless to those who differed fundamentally.[1] With him, controversy was chiefly exposition and the pointing out of mis-statements. There was little of direct argument. "Giant controversialist!" One can fancy the fate—there are stories on record as to the fate—of the pompous man who went to talk to him of controversy, as one great controversialist to another. One specimen of the class comes with notes, and books, and points for discussion on problems of education, but finds the Cardinal so absorbed with news about the "barley crop" in Norfolk that no other subject seems to interest him. Another presses him for a refutation of one of Mr. Gladstone's arguments against the Vatican decrees, but only succeeds in eliciting the reply that Mr. Gladstone is an old Oxford acquaint-

[1] Cf. *University Sermons*, pp. 200, 201.

ance, and has been very kind to him. And when the subject is insisted on, the conversation suddenly passes—his visitor knows not how—to the oaks of Hawarden and the exercise of cutting down trees. A third visitor finds himself engaged *in limine* in a discussion as to the number of stoppages in the 1.30 train as contrasted with the 3.40, and has unexpectedly to employ his conversational talent in explaining his cross-country route, and the lines by which he came. And then there is the Oxford story of Newman's guest who introduces the "origin of evil" at dinner, and at once produces a dissertation—full of exact knowledge, and apparently delivered with earnest interest as to the different ways of treating hot-house grapes, and the history of the particular grapes on the table before him. Such are the stories which are current:—not that really anxious inquirers who approached him with tact could ever have such a tale to tell; with them he took infinite pains. But where the pomp of controversy was invoked by tactless or self-sufficient persons, he remembered the proverb, "Answer a fool according to his folly."

And what of "learned theologian"? An unquestionable truth; yet we cannot help seeing the Cardinal's smile again. Who that has read it can forget the irony of his description of the typical learned man, the historian, or archæologist, or theologian, whose learning has overgrown and stiffened the freedom of his mind? It expresses the half-restrained irritation—half irritation, half amusement

—of Cardinal Newman himself after a two hours' walk and talk with Mr. Casaubon. It may be read in a lecture delivered at Dublin, and is, perhaps, so little known as to be worth writing down here.

Such readers are only possessed by their knowledge, not possessed of it; nay, in matter of fact they are often even carried away by it, without any volition of their own. Recollect, the memory can tyrannise as well as the imagination. Derangement, I believe, has been considered as a loss of control over the sequence of ideas. The mind, once set in motion, is henceforth deprived of the power of initiation, and becomes the victim of a train of associations, one thought suggesting another, in the way of cause and effect, as if by a mechanical process, or some physical necessity. No one who has had experience of men of studious habits but must recognise the existence of a parallel phenomenon in the case of those who have over-stimulated the memory. In such persons reason acts almost as feebly and as impotently as in the madman: once fairly started on any subject whatever, they have no power of self-control; they passively endure the succession of impulses which are evolved out of the original exciting cause; they are passed on from one idea to another, and go steadily forward, plodding along one line of thought in spite of the amplest concessions of the hearer, or wandering from it in endless digression in spite of his remonstrances. Now, if, as is very certain, no one would envy the madman the glow and originality of his conceptions, why must we extol the cultivation of that intellect which is the prey, not indeed of barren fancies, but of barren facts, of random intrusions from without, though not of morbid imaginations from within? And, in thus speaking, I am not denying that a strong and ready memory is in itself a real treasure; I am not disparaging a well-stored mind, though it be nothing besides, so that it be sober, any more than I would despise a bookseller's shop—it is of great value to others even when not so to the owner. Nor am I banishing—far from it—the possessors of deep and multifarious learning from my ideal university; they adorn it in the eyes of men: I do but say that they constitute no type of the results at which it aims; that it is no great gain to the intellect to have enlarged the memory at the expense of faculties which are indisputably higher.

Once more—"recluse!" He lived in the Oratory and saw little or nothing of the world. But where were the gloominess, the sternness, the unsociableness which the word suggests? As has been well said by a recent writer, his need of loneliness was fully balanced by his need of friendship. *Cor ad cor loquitur* was his motto, and it expressed the man. He loved to unbend among familiar friends. His sense of humour was of the keenest. His life-long habit, formed at Oxford, of living in intimacy with those whose objects were his objects, and who loved and understood him, had become to him a second nature. True, he despised the vanity of society. He felt the heartlessness of the world and withdrew from it. But he withdrew from the world only to give himself more fully to his friends. With his brilliancy and fastidiousness it might have been expected that the best society, with its ideal of exclusiveness and refinement, would in early days have had some attraction for him (so at least the late Canon Mozley seems to hint); but there was in him a far deeper force which made him shun all that approached to dissipation of mind, and put away all that savoured of ambition. But it was not in the spirit of a hermit. The sternness of a recluse, the austerity of his demeanour, the marked protest against the rest of the world which the conception conveys, were uncongenial to him. He was like his own St. Philip Neri. An intimate friend of his wrote, a few years ago, on his "naturalness," on the simplicity with which he laughed at his own failures—his "floors," as he called them. Though his natural refinement was intense, there was no trace of anything artificial or of affected reserve. "A. B. is a man one can't talk to in one's shirt sleeves," he would complain. Just as the abstraction of the mystic was not his, nor the pedantry of the controversialist, so the pronounced *rôle* of a recluse was foreign to his nature. He loved to be as other men. His prayer for himself and his friends was, he said, not for those heavy trials some saints have asked for — persecution, calumny, reproach —but simply that they might be overlooked, passed over as members of the crowd.[1]

And thus we get from the limits which must be placed on the meaning of "mystic," "controversialist," "learned theologian," "recluse," as applied to Newman, a glimpse of one aspect of his distinctive charm —a kind of social charm rare in all classes, especially rare in one whose life-work is greatly that of the student. Men of letters and men of science are often known to men of the world as "book-worms," or regarded with distaste and some alarm as "very *learned.*" And with a certain amount of ignorance implied in the tone of such unsympathetic judgments there is a grain of truth in them. Such men are often eccentric, and are wanting in the sense of humour which should teach them to avoid talking "shop,"

[1] *Sermons on Various Occasions*, p. 241.

and to find common ground of converse with the rest of the world. Newman was the antithesis to the "book-worm" or the "learned man" as conceived by the man of the world. Full though he was of knowledge gained by observation and reading, he could put it entirely aside on occasion. He valued intercourse with his fellows more than mere study as a means of improvement. "Given the alternative," he once said, "in a University, of social life without study, or study without social life, I should unhesitatingly declare for the former, not the latter."[1] Life was for action, and action was determined by character. All his intellectual efforts were guided and limited by this thought. His sermons, his lectures, his philosophy at Oxford were all designed to meet the practical difficulties of those to whom he was a spiritual father. There was no rhetoric for rhetoric's sake; he never preached abstract dogma except as helping the spiritual life, nor taught philosophy as a speculative science, but solely as a practical help to those in doubt.

And this brings me to another point which I can only touch on briefly. The word "philosopher" has been used of him less often than the epithets I have referred to. It has been used by some of the best critics; yet it has been, by implication, denied by men who were in close contact with him. Dean Stanley in his well-known estimate of the Oxford movement never once refers to the Oxford University sermons, which were, at that time, the embodiment

[1] This sentiment is also expressed in the *Idea of a University*, 2nd edition, p. 205.

of Newman's philosophy. And one who opens these sermons will find nothing in the form of a philosophical treatise; nothing about the origin of ideas, about the categories, about the distinction between the pure and the practical reason. Yet those men of acute and religious mind who went to hear him, in doubt and trouble as to man's right to confident belief in the very being of a God and in the hope of immortality, came away reassured. Does philosophy require a formal and technical treatise, completely elaborated, on the human faculties and on metaphysics? If so, Newman was no philosopher. Is he a philosopher who takes in at a glance the root-problems as to what practical beliefs are reasonable in matters of deepest moment to each individual; who treats these problems in such a way as to help those in need, the deepest thinkers if so be; who treats them informally, suggestively, incompletely, seldom using technical language; who almost professes that he is not philosophising but only reminding us of the asseverations of sober common sense; who refrains from entering on questions which cannot help the action of practical life, but who gives to more systematic writers the groundwork, if they care to build on it, of a philosophy of faith, unsurpassed for breadth and depth, which he does not fully elaborate himself? If such a man is a philosopher —a religious philosopher—Newman was a great philosopher. His philosophy was like the rest of his work, the expression of his personality. It was the expression of his own deep reflections, as they came to him; of answers almost as he would have given them in conversation. When a conclusion was obvious he had not the pedantry to draw it. When it would offend some and help others, again he would not draw it. He gave the materials for it which would be of service to the one class; he refrained from making the statement which would scare the other. Where a professional philosopher would press for a logical explanation, he would perhaps suddenly "shut up," and break off an argument which had really done its work, and pass on to something else instead of engaging in fruitless logomachy. When he had shown in the *Grammar of Assent* some of the strongest instances of clear and confident religious conclusions, which certain minds attain to without recognising more than mere suggestions of their real premises, he foresaw the indignant objections of the incurable logician. But he had really said enough for his purpose, which was to show that such inferences in untrained minds may be practically reliable; and that was sufficient. He did not want to argue with the logician; he wanted to satisfy the simple mind that it was on the right road. So instead of an elaborate answer we find the following words: "Should it be objected that this is an illogical exercise of reason, I answer that since it actually brings them to a right conclusion, and was intended to bring them to it, if logic finds fault with it so much the worse for logic."[1]

In a similar spirit—though this is not an instance

[1] *Grammar of Assent*, 5th edition, p. 403.

from his philosophy—when years ago he had strung together a *catena* of Catholic doctrines from Bull, Andrewes, and other Anglican divines, old Oxford men relate how he foresaw the objection, "But other passages from them tell a different tale." This opens an endless argument on Anglican inconsistency—endless and hopeless. It was enough for him to have got a rough *catena*—enough for the past, as much as could possibly be expected. He had never thought, as more sanguine men had, that Anglican tradition could be proved consistent; all he hoped was to show a tradition, feeble enough at times, damaged by Protestant influences, yet never actually broken. Let the future be consistent. Let the dead past bury its dead. But he could not say all this in hearing of the Puseys and Palmers who thought otherwise. He must not break up his party by his own pessimism. And so he gave the following characteristic reply: "To say this is to accuse them of inconsistency, which I leave it for their enemies to do."

And so on throughout. What Döllinger styled Newman's "subjectivity" in philosophy, though the present writer does not believe that it diminishes the real objective value of his thought, was, in the sense of personal element, most marked. A recent critic has spoken of the *Grammar of Assent* as a treatise showing how things may be taken for granted. There cannot be a greater mistake, though the subjective mode of expression in some passages partly accounts for it. Newman shows that all begin with first principles which cannot be logically proven.

He sees in himself religious first principles of which his nature assures him. He sees that those who cry out "You are taking them for granted" are themselves assuming a number of other first principles. A man who denies that human nature is normally Christian assumes it to be something different. He starts with one conception of human nature as the Christian starts with another. A man who denies that conscience reveals sin, in the Christian sense of the word, *starts* with his own different impression of what conscience conveys, and proceeds to account for his impression as being due to an offence against society, or against law, or to an inherited feeling resulting from past experiences of general utility. Cardinal Newman's conclusion is not "We all assume unwarrantably," but rather "*You* say I assume; I can at once retort that *you* assume; but in fact I do *not* assume; I see with certainty."[1] Or, as he expressed it in a letter to myself written during his last years, "The religious mind must always master much which is *unseen* to the non-religious. . . . I can't allow that a religious man has no more evidence necessarily than a non-religious."[2]

The contrast between the arbitrary assumptions of the Agnostic and the first principles which a religious mind adopts rightly and with certainty, and the tests whereby they may be distinguished, were subjects which exercised his mind, as we see from his last

[1] Cf. *Development of Religious Error*, p. 459.

[2] The Cardinal gave me permission in 1885 to make public use of any part of this letter, which is for the most part a discussion on the nature of religious knowledge.

publication in 1885, on *The Development of Religious Error*, to the very evening of life. But it would carry me too far to attempt here an analysis of that essay.

The personal element then, both in style and in matter, is most prominent. In the former this is the result of his object and his method, of helping others by his own personal influence, and by putting *himself* before them. In the latter it is an illustration of the principle which he maintains, that "egotism is true modesty." A strong man in fully revealing his own mind—its struggles and its victories—aids weaker minds in time of trial and difficulty.

Briefly it may be said that two points give the key to much of his work and influence, whether in philosophy, or in preaching, or in religious controversy, or in the guidance of individual consciences,—the power over others of his personality, and the exercise of that power with absolute simplicity to make men better than he found them. And as the peculiar power of his personality was that it appealed to such different minds, so, according to the bent and genius of each, his influence as a whole was most various. His was not simply a spiritual influence, as John Wesley's; not merely that of the dry light of philosophy, as Kant's, or Coleridge's in our own country; nor of a brilliant converser and critic, as Johnson's; nor of intellectual and imaginative power, as Carlyle's; nor of the religious poet, as Keble's; nor of the Christian counsellor to the men and women of the world, as Fénelon's or St. Francis of Sales'. It was to each man one or more of these kinds of influence; and thus it was to all a combination of them.

Some of the most remarkable published testimonies to his early power over others come from men as different from each other as Mr. J. A. Froude, Principal Shairp, Dean Church, and Mr. Mark Pattison. While he influenced intellectualists like Pattison and Froude, and men of high mental gifts like Church, intellect was not in the least a necessary qualification for the most intimate friendship with him. This fact, which aroused Mr. Mark Pattison's supercilious contempt, was part of Newman's peculiar strength. Littlemore was no assemblage of intellectual lights; it was a community of religious and devoted friends—some, as Dalgairns, men of special mental gifts, others not so. Men living in the great world also, taking part in politics or in public affairs, leant on him and appealed to him, as well as those whose life was in abstract thought or religious seclusion. To mention only a few and life-long friends, Lord Blachford, Lord Emly, and Mr. Hope Scott were as thorough in their personal allegiance to him as Dr. Pusey or Dean Church. He himself has described that assemblage of qualities which constitute the perfection of University refinement, which make up the idea of a "gentleman," if not exactly in the popular English sense, still in the highest sense of the perfection of the intellectual and social nature.[1] He tells us that men may have those

[1] The well-known description I refer to comes in *Idea of a University*, 2nd edition, pp. 305-309.

qualities and yet not be Christians; or they may have them and use the attractiveness they give simply for good. "They may subserve the education," he writes, "of a St. Francis of Sales or a Cardinal Pole; they may be the limits of the virtue of a Shaftesbury or a Gibbon. Basil and Julian were fellow-students at the schools of Athens; and one became a Saint and Doctor of the Church, the other her scoffing and relentless foe." Newman had the qualities he describes,—they were a great part of his magnetism; they pervaded his writing and his conversation; and he used the influence they gave as St. Francis or Basil would have used it, but with greater variety of gifts than either, and over a more heterogeneous collection of disciples.

Beginning, then, at Oxford among young men, his equals in age many of them, passing into the comparative obscurity of the Birmingham Oratory, living there unseen by the world at large, holding for many years no position of official importance, his personality, in a manner so subtle that it is hard fully to account for it, made itself felt over the whole country. Leading the simple consistent life of a priest, ever ready to help those who came to him or wrote to him for advice, shunning the crowd, welcoming each individual, helping each according to his character to love God and to realise the true end of life, never seeking influence for his own sake, thinking only of those he was helping, grateful for their trust, but deeply feeling its sacredness before God and his responsibility for the use he made of it, throwing himself into the position of each of those who consulted him as if each were the only one, he gained steadily in immediate influence as life went on; while the power of a devoted life, as a witness to the unseen world, made its way to the crowds who form public opinion. It would be hard to estimate the number of those who have sought his help, during the last forty years, on their road to the Catholic Church; and many more have been guided by him in other matters. In his measure, and allowing for the difference of gifts and circumstances, he carried out the kind of work done by his own St. Philip, which, early in his Catholic life, he had spoken of as the only work he had a call to do. The Cardinal's chief instruments were writing and correspondence, the Saint chose direct conversation; but the spirit of the work was the same in both cases. As St. Philip, by his love for those who leant upon him, and by his personal character, drew all men to him for guidance and advice, winning respect and esteem from Jews and Infidels as well as members of the Church, so did Newman, by the power of his personality, find himself the centre of influence among vast numbers, priests and laymen, non-Catholics as well as Catholics. The simple priest was by the popular voice called Apostle of Rome; the English Oratorian was, as a representative critic has expressed it, canonised at his death by the voice of the English people.

"Whether or not," he wrote early in his Catholic life, "I can do anything at all in St. Philip's way, at least I can do nothing in any other. Neither by my habits of life, nor by vigour of age, am I fitted for the task of authority, or of rule, or of initiation." And what was St. Philip's way? Let us read Newman's beautiful account of it. It describes his aspiration in 1852; it describes the spirit of his work done in the Catholic Church forty years later.

He lived in an age as traitorous to the interests of Catholicism as any that preceded it, or can follow it. He lived at a time when pride mounted high, and the senses held rule; a time when kings and nobles never had more of state and homage, and never less of personal responsibility and peril; when mediæval winter was receding, and the summer sun of civilisation was bringing into leaf and flower a thousand forms of luxurious enjoyment; when a new world of thought and beauty had opened upon the human mind, in the discovery of the treasures of classic literature and art. He saw the great and the gifted, dazzled by the Enchantress, and drinking in the magic of her song; he saw the high and the wise, the student and the artist, painting, and poetry, and sculpture, and music, and architecture, drawn within her range and circling round the abyss; he saw heathen forms mounting thence, and forming in the thick air:—all this he saw, and he perceived that the mischief was to be met, not with argument, not with science, not with protests and warnings, not by the recluse or the preacher, but by means of the great counter-fascination of purity and truth.

He was raised up to do a work almost peculiar in the Church: not to be a Jerome Savonarola, though Philip had a true devotion towards him and a tender memory of his Florentine house; not to be a St. Carlo, though in his beaming countenance Philip had recognised the aureole of a saint; not to be a St. Ignatius, wrestling with the foe, though Philip was termed the Society's bell of call, so many subjects did he send to it; not to be a St. Francis Xavier, though Philip had longed to shed his blood for Christ in India with him; not to be a St. Caietan, or hunter of souls, for Philip preferred, as he expressed it, tranquilly to cast in his net to gain them; he preferred to yield to the stream, and direct the current—which he could not stop—of science, literature, art, and fashion, and to sweeten and to sanctify what God had made very good and man had spoilt.

And so he contemplated as the idea of his mission, not the propagation of the faith, nor the exposition of doctrine, nor the catechetical schools: whatever was exact and systematic pleased him not; he put from him monastic rule and authoritative speech, as David refused the armour of his king. No; he would be but an ordinary individual priest as others, and his weapons should be but unaffected humility and unpretending love. All he did was to be done by the light, and fervour, and convincing eloquence of his personal character and his easy conversation. He came to the Eternal City and he sat himself down there, and his home and his family gradually grew up around him, by the spontaneous accession of materials from without. He did not so much seek his own as draw them to him. He sat in his small room, and they in their gay worldly dresses, the rich and well-born as well as the simple and illiterate, crowded into it. In the mid-heats of summer, in the frosts of winter, still was he in that low and narrow cell at San Girolamo, reading the hearts of those who came to him, and curing their souls' maladies by the very touch of his hand. . . .

In the words of his biographer, "he was all things to all men. He suited himself to noble and ignoble, young and old, subjects and prelates, learned and ignorant, and received those who were strangers to him with singular benignity, and embraced them with as much love and charity as if he had been a long while expecting them. When he was called upon to be merry he was so: if there was a demand upon his sympathy he was equally ready. He gave the same welcome to all, caressing the poor equally with the rich, and wearying himself to assist all to the utmost limits of his power. In consequence of his being so accessible and willing to receive all comers many went to him every day, and some continued for the space of thirty, nay, forty years, to visit him very often both morning and evening, so that his room went by the agreeable nickname of the Home of Christian mirth. Nay, people came to him not only from all parts of Italy, but from France, Spain, Germany, and all Christendom; and even the Infidels and Jews who had ever any communication with him revered him as a holy man." The first families of Rome, the Massimi, the Aldobrandini, the Colonna, the Altieri, the Vitelleschi, were his friends and his penitents. Nobles of Poland, grandees of Spain, knights of Malta, could not leave Rome without coming to him. Cardinals, archbishops and bishops were his intimates: Federigo Borromeo haunted his room and got the name of "Father Philip's soul." The Cardinal-Archbishops of Verona and Bologna wrote books in his honour. Pope Pius the Fourth died in his arms. Lawyers, painters, musicians, physicians, it was the same too with them. Baronius, Zazzara, and Ricci left the law at his bidding and joined his congregation, to do its work, to write the annals of the Church, and to die in the odour of sanctity. Palestrina had Father Philip's ministrations in his last moments. Animuccia hung about him during life, sent him a message after death, and was conducted by him through Purgatory to Heaven. And who was he, I say, all the while, but an humble priest, a stranger in Rome, with no distinction of family or letters, no claim of station or of office, great simply in the attraction with which a Divine Power had gifted him? And yet thus humble, thus un-ennobled, thus empty-handed, he has achieved the glorious title of Apostle of Rome.

And, in drawing to a conclusion, the present writer feels how much he has not even touched on which was essential to the Cardinal's influence. That unique gift which made one who was no orator the greatest preacher of his age; his faithfulness to his friends—"faithful and true," as he loved to say of Our Lord; his power of resentment of injury done to those he loved, or to his cause; the attractiveness which came of his sensitiveness, even of over-sensitiveness; the combination of far-seeing and dispassionate wisdom with keen and quickly-roused emotion; his tenderness for and sympathy with the distressed in faith, which made on-lookers, even fear, at times, lest, in meeting them half-way, he was losing sight of the very principles he was in reality protecting; the very "defects of his qualities," which his closest friends loved almost as they did his virtues—which made him so truly human amid his greatness; these were all part of him. And the thought of them makes me fall back upon the description with which I began as the only true one, that as Nirvana is Nirvana, so Newman was Newman.

PHILALETHES

SOME WORDS ON A MISCONCEPTION OF CARDINAL NEWMAN

It is not to be expected at the present hour that the question of miracles should receive very patient or serious consideration from those to whom the judgment of what has been called the Zeitgeist is a final test of truth. The present age, instead of learning effectually the one true lesson which Agnosticism suggests — how much there is in the supernatural region which we can neither prove nor disprove — has passed rapidly to a new Gnosticism, and considers direct Providence or Miracle not only unproved, but utterly at variance with the conclusions of physical and critical science. Consequently the title-page of a work published not long after Cardinal Newman's death, "Philomythus, an Antidote against Credulity. A discussion of Cardinal Newman's 'Essay on Ecclesiastical Miracles,' by Edwin Abbott, D.D., late Head-Master of the City of London School," is not calculated to astonish any one. Nor would the present writer have been surprised to find in it a stringent and even contemptuous criticism of Cardinal Newman's conclusions. But the wholesale condemnation of the man, which it contains, the systematic, though no doubt unintentional, misrepresentations by which this condemnation is supported, the charges which involve nothing less than accusations of habitual dishonesty in dealing with evidence, are graver matters. These charges are avowedly based on only a "partial examination" of the Cardinal's works;[1] they are preferred with an intemperate violence of language—"foulness and falsehood," "immoral shiftiness," "insolent aggressiveness," are specimens of the phrases thrown about —and they are such in their details as would have been simply impossible to one who knew either the man or his works intimately, however much he dissented from the views which those works contain. Coming from a writer of known antecedents they can only be regarded as remarkable instances of the heating and blinding force of a strong bias. The union of Christianity with belief in the miraculous is in this writer's eyes the most disastrous obstacle to the cause of religion; Catholicism is committed to that union: Newman is the most influential name among Catholics in this land. Little dreaming—apparently not able to comprehend—the extent and depth of reflection. the wide vision from different points of view, which were characteristic of the man he assails, he seizes on the work whose title promises to be most directly to his purpose—the *Essay on Ecclesiastical Miracles* —and goes through it, without to the end under-

[1] See *Philomythus*, p. 44.

standing what Newman's attitude towards miracles was. He treats his phrases and sentences as a man unacquainted with the art of watch-making would behave, if by way of ascertaining how a watch was constructed, he should hastily pull it wheel from wheel, and should suppose that scrutiny of some of the fragments taken at random, would explain to him the mechanism of the whole. By a similar process of hastily setting down passages from Newman's writings, without taking the pains to enter into his mind or to understand their organic connection, the writer has accomplished the feat of covering most of his 259 pages with an assault not on Newman, but on a lay figure, first constructed and then demolished by himself. True, he has clothed it in some of Newman's language, but as in the case of most persons who are burnt in effigy, the clothes are the only, and not very essential, point of resemblance.

I should have thought that—quite apart from any other reason—one broad consideration would have suggested to this critic that there must be a flaw somewhere in his theory. Newman lived a long life; he was often misrepresented; all did not share the extraordinary enthusiasm of his Oxford disciples. There is perhaps at the present moment in some quarters a reaction from the almost universal admiration which has lasted in England since the publication of the *Apologia*. There is in some quarters a tendency to impatience at what is thought to be his over-subtlety, his subjectivity, his rejection of broad and bold statements as inexact, his over-scrupulousness, his strong feeling—repugnant to an age in which critical and physical science have done so much—that the highest knowledge is independent of the intellectual achievements of any particular time, and finally, at the superstition attributed to the creed he ultimately adopted. Such a tendency is only a return to a view commonly taken of him years ago at Oxford by a certain school; but those who maintained it and who had also the opportunity of knowing him, pronounced, both intellectually and morally, a judgment quite inconsistent with the statements in this book. No one could be more opposed to his conclusions or to his subjectivity than J. A. Froude; no one has been less in sympathy with the subtlety—the "tortuousness" he called it—of Newman's sensitive intellectual nature than Dean Stanley; few men had less doctrinal sympathy with Newmanism than Principal Shairp, the friend of Tait. Yet read Froude's testimony to the moral depth of Newman's teaching and to the nobility of his personal character in the *Short Studies;* read Stanley's words in reference to the ethical elevation of his sermons in his Essay on the "Oxford School"; read the noble tribute paid by Shairp to his influence on the moral tone of Oxford, and you realise that those who least agreed with him entertained, where they had any right to speak from real knowledge, a conception of him utterly opposed to the conclusions of this book. Kingsley was allowed by his own admirers to have overstepped the mark; and this writer, by the pertinacity and detail of his accusations, oversteps Kingsley. He is running counter to a judgment universal among those who have had a claim to speak; and in personal judgments, as in religious, it is dangerous to violate the rule "*quod semper, quod ubique, quod ab omnibus.*" The modern Yankee has, I believe, expressed the same truth in language no less forcible, if less dignified: "You can take in some of the people for all of the time, and you can take in all of the people for some of the time; but you can't take in all of the people for all of the time": and consequently the very first impression produced by many of Dr. Abbott's charges, once their gravity is understood, is that parts of his book *must* be either not serious or not fair. He must be prepared to find them read by very many in much the same spirit as Whately's ingenious *tour de force*, which establishes the fact that Napoleon I. never existed.

However, Newman's writings are not familiar to the majority, who are, consequently, at the mercy of such a writer as this. I have already pointed out how little real knowledge there was in the chorus of admiration which we heard at the time of his death; and in such circumstances the crowd is ready to pass rapidly from the cry of "Hosanna" to that of "Crucify him." It seems necessary, then, to note in some salient instances the contrast between the real Newman and the mythical figure depicted in these pages.

The writer's general view may be summarised thus. Newman's religion was primarily one of fear;[1] there was scarcely any element of love in his religious temper[2] or in his faith.[3] His "conscience was a horror,"[4] his expressions of self-distrust were signs that he suspected himself of being shifty and insincere, and it is a serious question whether he was not really hollow at heart,[5] though the writer finally refuses to believe this. He is represented as throwing himself into the superstitions of the Catholic Church as a means of escape from the terrors and horrors of his conscience. So much for Newman's fundamental religion. But the bulk of the book is directed towards showing *how* he advocated the beliefs to which his fears had led him; and here he is described as using language with scarcely any regard for truth, with special pleading, systematic, habitual, and barefaced, though extremely clever and effective with the dupes of his fascination.[6] His great object was to deceive others, having first deceived himself, into thinking that his conclusions were logically tenable.[7] With this end he devised his theory of belief;[8] with this end he altered or suppressed inconvenient phrases in the evidence for facts he wanted to prove.[9] With this end he cultivated for the purpose of obscuring the truth, a use of words "verging on immoral shiftiness," and studied all the arts of rhetorical deceit,[10] which the writer exposes at great length. He was habitually un-

[1] *e.g.*, p. 35. [2] p. 38. [3] p. 81. [4] p. 37. [5] pp. 41, 42. 82.
[6] Cf. chapters 8 and 9, *passim*. [7] *ibid.* [8] pp. 74 *seq.*
[9] pp. 4 *seq.*, 14, 207. [10] pp. 211 *seq.*

truthful with himself,[1] and his great power in the use of language furnished a "grace" of expression "calculated to conceal the underlying foulness and falsehood" of his method. This is, I think, a true summary of the indictment, which is however qualified by occasional assertions which are incapable of being reconciled with the detailed charges in the book, that he was aiming at sincerity, and that he was striving with all his might to be honest. If he was striving he is certainly not represented as striving with any success. So much, then, for the general accusation, of which his view of miracles is a particular instance. Newman was bent on accepting miracles however weak the evidence; and if the evidence would not do as he found it, with careful carelessness he omitted or altered words in the documents he cited, so as to make it appear stronger than it really was.

At the root of all this is a great psychological mistake, which must be shortly noticed before special instances are considered. The writer when preparing his brief takes note of certain peculiar intellectual gifts in Newman; but he quite misses the guiding principle in his employment of these gifts. He sees mental peculiarities, but he misses the candid and deep intellectual insight which was essential to their true nature; and consequently he identifies these gifts and qualities with a character diametrically opposed to Newman's. He sees truly an extraordinary subtlety of mind, great rhetorical power, a changeableness in

[1] pp. 211 *seq.*

the use of words, a power of evasion in argument, a method which leads him on occasion summarily to put aside detailed considerations that tell against his conclusions, a conception of an ever-present Providence, which to thinkers of a certain order must appear superstitious. But while the man who had these characteristics was beyond all things truthful with himself, and sensitively alive to every fact which told against his conclusions, while he used his intellectual gifts in analysing, arranging, representing to his readers the perplexed and intricate web of the universe of spiritual and phenomenal fact as he saw it, with its apparently irreconcilable contradictions;—though at the same time he indicated the direction in which he looked for the harmony which he believed to be real though unperceived;—the writer of this book pictures him as intent only on bending facts to his purpose and doing the work of a special pleader. Yet this conception of Newman contradicts what is plain on the very surface of his writings. Far from taking pleasure in representing evidence as persuasive, he is constantly reminding us of its insufficiency, as contrasted with the numerous considerations *not* in evidence, which determine our deepest convictions. His own most intense belief was in God's existence; and yet to him it was most fraught with difficulty, most hard to justify by evidence.[1] He disparages the argument from causation;[2] he is not satisfied with the argument from design;[3] he looks on the world at large (apart from

[1] *Apologia*, p. 239. [2] *Grammar of Assent*, fourth edition, p. 66.
[3] *University Sermons*, p. 70.

the human conscience) as "giving the lie" to this great truth of which his whole being was full.[1] Again, the Catholic Church was to him a great fact which, as viewed in the light of the anticipations raised by conscience, was in some sense its own evidence. Yet, instead of idealising its history to make it persuasive, as some ecclesiastical historians have done,—finding Popes perfect, scandals absent, popular Catholic religion admirable,—he notes with cold scrutiny all the flaws in the "earthen vessels" in which the treasure of faith has been preserved. Popular religion must be, he has said, corrupt.[2] *Malaria* is at the foot of St. Peter's rock.[3] Popes themselves have been, on occasion, he sees, a scandal to Christendom. Catholics are often apparently no better—perhaps apparently they are worse—than the non-Catholics by whom they are surrounded.[4] Similarly when defending the simple unquestioning faith of a Christian in God and Christ, he sees each point that can be urged against it—how it seems to violate the primary laws of inquiry and reasoning, how hard at first sight it is to distinguish it from bigotry or senseless credulity. Indeed, so far is he from being a special pleader that, by comparison, Mr. Leslie Stephen's estimate seems discerning, that he held that the human mind can prove contradictory positions, and was thus a sceptic. This view, at least, recognises a marked feature in his method which the other simply fails to account for.

[1] *Apologia*, p. 241. [2] See also *Difficulties of Anglicans*, i. pp. 229 *seq.* [3] *Ibid.* ii. p. 297. [4] *Essay on Development*, p. 322.

No doubt, here and there, the connecting link and true interpretation of his deepest convictions, and of the facts which seemed to tell against them, broke upon Newman with comparative clearness; and then his rhetorical gift gave him unsurpassed power in presenting forcibly to others the trains of thought which had come to him through years of struggle with difficulty. And a part of this peculiar power lay in a very delicate appreciation of the effect of each of his words on the reader's mind. He made his reader feel the difficulty which had so long troubled himself, and then brought the solution home with well-calculated force. But to confuse the pathway he made, and showed to others, from fact to fact, each recognised with scrupulous exactness, and from these facts to ultimate convictions, due to what were to him an overwhelming crowd of unmistakable truths witnessed by the human conscience and by experience, with a clever and shifty progress towards a desired conclusion, with little care for exactness as to fact, and great readiness to see things as he wished, is one of the most curious identifications of opposite methods and opposite intellectual and moral temperaments which the present writer has ever met. The very lines on Newman's face, the very expression of his features told of what his writing bears detailed witness to,—his critical, careful, conscientious recognition of all that was perplexing and apparently contradictory; as the smile which would break forth now and again had in it something which spoke of the vision of the unseen, which promised an ultimate solution, in another world, but never in this.

And even if this vision appeared to some—as to J. A. Froude—to be mixed up with the delusions of superstition, and calculated to vitiate his conclusions, the devotion to truth which characterised both his critical and his mystical side could not even by them be unnoticed, if they knew really the man or his writings.[1]

And with the clue afforded by the habits of thought I have been considering, it is easy to understand that what this writer takes for something like "immoral shiftiness" in language was really only the attempt, in view of the extraordinary delicacy of his insight into the complex problems he considered, to express more and more accurately truths which he always held to transcend words. Truths simple to others were complex to him, because he recognised all the assumptions, prepossessions, and previous questions which they involved. His self-criticism and the criticisms of others perpetually led him to verbal alterations. Many such have a history well known to persons now living, which I cannot here enter into, but which throws an amusing light on the elaborate and suspicious exposure in this book of artifice, where no artifice whatever was intended. His subtlety was the subtlety of the highest and most critical fastidiousness, and his changes of expression all had a definite drift towards a conclusion more and more clearly seen, but which he never hoped to express quite to his satisfaction. His power of evasion was used in protection of the true proportion of an argument as a whole. Truth

[1] "Newman's whole life had been a struggle for truth" (Froude, *Short Studies*, iv. p. 326).

would suffer, and not gain from undue space being devoted to what was minor and irrelevant. And the same sense of due proportion led him to feel that difficulties in the details of a proof which was overwhelming in the mass, should be put aside. These peculiarities in Newman's method were really inseparable from a very fine sense of fact; though some of his facts would be, in the eyes of a sceptic, the delusions of mysticism. And if they were used to prevent irrelevant facts from being unduly prominent with his readers, this was due not to deception, but to an extraordinarily wide and candid vision in himself.

Passing now to the broad and definite charges preferred in the book, it is a significant fact at starting that the author has curiously missed the object of the very essay he is criticising, and ought to be well acquainted with, the *Essay on Ecclesiastical Miracles.* He has treated it as what he expected to find it—as a polemical and critical essay professing to justify belief in miracles in general, and in certain miracles in particular. Now I think that any one who has read the essay without this initial preconception will have seen that it is not a polemical, but in some sense a philosophical essay; that it is not designed to prove the miraculous or particular miracles to the world at large, but rather to trace the relations of belief in the miraculous to various ethical tempers, and various conceptions of Christianity: and, still more, to exhibit in concrete instances, the attitude towards the evidence for miracles which is natural and logical for one who accepts the Catholic view of

God's active Providence in the visible church, with all its corollaries.

But before enlarging on this, I must deal with the previous questions of which I have spoken. First, as to the statement that Cardinal Newman's religion was a religion of fear—that "the love of God as it is described in the New Testament appears to have been either absent or quite latent in him," and that the absence of love "was not compensated by any profound trust in God's infinite justice and righteousness" (*Philomythus*, p. 38),—it is contradicted so fully throughout his sermons and other ethical writings, both Anglican and Catholic, that it becomes a curious question which of them his critic has studied carefully. A recent writer confronted him with a passage from the *Dream of Gerontius*, and the critic, to whom the passage was evidently new, replied that that only referred to an anticipation of the love of God in the next world. That Newman recognised that there is no realisation of what God is without fear—and deep fear—is true enough. But it was this very realisation of what God is which gave to Newman's love a depth and intensity which it could not otherwise have had. His fear was a necessary condition to a love as much deeper than the easy-going confidence advocated in these pages, as God is, even to our finite apprehension, lovable beyond the best of men. His position is exactly defined in his sermon on "Love the one thing needful," in which, after describing "a system of fear," he says "it is not religion, which really consists not in the mere fear of God but in His love;

or, if it be religion, it is but the religion of devils." I do not think it will repay us to dwell long on a charge which can only be refuted as fully as it really admits of being refuted by more extracts than I have space for. I will content myself with setting down one passage from his sermons which gives some indication of the feelings which possessed him.

The contemplation of [God] and nothing but it is able fully to open and relieve the mind; to unlock, occupy, and fix our affections. We may indeed love created things with great intenseness, but such affection when disjoined from the love of the Creator is like a stream running in a narrow channel—impetuous, vehement, turbid. The heart runs out, as it were, only at one door; it is not an expanding of the whole man. Created natures cannot open to us or elicit the ten thousand mental senses which belong to us, and through which we really live. None but the presence of our Maker can enter us, for to none besides can the whole heart in all its thoughts and feelings be unlocked and subjected! "Behold," He says, "I stand at the door and knock; if any man hear My voice and open the door, I will come unto him, and will sup with him, and he with Me." "My Father will love him, and We will come unto him, and make Our abode with him." "God has sent forth the spirit of His Son into your hearts." "God is greater than our heart, and knoweth all things." It is this feeling of simple and absolute confidence and communion which soothes and satisfies those to whom it is vouchsafed. We know that even our nearest friends enter into us but partially, and hold intercourse with us only at times, whereas the consciousness of a perfect and enduring presence, and it alone, keeps our heart open. Withdraw the object on which it rests and it will relapse again into its confinement and constraint; and in proportion as it is limited, either to certain seasons or to certain affections, the heart is straitened and distressed. If it be not over-bold to say it—He who is infinite alone can be its measure. He alone can answer to that mysterious assemblage of feelings and thoughts which it has within it.—(*Parochial Sermons*, vol. v. p. 318.)

What is to be said of this? Did St. Augustine himself ever convey the sense of deeper, more absorbing, more overwhelming love of God; or of more trustful confidence in His guidance and protection? And this is the man of whom "absence of love" is gravely alleged.

Let us now turn to the question of Newman's theory of religious belief. The writer seizes on the phrase "belief on a probability," which Newman has used in the *Apologia* and elsewhere, and of which I shall have something to say presently. He sees in it only an artifice for justifying belief in any superstition, for which *any* reason can be alleged. Consequently he springs to the conclusion that it is a very dangerous doctrine—whatever it may be. There is no love in Newman's belief, he maintains; and religious certainty is not with him connected either with moral action, or with religious love; it is all a matter of probability. What is to be said of this? The student of Newman knows that he has been charged with connecting faith *too closely* with moral goodness and its reward; that his theory of probability is an attempt to analyse not only a *connection* between Faith and Love, but the proposition that Faith is in a true sense *based* on Love. "Love is the parent of Faith," he writes in Tract 85. And his critic, resting on a few isolated passages which he has not understood, blames Newman for denying what he may be considered to have affirmed almost too emphatically. I will place Newman's account of himself and his critic's account of him on these matters in parallel columns, italicising portions. And I will take my representation of Newman's mind from his most suggestive volume on the subject—the *University Sermons*—which he devoted almost exclusively to the analysis of religious belief and the investigation of its basis, as I have said elsewhere, though the author seems to be unaware of this, and amusingly corrects my word "exclusively," and suggests that I meant "extensively" (p. 2).

PHILOMYTHUS.

The emotions of *Hope, Love, Faith, seem to be altogether out of court*, to have no place, no right to say a word, in the formation of religious certitude, *nor is the "acting" to be moral action*, beneficent action, that kind of action which appears to be contemplated in the words, "If any man do his will he shall know of the doctrine whether it be of God." *It is to be a piling up of probabilities, a supplying oneself with a logical basis* (p. 81).

CARDINAL NEWMAN.

The safeguard of Faith is a right state of heart. This it is which gives it birth; it also disciplines it. . . . It is *holiness, or dutifulness*, or the new creation, or the spiritual mind, however we word it, which is the quickening and *illuminating principle of true faith*, giving it eyes and hands and feet. It is *Love which forms it out of the rude chaos into an image of Christ.* . . . . "Ye believe not because ye are not of My sheep, as I said unto you. My sheep hear My voice, and I know them, and they follow Me." . . . . *What is here said about exercises of Reason in order to believing?* What is there not said of *sympathetic feeling, of newness of spirit, of Love?*—(*University Sermons*, new edition, p. 235.)

Take again the following:—

PHILOMYTHUS.

We are to believe in God and in Christ on the same

CARDINAL NEWMAN.

It is written in the Prophets, "And they shall be

grounds as we are to believe in the liquefaction of St. Januarius' blood; only in the former case the probabilities are by some mysterious process (not illustrated by anything in Nature) converted into a "certitude," whereas in the latter case they remain untransmuted, merely "beliefs" or "pious opinion." . . . . Practical atheism being that state of mind in which a man believes in God *without a basis of Love*, Newman, if in his heart of hearts he had adopted this theory, would have been a practical atheist (pp. 81-2).

all taught of God." Every man, therefore, that hath heard and hath learnt of the Father, cometh unto Me. It is the new life and not the natural reason which leads the soul to Christ. Does a child trust his parents because he has proved to himself that they are such, and that they are able and desirous to do him good, or from the instinct of affection? We believe *because we love.* How plain a truth! What gain is it to be wise above that which is written? Why, O men, deface with your minute and arbitrary philosophy the simplicity, the reality, the glorious liberty of the inspired teaching?—(*University Sermons*, p. 236.)

I have said enough on this head. One who has so "partially examined" Newman as to attack him for denying what were central and emphatic points in his teaching, cannot claim to be followed throughout the innumerable detailed mistakes which arise from his initial error, and which further reading would have enabled him to correct for himself.

It may be worth while, however, briefly to indicate what appears the source of the writer's missing what most readers of Newman are familiar with. On the first point—the absence of love in Newman's religious *ethos*—he implies[1] that he is to some extent open

[1] See p. 44.

to correction from those who know Newman's works better than he; though we may remark that it is an unusual course to bring such heavy charges against a man on an avowedly uncertain basis. But on the other two, which are concerned with his theory of certitude and on which the writer proudly says that he does "not speak under correction" (p. 45), a word more must be said. Newman was dealing with a question which from the days of the Academics has vexed thoughtful minds, the question how to justify theoretically our practical certainties. Of course the religious application of the question was the most prominent; but as any reader of his varied and suggestive treatment of the subject will see, the *difficulty* concerned all knowledge; and in its religious application the primary truths of Theism and the supernatural rather than the details of dogma were uppermost in his mind. In the two great works in which he expressly deals with the subject—the *Grammar of Assent* and the *University Sermons*—this is especially evident. Beginning with the difficulty of ascertaining sufficient logical grounds for the confident belief each man has in such truths as the fact that unexplored parts of Greenland exist, or even that Great Britain is an island—for the nature of the proof is for most persons cumulative, and each reason by itself is theoretically liable to error—and rising to our belief in God, he treats the subject with that "sure and piercing judgment" which Dean Church has happily described as his characteristic. The fundamental question is: Is certitude a possible thing at all?[1] His language varies a good deal, and the careful reader will see that the difficulty haunted him through life; but he got nearer and nearer to its solution, his last words on the subject being published in the *Contemporary Review* in 1885. There are here and there modes of expression which to one unfamiliar with his writings seem paradoxical. And again the occasional prominence of psychological observation as to how the mind *does* act, when the reader is anxious to know how it should act, has caused some thinkers to miss a great deal which he contributes, by implication, to the deeper problem. The difficulty which begins in the possibility that in recalling and analysing the grounds for belief in such indubitable facts as the insular character of this country, memory may err as to any one of the recollected facts or proofs which are essential to its justification, and the testimony on which we depend may in any one case be false; that this may theoretically be so in any case, and therefore *theoretically* in all cases; and that consequently a belief really certain is *theoretically* based on probable reasoning, finds its parallel in Faith and religious conviction, in which reasons for trust and confidence may not be fully expressible or theoretically justifiable by the individual. And again in the special case of religious belief, admitting that goodness and love are an essential part of its deepest basis, the question arises: May not a belief so grounded be only delusive fanaticism? How distinguish merely

[1] *Grammar of Assent*, fifth edition, p. 228.

emotional love which leads to delusion from that religious love which claims to represent the outcome of our highest reasonable nature? (cf. *University Sermons*, new edition, p. 236 *note*). Of this fundamental question his critic gets no real glimpse. He sees only in Newman's theory an attempt to get some principles which will justify him in accepting the liquefaction of St. Januarius' blood and the whole mass of the superstitions of Rome. Thus he grasps at isolated statements in ignorance of Newman's mind, draws his own conclusions, and must inevitably find himself confronted (as we have seen) with words of Newman's directly contrary to conclusions which are based on a complete misapprehension. He sways backwards and forwards, treating "probability" at one moment as belief consciously reflected on as doubtful,[1] when Newman is all the while trying to explain how we are conscious of *certainty* or of undoubting assent, and at another as "provableness,"[2] when Newman is showing that complete explicit proof is just what we cannot attain.

The writer never sees that he is cutting the ground from under his own feet by his assault; that Newman is really inquiring with great delicacy into the nature of that very Faith and Love which his critic professes to be the basis of his own Christianity, but fails to justify against the Agnostic. Newman as the reflective thinker, as the man to whom himself and his Creator were ever the two most luminous of realities (*Apologia*, p. 5), as the man who is

[1] pp. 53, 69, 74, 79. [2] p. 71.

bringing all his gifts of profound analysis and religious imagination to justify belief in God and Immortality, never enters into the limited range of this writer's vision; and while the great Oxford thinker's own mind and soul are concentrated on securing from assault those primary truths on which the religious life of every Christian depends, the critic can only see an artificial theory, planned with the express purpose of tricking unwary souls into believing in miraculous Madonnas with moving eyes, or giving their confidence to priests intent on fraud and extortion. He only once catches a glimpse of the very necessity of justifying, for the satisfaction of those in whom questions inevitably arise, that loving trust which is popularly called Faith; and then simply remarks that to "entertain questions of this kind leads to insanity."[1] He does not see, with the full tide of Agnosticism at his door, what Newman foresaw fifty years ago, that the question will force itself upon many a religious mind—Is my loving trust a groundless delusion? Is it a sentiment corresponding to no reality, as the Agnostics say? And where Newman with patient anxiety devotes volumes to this question, the critic, hardly looking at his solution in its fundamental application, but scared beyond words at the superstitious horrors it will be made to sanction, endeavours with blind violence to dislocate and disable words and sentences

[1] The writer says this with reference to the case which Newman so often places as parallel to religious Faith of personal trust;—belief that a certain course of action is inconsistent with this or that person's character. (See *Philomythus*, p. 62.)

whereby Newman meant to convey principles with which no Christian can dispense, however little many may consider them applicable, as Newman ultimately did, to belief in the Catholic Church. All the deep, candid, careful analysis of the springs of Faith, all the subtle introspection into the ultimate unconscious basis of every degree of belief; all the fine comparisons and contrasts between the definiteness and shallowness of the unbelieving view of the world, and the imperfect form and yet conscious depth of the religious view; between the conclusions of mere logic and the conviction of the whole man; between vivid living belief and deep restful certitude; between the credulity of superstition and the confident faith which is protected by love; between the formal dogmatism of bigotry and the teachableness of faith, and the wide, calm, all-seeing vision of the spirit of wisdom—all this remains unnoticed, as this writer blunders on, eagerly moving his single eye, looking for St. Walburga's oil in one corner, Papal infallibility in another, Newman's own hollow heart in a third. Oh, the pity of it! The handiwork which Newman fashioned so delicately and with such infinite pains, adding each year to the very end a finishing touch—new thoughts and new words as fresh truths broke on him, or old truths were seen better—all the beautiful and delicate ware utterly and hopelessly smashed by the invader, as he advances with bovine stride, wholly unconscious of the value of the Dresden figures, of the antiquity of the Crown Derby, of the history of the Worcester vases, of the irredeemable and Philistine destruction he is perpetrating in his wild-goose chase after superstitions and deceptions. "Sad work, my masters, sad work!"

Turning now to Newman's Essay on "Ecclesiastical Miracles," it is, as I have said, a work on quite a different plan from this critic's conception of it. It is in some sense a psychological investigation which must be read in connection with his general Oxford teaching, on the relations of certain preconceptions to the view which is naturally taken of the evidence for miracles. Newman admitted in great part Hume's contention as to the antecedent improbability of all miracles whatsoever. He saw, however, that once the Scriptural miracles are believed—once miracle is admitted at all into the category of established fact—*logically* the deep incredulity which from Hume's standpoint was not unreasonable, must give way. He contrasts the two views of Christianity which were current at the time he wrote—the one allowing the Scripture miracles, allowing that a mass of supernatural agencies and interferences had set the Christian scheme afloat, and maintaining that the Creator had afterwards, so to say, retired from His creation; the other viewing the great outlines of Church history as providential, looking on Catholic sanctity, and the activity of Catholic life, and the great fact of the Catholic Church as tokens of the presence of God among us, and contemplating alleged miracles throughout the history of Christendom, as possible instances, *primâ facie*, of His active Providence. The former view he held to be illogical. Denying so much, it should deny more. Or, admitting so much, it should admit more. He indicates the two conceptions of the universe which are philosophically tenable—of fixed and uniform law on the one hand, evolving steadily, consistently excluding any direct supernatural action: and, on the other hand, the conception of Providence as ever controlling the universe, by fixed laws as general rules, but not without power and will to direct or modify the working of the laws it has made. And these two conceptions, which should logically be in permanent opposition, were, he shows, by the inconsistent school to which I have referred, *both* adopted—one in reference to the Christian scheme in the present, the other in reference to the rise of Christianity and the Scripture miracles which they accepted. Finally, if the providential conception be consistently adopted, if all that is involved in allowing the truth of the Scriptural miracles is realised and the Catholic position accepted, the weight lawfully attaching to evidence for miracles in general, and for special miracles in particular, is materially affected. On the other hand, the nature of alleged miracles is considered by him, and the dangers of credulity and the risk of deception are taken into account. And suggestions as to the reasonable attitude of a Catholic in view of all these considerations, form the scope of the rest of the Essay.

This, then, is the fundamental purpose and plan of the Essay—not to *prove* the miraculous nor to *prove* individual miracles—for this would involve on Newman's principles a previous proof of the divinity and true character of the Catholic Church—but to sketch the actual views of the evidence in question as a psychological study; to sketch the reasonable views according as one or another set of first principles is adopted as a logical study; and then more fully to apply the Catholic first principles to individual cases, for the benefit primarily of his Oxford disciples, as a chapter in the Catholic theology which the Tracts had been developing. With the same dramatic power with which he drew out in his Dublin Lectures the contrast between heathen and Christian in ethical temper, or with which he depicted in the *University Sermons* the alternative views of sound reasoning adopted respectively by the man of the world and by St. Paul—the wisdom of the world and the foolishness of the Gospel—he depicts in the Essay on "Ecclesiastical Miracles," the "ethical incredulity" of Douglas and Middleton, he enters into the logical incredulity of Hume, and he draws out, more fully, the lawful effect on our attitude towards the evidence for miracles, of a belief—which so many readers will refuse to entertain as worth serious consideration—in a visible Church under an active Providence. "Our view of the evidence," he wrote, "will practically be decided by our views on theology."

His critic, quite missing this central point, is throughout beating the air. He is in the difficulty of having to deal with an apparent contradiction. He thinks that he must have his eyes eagerly open to detect Newman's sharp practice in proving his monstrous superstitions; and then he is disconcerted when he finds time after time that Newman, after all his cunning and special pleading on behalf of a miracle, draws a very hesitating conclusion as to the amount of credence to be attached to it. Thoroughly exasperated, the critic concludes that "all his inquiries were farces."[1] But he has no dream of the true fact—that the logical plan of the Essay is such as to make Newman comparatively *indifferent* whether or no he ends by establishing this or that particular miracle beyond question. The author repeatedly says that Newman in selecting his nine miracles ought to have chosen the best attested, and must have meant to do so.[2] He laughs at miracle after miracle as a specimen of what professes to be proved by "cogent and complete" evidence. But to have so selected his instances would have been to have reasoned on quite different lines from those chosen by Newman, who expressly says (p. 228), "It does not strictly fall within the scope of this Essay to pronounce upon the truth or falsehood of this or that miraculous narrative;" and he adds as his reason for looking into the evidence at all in individual cases "to throw off the abstract and unreal character which attends a course of reasoning."

He chose, then, certain well-known miraculous stories, chiefly from the history he was editing, *avowedly* on the ground, not that they were better

[1] *Philomythus*, p. 156.

[2] Near the end of the book he intimates a doubt, however, whether Newman "recognised the duty" of doing so at first.

established, but that they were "more celebrated than the rest" (p. 134). Their finding their way into the pages of history no doubt marked them off from mere fables, and gave them a certain *primâ facie* claim; but no more than this. He probably did not know at starting how he should stand in reference to this or that one, when he should have sifted the evidence in each case. But they afforded the opportunity of exhibiting, in the case of conspicuous instances, the application of the principles he had sketched as logically following from the Catholic position; and these were applied with singular delicacy and candour.

One more point must be noted briefly. Whereas, generally speaking, Newman, in commending one or another miracle to a Catholic's belief, has no thought beyond that sort of belief which is a basis of devotion, his critic never grasps this as a real state of mind, and often assumes that such devotional belief must have a depth and certainty almost parallel to belief in God. In words he recognises "pious opinion," but he never gets any true insight into that attitude of mind which has so large a share in all Catholic devotion—the imaginative dwelling on tokens of the unseen, whose genuineness can never be proved to demonstration, and *may* be seriously doubted. He says in one place[1] that, surely, doubt as to the authenticity of a relic must make devotion to it impossible,

[1] "If in any of these 'devotions' the thought of 'probability' steps in, must it not be fatal?" he writes, after quoting Newman's statement, "Who can really pray to a Being about whose existence he is seriously in doubt?" (*Philomythus*, p. 236.)

just as doubt of God's existence makes prayer impossible; a most curious evidence of what I am noting. The difference is this, that while devotion to the relic involves the thought of God as the ultimate rest of the mind and heart, which thought remains even if the relic is not what it was supposed to be, prayer to God begins and ends in Him. This applies to other objects of devotion—to possible miracles, to providences. A lover who knows that he is loved dwells on what he takes to be a token of love—of a feeling of whose existence he is certain. Suppose he is mistaken—suppose Edith Plantagenet had not seen Sir Kenneth, and had dropped the rose by accident—still his feeling as he kisses the rose is not futile or given in vain. He passes, through the token which is more or less probable, to the love which is (I am supposing) certain. And so a Catholic dwells on that which bears evidence of being providential, or even miraculous, passing through the sign of which he may not be certain, to the constant presence of Providence of which he *is* certain. And devotion may remain when all thought of authenticity is gone. Hallowed shrines may raise the heart to God, as scenes of historic worship, after the legends which had clustered round them have been, for the individual, disproved. They may help devotion, not as Edith's rose which she dropped, but as her picture, which the knight has gained possession of without her knowledge;—which enables him to imagine that she is present while he knows that she is absent. If "belief"—when there *is* a belief—meant absolute certainty, no doubt the dangers of credulity would be present; but it does not: and its primary object is not intellectual, but devotional. The ultimate rest of the lover's confidence is the love of another; and the ultimate rest of a Catholic's unalterable conviction in such matters is that Providence of which the particular instance or token is a suggestion, and may or may not be a manifestation.

So much for the primary mistakes which make the bulk of this book simply beside the mark. The author expected to find a work of one kind; Newman proposed to write a work of quite a different kind; and to the end his critic cannot get over his indignation at being baulked of his prey—at finding Newman refuse to make test cases, for him to criticise, of particular ecclesiastical miracles. An example of this is worth giving before concluding this part of the subject. Having furiously demolished (as he supposes) the evidence for the miracle of the Thundering Legion—the thunderstorm which Eusebius and Tertullian refer to as supposed to have come in answer to the prayers of the Christian soldiers of Marcus Aurelius—he reaches Newman's own conclusion, that the thunderstorm *occurred*, but "whether through miracle or not we cannot say for certain, but more probably not through miracle in the philosophical sense of the word. All we know and all we need know is that 'He made darkness His secret place, His pavilion round about Him, with dark water and thick clouds to cover Him. The Lord thundered out of Heaven, and the Highest gave His thunder, hailstones and coals of fire. He sent out His arrows and scattered them, He sent forth His lightnings and destroyed them.' " The critic, who endeavours all through to give the impression that Newman is selecting miracles whose evidence he thinks "cogent and complete," and who had been longing to turn over the page and find Newman quite sure that he had got hold of a miracle, is highly irritated at this conclusion, and writes as follows:

> Now this would be all very well for the conclusion of a sermon, but it is not well, it is very ill, for the conclusion of an "inquiry" into a particular miracle, which if it can be proved true by "cogent and complete evidence" will afford a basis for "recommending" a great number of other ecclesiastical miracles to the "devout attention of the reader." For the serious "inquirer" into one of the alleged nine great historical miracles of post-Apostolic Christendom it is mere trifling to be told that "*all he need know is the truth of Psalm* xviii. 11-14." But the fact is that Newman *is* trifling. All his proposed inquiries are farces, and this is but one among many proofs of their farcical nature.

And yet if this writer had taken more pains to understand Newman, he would have seen that the passage is simply an illustration of a view which Newman had thought out very carefully. What he means—and what is so beautifully expressed in the citation from the 18th Psalm—is that the important point at issue is *not* between what is philosophically speaking an interruption of a permanent and fixed law and what is not; but between the conception of an universe whose *phenomena* proceed uniformly by blind necessity, and an universe in which Providence, in ways of which we can know little or nothing, is accessible to our prayers and guides the course of events. The storm was, he says, probably an answer to prayer; and that is the important thing. The question as to whether this involved an actual breach of a law otherwise universal, or could be effected by means which Providence habitually employs, is a far less important one, as being mainly a speculative and not a practical one. Had the writer understood this —and it is a view with which any thorough student of Newman is familiar—he would have seen that the remark "all we need know," etc., far from showing that the inquiry was "a farce," has a most definite and clear meaning.

That Providence *versus* blind necessity *is* the primary issue—that far from the idea of fixed laws being the product of "exact thought," which is superseding the antiquated idea of Providence, the two conceptions have always been rivals, entertained by opposite schools, is a view which runs through several of Cardinal Newman's unpublished *memoranda* on religious philosophy, which were by his desire placed in my hands after his death.

In a *memorandum* dated Sept. 13, 1861, for example, he writes thus:

To my mind it is wonderful that able men like [A. B.] should take for granted that the notion of fixed laws is a new idea of modern times which is superseding, and to supersede the old idea of a Providence—referring to Mr. Darwin and Mr. Buckle who [are] developing the new truths in the physical and moral worlds. Why, it is the old idea of Fate or Destiny which we find in Homer. It is no new and untried idea, but it is the old antagonist of the idea of Providence. Between the philosophies of Providence and Fate there has been a contest from the beginning. Fate may have new and better arguments now, but Providence has been able to stand against it for 3000 years, and there is no reason why it should not keep its ground still, though the philosophy of Fate may still have followers.

And the relation of miracle itself to the ordinary course of nature—its respect, so to say, for the laws it supersedes, is referred to in a *memorandum* dated Sept. 3, 1865.

Some miracles, as the raising the dead, certainly are not a continuation or augmentation of natural processes, but most are: *e.g.* there is said to be something like manna in the desert ordinarily, and the sacred narrative mentions a *wind* as blowing up the waters of the Red Sea—and so in numerous other miracles. It is a confirmation of this to look at Gibbon's "Five Causes of Christianity." We do not deny them, but only say they are not sufficient—*i.e.* the spread of Christianity was something more than natural.

Once more, in September 1861, we have the following expression of a view somewhat similar to Dean Mansel's—that *philosophically* miracle is only parallel to the interference of human volition in the blind sequence of physical cause and effect:

Is not human volition in its action upon mechanical processes, a miracle? I put out my hand and stop the pendulum of a clock. The clock stops. Again, I am falling. I catch hold of a beam, and I stop the action of gravity. Here is a force, volition, which impedes, or strengthens, or quickens, as the case may be, the operation of physical laws. . . . Now, what is a miracle in theological science but the interference of such an extra-physical cause, viz. of a Being, not hypothesised for the occasion, but known already to exist as a moral governor by means of the conscience? Again, as the hand of a showman may be so introduced into clockwork or the like as not to obtrude itself on our notice in the effects it produces, so divine interpositions may really take place, yet without a manifest *criterion* of their occurring.

The space I have occupied warns me to a conclusion. And yet there is another feature of Dr. Abbott's book which its critic cannot leave unnoticed. The great contrast in intellectual temper accounts in part for the writer's failure to understand the Cardinal intellectually. But, even if his work be looked at only in the details of its literary criticisms, the failure to represent at all accurately the Cardinal's arguments and authorities is a very serious blemish, which marks its character still more pointedly as a partisan indictment. I have already pointed out some instances of this (*Spectator*, April 25, 1891); and the *Guardian* (May 20) has mentioned others. I will give one specimen here—briefly, as my limits require.

Mrs. Humphry Ward has been content, in dealing with the controversy, to cite this writer's criticism on Newman's treatment of the Thundering Legion as a case plainly showing his unreasoning credulity. I, on the other hand, am quite content that any one who wishes to form an opinion as to the worth and spirit of this work, and the temper of the Cardinal's book, should do no more than read carefully the twenty pages (pp. 241-60) in which Newman deals with this story, and the five pages (152-6) in which his treatment is criticised in *Philomythus*.

Let it be borne in mind that the critic throughout

takes no absolute line against belief in answers to prayer, or in special Providences, and that his criticism on Newman is that he does not deal honestly with *facts*, and that he makes out facts to have occurred which never *did* occur.

This being so, let me put down the logical order of Newman's section on the Thundering Legion. (1) He gives the testimony of Apollinaris and Tertullian, and the words of Eusebius, in which that testimony is introduced, to the effect that the thunder-storm came in answer to the prayers of Christian soldiers. (2) *He dismisses their evidence on account of its inaccuracy*, "the evidences *as* evidences are not true" (p. 243). (3) He examines the evidence in both cases, showing that its inaccuracies are not fatal to the broad facts of the story being *possibly* true. (4) He finally puts the statements of Tertullian and Apollinaris out of court as reliable evidence for the facts as a whole, and proves the storm and its effects by reference to pagan authorities and monuments, etc. (pp. 248-50). (5) Allowing (on these authorities) that there was a storm which scattered the enemy and delivered the Romans from drought, he says that "from the general history of the times" (p. 250) we may be sure that there were Christians in the army, and we "may be sure also, even before we have definite authority for the fact, that they offered up prayers for deliverance." (6) Then he accepts the statements to *this* effect of Eusebius, Apollinaris, and Tertullian, *not on the sole ground of their evidence* (which he has already described as untrustworthy), but as a confirmation of what was practically certain beforehand. So little weight does he attach to their words *as* evidence that he contemplates in a foot-note Moyle's suggestion that there were few or no Christians in the army (p. 251); and instead of setting the evidence of Tertullian and the rest against this he says, "This is an objection which, if valid, strikes deeper than any of those which I have noticed in the text." No doubt his own conclusion is that Moyle's objection is probably unfounded, and that "on the whole, we may conclude that the facts of this memorable occurrence are as the early Christian writers state them"; a conclusion substantially identical, it will be remembered, with Bishop Lightfoot's; but throughout is maintained Newman's plan of setting down the evidence "for and against," and leaving his readers to draw their conclusion from it. Throughout we have the union of readiness to give a providential *interpretation*, with caution in accepting for certain convenient *facts*.

Be it noted that the whole evidence for the remarkable fact of the thunderstorm and its effects is based on the heathen writers and monuments, whereas the whole criticism in the work before us is on the evidence of *Tertullian and Apollinaris, which as evidence for the main facts Newman has expressly dismissed, and on that of Eusebius, on which, in itself, Newman lays no stress.* The impression which the reader of the book gets is that their evidence, which Newman really treats as in great measure unreliable, is his main or indeed his sole ground; and that, when he finally accepts the main facts *as* they state them, he means *because* they state them. Whereas in reality he bases the startling facts on pagan evidence, and the coincidence of Christian prayer mainly on antecedent considerations. That the storm came in answer to the prayers of Christians, assuming that there were Christians in the army who prayed, is no doubt a pious belief which to many minds is unreasonable. But what has it to do with perverting *facts?* It no more enters on ground challengeable from the point of view of history, than does the belief in answers to prayer for personal help and guidance which has ever been common among all kinds of Christians.

In conclusion, after this imperfect estimate of a most misleading book, let me say that if the author had written with a little more of Cardinal Newman's candour and accuracy, his work might have been a contribution to problems of real difficulty, which even those who rejected its conclusions could read with profit. Catholics may welcome Dr. Martineau's contributions to the philosophy of Theism much as they dissent from his views of Scripture criticism. They can be grateful for Professor Green's constructive philosophy, while they reject his destructive religious creed. They can regard with gratitude the work of a Lightfoot or a Westcott, though they adopt in fact a different standpoint from those critics. But such a work as this, inaccurate in statement, partisan in character, and based throughout on the travesty of a misconception of the man whom its author assails, can satisfy no one, except other blind partisans, who welcome any attack on views they dislike, caring more for statements in harmony with their prejudices than for statements accurate in fact. As a serious contribution to the important matters it reviews it can have no value, whether for those who agree with the author's conclusions or for those who do not.

THE WISH TO BELIEVE

DIALOGUE I

Bernard Darlington and Edmund Ashley became acquainted for the first time during their residence together for some ten days at a small hotel near Lake Coniston, on the borders of Cumberland. They were men whose calling and religious tenets would have led one to expect great dissimilarity in their character; but who had, in reality, many sympathies in common. Darlington was by profession a barrister. When an undergraduate at Muriel College, Oxford, he had been thrown in contact with men of keen and eager mind, whose principal ambition it was to keep pace with what is called the thought of the day; and who had sufficient powers of argument to enable them to say a good deal that was difficult to answer in favour of advanced opinions on things in general, and on religion in particular. He had constantly heard those around him speak of the absurdity of expecting *certainty* on questions connected with another world, when all the arguments producible in favour of religious belief had by many of the very greatest minds been long since weighed in a balance and found wanting. This idea had been for many years a first principle with him, and seemed indeed only the veriest common sense. "Who am I," thought he, "that I should pretend to be positive as to the conclusiveness of arguments which Hume and Gibbon, Huxley and Spencer have felt to be inconclusive?" Questions as to the immortality of the soul, the Divine origin of Christianity, and the like, should, he thought, be left alone by a sensible, rational man. The controversies in their regard might, indeed, have an historical interest, but no more. Dispassionate judges held them to be incapable of solution: and the idea of certainty in their regard had only arisen from the passionate craving which exists in some minds to have definite knowledge and grounds for hope as to the future, which, in days when emotion was strong and reason not very circumspect, led many to catch at any theory, however insufficiently proved, that professed to satisfy their desire. Some great intellects of mystical and ideal tendencies were led by this same desire to create systems of belief which should answer to the need of their own hearts, and should at the same time serve as a sanction for their moral code. To aid them in their endeavour they had invoked those myths and traditions of the past which in a more or less confused way express the anticipations, hopes, and fears of nations in the course of their history, and the speculations of the popular mind; and out of these raw materials of emotion, desire, and tradition, supported by a certain measure of plausible argument *à priori*, they constructed their several religious theories. The mass of mankind get their knowledge from the teaching of experts, and when master minds professed aloud their belief, the multitude felt that there must be ample warrant for it, and hence it soon spread; and as faith is in its very nature unquestioning, once gained, it was not readily abandoned. Then, when religion in one shape or another had thus become considerably diffused, common consent seemed to be a confirmation of its truth. There was, moreover, much in the nature of the human mind and of the world in which we live to strengthen religious belief as soon as it had come into existence. Man's natural feeling of helplessness and dependence amid the powers of nature harmonised well with the account which had been given him of certain potent and invisible personalities having control over the universe; while the idea of prayer and of its efficacy in securing Divine protection was readily welcomed as lessening the feeling of impotent dread which must have arisen in the human mind, should these vast powers have been deemed to act blindly, and without regard to our own wishes or happiness.

Such was, Darlington considered, in outline the origin of all religions—from the systems of Moses, Zoroaster, and Buddha, to those of Christ and Mohammed—and the foundations on which they rested needed only to be looked at that it might appear how weak and unsubstantial they were. There might *very likely* be much truth to be found as it were "in solution" among the various creeds; but the idea of religious *certainty* was, he said, "utterly incompatible with exact thought"; a phrase, we may remark by the way, which is often made to do duty for a great deal of the thing which it signifies; which magnificently condemns as unworthy of notice many arguments which require for their refutation considerably greater power of "exact thought" than is possessed by him who disdainfully dismisses them. Darlington was, then, what is commonly called an Agnostic, using the word in its wider sense. He had been educated without any deep concern about religious subjects, and had believed rather because he never questioned himself about his belief than deeply or after reflection; and therefore it had not cost him much to abandon a Christianity which in him had never amounted to much more than an external profession.

Ashley was a Catholic priest; the Professor of Moral Philosophy at Sandown College. He had been a Catholic all his life, and had never been touched by the wave of scepticism which is sweeping over the non-Catholic world in England. He had arrived at that time of life at which the opinions are generally fixed and set; so that now, although he might understand a point of view differing from his own by force of imagination, there was little fear of his own belief being in any way shaken. He had, however, great powers of sympathy, and was readily drawn to Darlington by the perception in him of a natural temperament both attractive in itself, and especially so to him by reason of its similarity to his own. Both of them had a strong love for scenery, which, in the Lake country, was a sure bond of union; both were men of active minds and keen interests; and though one was by profession a dealer in syllogisms and the other a barrister, neither was given to that argumentativeness which so often makes able men disagreeable. They conversed a great deal, but rather with a view to gaining information than to disputing. Religion was naturally a subject of interest to both; to one as the great centre of the outgoing phase of civilised thought; and to the other as the foundation of his whole life, and man's most important possession. Father Ashley found in his new acquaintance, in the course of their rows on the lake and rambles among the hills, so much of natural religious feeling, and so fair and candid a mind, as to make him form great hopes that some day or other he might come to a knowledge of the truth. Rightly judging, however, that much more than mere argument is required for conversion, he asked him to come and spend a few days at Sandown after the students had reassembled at the end of the vacation, in the hope that the sight of the practical working of Catholicism and its influence over the lives of the boys, so far as these might be seen even by a casual visitor, might arouse within him a still greater interest in the subject, and spur him on to more active inquiry. In the course of their conversations it transpired that Walton, an old college friend of Darlington's, and a convert to Catholicism, was now a priest in the immediate neighbourhood of the college. He had been driven by the free-thinking spirit at Muriel in a direction exactly opposite to his friend. Dismayed at seeing so many cherished convictions, of whose truth he was deeply conscious, called into question and cleverly combated, he soon began to feel the difficulty —nay, the impossibility—of holding to the principle that each separate belief had to be proved by him on its own merits against men of far superior knowledge and logical *acumen.* He felt that life was not long enough for a work of this kind; and again he was often most dissatisfied with his own advocacy of the various doctrines. "Surely," he said to himself, "life is meant for action, and it cannot be right that the very foundations and springs of well-doing should be in constant danger of giving way. All my efforts are spent in securing *them,* and very insecurely after all. How can I go on doing good when at every step the very thoughts I rely upon as proving my course to be worth pursuing are cleverly attacked as being so many illusions, and when I feel my own knowledge to be in many cases so imperfect that I am ashamed to rest my belief on it?" This feeling led him by degrees to recognise the voice of God in the Catholic Church, speaking absolutely and categorically, and relying not on processes of argument, but on its own Divine mission and inspiration. He recognised that the Church was God's vicegerent on earth. He had studied her in her various aspects, her moral and ascetical theology, her official pronouncements, her practical system, and he found in them all a profound knowledge of human nature, and an uncompromising and elevated moral tone quite unlike anything he had seen elsewhere. He was not at all blind to the human weakness of her members, or the scandals of her history; but the system, and the representatives of the system—those who had taken full advantage of the assistance it offers to mankind—gave to the Church in his eyes a stamp of Divinity. *Vera incessu patuit dea.* And when his mind had taken this step, he felt that his old belief in the primary Christian truths rested on a new and secure basis. It was no longer his own reasonings from the nature of things or from Scripture, but the voice of God speaking through His chosen oracle which sanctioned his creed; and this being recognised, the mazes of human speculation were powerless to mislead him any more. Indeed, when he had once satisfied himself that he had found a living guide and teacher, he considerably lost his intellectual interests, which had ever been concerned more or less with inquiry into religious subjects, and betook himself on his reception into the Church to active missionary work as a priest. Darlington had been grieved at the very opposite courses he and his friend had taken. "You will never convince me, however, Walton," he said. "Your change is no argument to me, much as I believe in your ability. You were *determined* to believe; you were not dispassionate, so you are no fair judge. You wouldn't give up your pet ideas, though, if you had been really fair, you should have done so. Your wish to believe was father to your thought."

"I was determined to get at the *truth*," replied Walton. "I believed Christianity to be the truth, and I was resolved, if there was a way to seeing its truth more clearly, that I would find it; and I *have* found it."

Darlington arrived at Sandown at about eight o'clock on a Thursday evening, some six weeks after the vacation had terminated. He was favourably impressed on entering the college, which was on a far larger scale than he was prepared for. The stone cloisters, pointed arches, and Gothic windows and doors, gave it quite the appearance of a mediæval monastery. The professors had finished dinner when he arrived, but Walton had been asked to meet him, and they dined together with Ashley in the professors' "parlour," a spacious room, simply but tastefully furnished with an oaken sideboard and chairs, a large mantel-piece of carved stone, designed by Pugin, standing over the fireplace. After dinner Ashley presented Darlington to the President, who asked him if he would wish to attend the "benediction" service which was about to commence. He expressed his willingness, and was ushered into the chapel, a small edifice built in the Gothic style of the elder Pugin, and adorned with much handsome carving in wood and stone. He was a good deal struck by the serious and earnest demeanour of the boys, both older and younger. They all seemed, without any undue affectation of fervour, to be quietly conscious that they had a serious duty to perform, and to perform it as though they meant what they were doing. At the end of the service one of Bishop Challoner's solid and practical discourses was read, as the subject for the next morning's meditation, and then all turned round to the statue of Our Lady, which was so designed as to appear to offer the prayers of those in the chapel at the throne of grace, and sang the beautiful hymn, "Maria, mater gratiæ, dulcis parens clementiæ, tu nos ab hoste protege et mortis horâ suscipe." After all was over, a certain number of the "professors," principally the younger ones, adjourned to the parlour to have tea, and invited Darlington and Walton to join them there.

"Certainly," said Darlington to Father Davenport, the procurator, as they entered the parlour together, "your liturgy and ritual are extremely beautiful. I think the idea of devotion to the Virgin Mother so touching. The ideal of a tender mother with human affections, to whom you have recourse as to one who can readily understand you and sympathise with you in your troubles, who has no heart to refuse to plead for you and help you, is to me a most beautiful conception."

"And yet," said Father Davenport, "it is so often a difficulty to outsiders! It is one of the commonest stumbling-blocks in the way of conversions."

"I think it very beautiful," pursued Darlington. "I declare, when you all turned round to the statue at the end of the prayers and sang that hymn to the Virgin, the idea of trust and confidence in the invisible Mother who intercedes for you and protects you all, was so strongly expressed that it quite moved me—let me see, what are the words?"

Father Davenport repeated them. "Yes," continued Darlington, "with the two 'amens' at the end, one like the echo of the other. It affected me very much."

"Ah! my dear friend," said Ashley, who came into the room while he was speaking, "a man who has the soul to feel all that should be a Catholic. He is out of place anywhere but in the true Church."

Darlington smiled. "I am afraid a good deal more is wanted for my conversion than that," he said; "you would hardly have me *believe* in a doctrine simply because I think it beautiful and consoling?"

"No," said Father Ashley, "but a man who has insight into and perception of the Divine beauty of Catholic doctrine, must, I think, be on the high road to the perception of its *truth*. His admiration for it is surely a grace of the Holy Spirit, and if he is not unfaithful the rest will follow."

"Won't you sit down?" said Father Davenport. They had been standing while they were talking, and Darlington perceived on looking round that the other professors were gradually settling themselves down in knots of two or three at different parts of the long table. Walton was seated at a little distance from them, intent on something in a newspaper. Darlington and Ashley sat down.

"Let me give you a cup of tea, Mr. Darlington," said Father Davenport; "we are rather proud of our tea and of our cream too."

"I shall be very glad to try it," replied Darlington. "I think that good tea is the most refreshing drink that ever was invented. No sugar, thanks. Of course," he continued to Ashley, "you express the thing differently from me, but I think we mean pretty much the same, and you are not the first man whom I have heard talk in a similar way. That manner of speaking and thinking, which I perceive in so many religious people, as though the fact that a doctrine is consoling makes it also true, is, I think, at the root of a good deal of my scepticism. It makes me suspect the whole basis of their belief."

"But I think you are wrong," said Ashley. "We may say that the intrinsic beauty of a doctrine is an *additional* sign that it comes from God, but none would maintain that all doctrines which are beautiful are true. Take the Pagan myths; many of them were the creations of highly poetic minds; but certainly none of us believe in Elysian fields, however pleasant a prospect they might be."

"Perhaps I expressed myself too generally," said Darlington. "I don't suppose that Christians would expressly *maintain* that a doctrine which is beautiful is therefore true. But still I must say that all my observations have tended to convince me that in very many cases their real state of mind falls very little short of that. They have *some* additional reasons, no doubt, but very insufficient ones; and their chief motive for believing is because belief is consoling and desirable. Do you remember Gibbon's account of the belief of the Christians of Rome under Pope Gregory the Great? He says that their temporal dangers and misfortunes, from the constant invasions of the Lombard and various other causes, led them to lend a ready ear to the hopes which the preacher held out to them of a happier state of things beyond the grave. Well, it seems to me that this is the state of many nowadays. They are not happy in this world, and so they readily believe on very insufficient evidence tidings of another and a more satisfactory future life, and doctrines connected with it which tend to console them."

"Should you say that the doctrine of hell tended to comfort or console?" put in a youngish man who had been listening to the conversation.

Darlington hesitated. "It is not fair," he said, "to isolate a doctrine from the system to which it belongs. It is almost proverbial that hope, even though one pays for it with a certain measure of fear, is preferable to a dead level of hopeless dulness. I don't think you can dispute that the Christian view of the world, *taken as a whole*, giving as it does a *greatness* to life and a connection with a realised ideal, imparting to labour and privation, and all that would naturally be irksome, a value which far more than compensates for their unpleasantness, and holding out a hope for the gratification in the future of all our highest and deepest yearnings, is, in spite of everything on the other side, a far preferable and more consoling one to a mind which is dissatisfied with the present, than the prospect of dull repetition of past experiences until, in the end, annihilation arrives."

"Surely," said Father Ashley, going back to the first question which Darlington had raised, "you cannot apply Gibbon's remark to the present age or to this country. He spoke of an exceptional state of things when the Romans were so wretched that they were ready to cling to any idea which afforded them a ray of hope. Not that I admit Gibbon's charge even with reference to the Romans, but I think there is even less colour for it nowadays."

"The exact circumstances may be different," replied Darlington, "but the general fact remains the same. Dissatisfaction was no doubt more widely spread then. But in one shape or another the *wish* to believe seems to me to be at the root of all religion still. One man turns to religion because he is *ennuyé* with the world; another clings to it because he has been brought up to it, and it is bound up closely with all the memories and associations of his childhood; another is attached to his creed because his ancestors died for it. Many become Roman Catholics because of the effect the gorgeous vestments, incense, and tapers have upon them. Newman himself admits that many can give no better account of the matter than that the Catholic religion is true because its fragrance is as perceptible to their moral sense as that of flowers to their sense of smell. In all these cases religion or a particular form of religion is embraced or adhered to from no rational motive, but simply because the believer wants to believe. As I said, the wish is father to the thought. Look at Moody and Sankey's converts—even the best of them. They had no new reason given them for belief. They were pleased and excited by the hymns and sermons. Mr. Sankey's performances on the harmonium constituted one of their chief motives. Religious belief gave them under the circumstances pleasant excitement, and so they believed—not because their intellects had received any new light —but because what they saw and heard made them *wish* to believe. I have seen so much of this that I am on my guard. *I* am quite alive to the consoling power of religion. I often suffer from great depression of spirits and *tædium vitæ.* I remember a schoolfellow of mine of a melancholy disposition, who used to go about crying out, 'Who will tell me of something to look forward to?' That is often my own feeling; and religious conviction would be the greatest comfort to me. But I am so alive to the fallacy of religious minds—the fallacy of believing because one *wishes* to believe—that I myself can never be a believer."

"Don't you think, Mr. Darlington," said the young man who had spoken before, "that the strong wish implanted in man's nature for religion may be worth something as an *argument?* Most of our appetites and cravings have a legitimate satisfaction; their existence seems to point to the existence of an object capable of satisfying them. Hunger is correlative with food, love with objects of love, and so forth; so it seems hard to believe that man has a thirst for religious knowledge, and yet that such knowledge is entirely unattainable."

"I don't think," replied Darlington, "that you are attacking exactly the position I have assumed, though doubtless I do tend to think religious certainty incapable of attainment. I do not speak of any natural or general craving for religion among mankind. What I say is that attachment to religion or to a particular form of religion on the part of an individual, and for reasons peculiar to his case, so often supersedes—and most unreasonably supersedes—argument. This would hold good even if I granted what you are saying. I am speaking merely of that common fallacy—believing what suits one, or is pleasant—creeping into religious inquiry."

"I don't yet see," said Ashley, "how you *prove* that the wish of the believer *is* father to his thoughts. After one has arrived by reason and grace at doctrines which are consoling, one may feel that they *are* consoling; but that is no proof that it is their consoling power which has made one believe them. If it is proved to me beyond doubt that I have come into a fortune of £10,000 a year, I may find the fact very consoling, but it would be very unjust in you to turn round on me and tell me that I believe it simply because it is consoling."

"I really could not give you in mood and figure an exact proof that it is as I say," said Darlington. "It is a matter of observation rather than of argument; and then, every one knows the tendency of human nature to believe what is pleasant. I think that it is at least a very remarkable fact that, whereas the evidences of Christianity are, to a great extent, common property and in everybody's hands, the people who are convinced by them are those who have what is called religious minds, or, in other words, who wish to believe. Lacordaire points out somewhere that, whereas Fénelon found in Scripture the strongest evidence of the truth of Christianity, Voltaire found in it only food for laughter. The proofs, such as they were, were open to both alike; but to him who had no prepossession in favour of belief they were quite insufficient. Take Hume and Johnson, again; both able men and capable of doing justice to the arguments on both sides. Hume was dispassionate and unprejudiced; Johnson had, as one sees at every turn in his life, strong emotional religious cravings. The calm and dispassionate man found the evidences for Christianity quite insufficient—and surely such a man is the best judge of their *true* worth. It is the same nowadays: your calm, clear-headed men of science think them quite insufficient and fallacious."

"I don't know that calm and unbiassed men are always the best judges," said Father Ashley. "No doubt bias is a bad thing, but I think that apathy is worse. If your unprejudiced men are apathetic, if their minds and hearts are in things other than religion, I had rather have a *prejudiced* man who is in earnest, and whose heart is in the matter. If I were a prisoner, I had rather my judge were somewhat prejudiced against me, than that he had neither bias nor sense of responsibility. The former kind of judge, if he is conscientious, has something in him to which one can appeal, and which may overcome his prejudice; the latter may condemn me through mere sleepiness or inattentiveness. You may reason away prejudice, but not apathy, as its very characteristic is that it takes no pains to attend to your reasonings."

Here a man, who had been an attentive listener for the last five minutes, but had not as yet spoken, broke into the conversation. He was somewhat stout, of middle age, and spoke with a resonant bass voice. He had been sitting alone at the other side of the table with a newspaper before him, but had for some time been making small pretence of reading it, as the conversation was evidently engrossing his attention. This was Father Walton, of whom we have already spoken.

"I think, Darlington," he said, "that your philosophy is at fault. You speak of the well-known tendency of human nature to believe what is pleasant. Well, I should say not only that such a tendency is not well known, but that it does not exist at all. I think the truth is exactly the opposite. If I am very anxious that a thing should be true, I find that I am slower, and not quicker, in believing it."

The others seemed to be waiting for him to explain himself.

"For instance," he continued, "many years ago I was weak enough to bet rather heavily on a horse which was running in the Derby. When the first report got out that that horse had won, I found that all my companions, who were not betting men, believed it at once; but I was not satisfied until I had seen it in print, and its truth was beyond the possibility of doubt. Yet I was far more anxious than the others that the report *should* prove true."

"That does certainly seem to be an exception to the rule," said Darlington. "But still you can't deny that, *as a rule*, men tend to believe what is pleasant. 'Thy wish was father, Harry, to that thought,' has passed into a proverb."

"I can't admit that it *is* a rule," replied Walton. "When boys here are anxious for a holiday, and have sent to ask the President to give one, I don't at all find that they over-estimate the reasons in favour of expecting it. The other day, in a French religious community where I was staying, they were electing a new superior, and I found many who expected their favourite candidate to fail, though there was really a good chance in his favour. It seems to me that there is no rule of the kind you suppose."

Here Father Davenport interrupted the conversation for a moment to replenish Darlington's cup with tea. Ashley, however, took the question up. Much as he wished to convince his friend, he could not see his way to accepting Walton's uncompromising denial of the former's principle.

"Surely you will not dispute, Walton," he said, "that there is a class of cases on the other side. I remember a very eminent physician who was so determined to believe that his remedies were effective, that if you told him they had not cured you, he simply answered that you were wrong and that they *must* have done so. It used to be quite an amusing scene with poor Bowring, whom you remember. Bowring suffered from very severe headaches, and Dr. R——, as I will call him (for

I don't want to mention his name), was confident that he could cure him in two days. At the expiration of that time Dr. R—— made his appearance, and said with a confident smile, 'Well, and how are the headaches *now?*' 'As bad as ever,' replied Bowring. 'Ah, then,' said Dr. R—— quite gravely, 'you did not take my prescriptions.' 'I took them most religiously,' said Bowring. 'Oh!' said the doctor in a tone of relief, 'then the headaches have gone.' 'But they haven't! I feel them still,' said poor Bowring. 'No, no,' said R——, 'believe me, they are gone. You have had so much of them that you can't help imagining that they are there still, but I assure you they are gone;' and it was impossible to convince him that they were not. Bowring had to pay his guinea for nothing, and to go to another doctor." [1]

Every one laughed. "Poor Bowring!" said Father Davenport, who had been listening to the story. "I can well imagine his distress of mind. I suspect he found food for a fortnight's grumbling in it."

"Well," continued Ashley, "I think *that* a strong case of believing because one wishes to believe. Dr. R—— had made up his mind that his medicine was to be successful, and therefore he would have it that it *had* been."

"I remember a case something like that," said

[1] All the anecdotes in this paper are substantially true, although reference to persons and places has been carefully avoided. Of course, their value as illustrations depends on their being true.

Darlington, "of old Mrs. Arton, the wife of one of our farmers in Yorkshire. She had manufactured some ointment which she believed to be an infallible remedy for bruises and sores of every kind. To the best of my belief it really retarded their cure very considerably. However, in the end nature's tendency to self-healing used to assert itself, and it was most amusing to see the old lady's triumph at the complete success of her ointment."

"I suppose," said Ashley, "she argued, 'post hoc, propter hoc.' The cure was subsequent to the anointing, therefore it was due to it."

"It was just the same," continued Darlington, "with her prophecies about the weather. They were invariably wrong, but this never in the least shook her faith in her own powers; and when a glorious, still, sunny day appeared after she had prophesied 'heavy rain and high winds,' she would gravely assure you that it was raining in some parts."

"Surely," said the young man who had spoken before, "the belief of some of the Tichborne tenants in the claimant illustrates what you are saying, Mr. Darlington. I should think there is little doubt that their strong wish to see their squire back again had a great influence in determining their belief."

"Or," added Ashley, "take a conceited coxcomb, who thinks all the world is admiring him. That surely comes from his love of admiration."

"I don't think we want for instances," said Darlington; "you must admit, Walton, that men have, at least in many cases, and under certain circumstances, a tendency to believe what is pleasant on very insufficient evidence."

"I admit," replied Walton, "that men often deceive themselves into *thinking* what is pleasant, where there is no danger of being brought immediately face to face with the fact that it is untrue: but I don't think that in those cases they seriously *believe*, though they may say they do. If they have the pleasure of the thought without the pain of finding out that it is untrue, it gives them for the time almost as much satisfaction as real and deep belief. But it is not belief—or at least it is not conviction."

"Dear me," suddenly interrupted Ashley, "what a very animated conversation is going on between Merton, Kershaw, and Gordon Brabourne! I suppose it is their usual topic—Roman *versus* Gothic in architecture and vestments."

"He doesn't mean what he says, Gordon," Merton was saying, a man with lively manner and pleasant voice, who sat at the end of the table. "If the Romans wore the present Gothic vestments, and the square ones were Gothic, Kershaw would see all sorts of defects in the square ones, and would discover all manner of hidden devotional and symbolical meaning in the many-folded robes so much loved by Pugin. Now, don't protest. You hold that the Roman Pontiff's infallibility extends to the shape of your *antipendium*, the carving on your pillars, and the cut of your albs; you know you do."

"Kershaw is a recent convert," explained Ashley to Darlington; "a splendid fellow, but a little extreme. He has just come back from Rome, and Merton chaffs him about what he calls his Roman fever."

"My dear Merton," replied Kershaw, "how can you talk so much at random? Whoever said it was a question of infallibility? All that I say is, that where Rome has set the example our duty is not to criticise but to imitate; that we do better by trying to appreciate duly the customs and usages of Holy Church, and to admire them as they deserve, than by setting up idols of our own creation in opposition."

"Rank heresy, Kershaw," said Merton. "As though the style of architecture in Rome were set up for our imitation, any more than the way the Romans cut their hair, or the shape in which they trim their beards."

"It seems to me," said Brabourne, the third speaker, "that if you insist on tracing these things to their origin, and making them more than a mere matter of taste, you should not forget that the present Roman architecture is originally Pagan—an introduction of the Renaissance. Gothic is the creation of Christianity."

"Besides," continued Merton, "Kershaw is not even content with making it simply a question of what is authoritatively held up for our *imitation*. He demands *interior assent* also. Roman architecture and vestments are not only to be *used* by every loyal son of the Church, but to be *admired* also. The duty of interior assent is not confined to decisions on faith and morals; matters of taste are likewise infallibly decided for us."

"You are very hard on me, Merton," replied Kershaw; "I never said that anything had been infallibly decided. I spoke only of my own taste in the matter, and it was you that insisted that it was grounded on the teaching of Rome; though I certainly do think that a priest shows a more becoming and loyal spirit if he is not content with obeying simply the letter of the law, but tries likewise to admire and like what Mother Church tells us to make use of, instead of looking in the first place to find out what he can criticise and run down without fear of formal heresy."

"Without fear of formal heresy!" repeated Merton; "what Mother Church *tells* us to make use of. Good heavens! I suppose you would agree with Ashburton; Ashburton, after he had been to Rome (shortly after his conversion), on his return to England used frequently to bring into church with him two large dogs with bells attached to their collars, which ran about during mass, making a most ungodly noise, because it reminded him of Rome."

"I am surprised the congregation allowed it," said Brabourne.

"It was a very small congregation," said Merton,

"and he was a considerable personage there, and a great benefactor to the mission, and so he was privileged. I remember asking him what he did it for, and he gravely assured me that it had a most devotional effect upon him."

"Nonsense!" said Brabourne.

"He did really," said Merton. "I suggested an idea which would make what he said more rational. I said I supposed that all that reminded him of Rome was so associated in his mind with his first fervour, that it had a great attraction for him. But he would not accept this explanation at all. He would have it that there was something in its own nature devotional in the sound of the collar bells of these animals as they ran about in the church."

Every one laughed except Kershaw, who said, "Well, if you are going to make a joke of the whole subject, I don't think I can do much good by arguing it out with you. Besides, I have to say the half-past five o'clock mass to-morrow for the servants; so I will wish every one good-night."

"I don't think he was sorry of an excuse to get away," said Brabourne, as Kershaw left the room. "He knows that when he gets on these subjects he has to fight against considerable odds; and then you are always so merciless with him, Merton."

"Yes," put in Ashley, from the other end of the table, "you are really too hard on him, Merton. Remember, Newman lays it down as one of the marks of a well-bred man that he is merciful towards the absurd."

"Well, I really think it does him good," said Merton. "I have no patience with men who talk as though the cut of your chasuble and the length of your cotta were matters authoritatively ruled by the Holy See. As though great Rome, who is so large-hearted and liberal wherever she can be so without compromising principle, who tolerates an Armenian and a Greek rite utterly unlike her own, would ever indulge in such petty tyranny over our artistic tastes."

"Kershaw will be a very different man ten years hence," said Brabourne. "Some converts are so determined to find ideal perfection in every stick and stone in Rome that their judgment as to things Roman is completely warped."

"To me," said Ashley, "there is something admirable in Kershaw's spirit, though I should not go the length he does. 'Love me, love my dog,' says the proverb. I think it shows true devotion to Rome to have an affection for all, even the smallest things, that remind one of her."

"Yes," said Merton, "but the proverb does not say 'Believe in me, believe my dog to be perfect,' or 'Condemn others for not believing it to be perfect.'"

"Surely," said Darlington, turning to Ashley and Walton, "Mr. Kershaw's frame of mind, as you describe it, is another instance of the very thing we have been talking about. His wish to find ideal perfection in everything Roman makes him think he has found it."

"I remember," said Brabourne, "an amusing instance of the same sort of thing when I took Compton—the Muriel man who was received two years ago—to Rome, just after his conversion. He had such an intense belief in the all-pervading piety of the place, that he gave a religious interpretation to everything he saw. We were strolling one day in the Campagna and lost our way. We wanted to find the Flaminian gate, and so we asked an old carter whom we met which was our way. He looked a surly fellow, and either found a difficulty in understanding our bad Italian, or did not feel in the humour for conversation. At any rate, not one word could we get out of him. I began saying, 'What a churlish old man that is!' but Compton was quite indignant with me for my shallow and uncatholic view of the matter. 'This comes,' he said, 'of living in a Protestant country, where all motives are secular and natural. Depend upon it, that man is under a vow of silence undertaken in expiation for some sin of the tongue.'"

"Well, I remember our friend Kershaw here used to talk," said Merton, "as though all the actions of a Roman were religious in object and motive, until at last I asked him point blank if he supposed that every man, woman, and child in Rome was a person of interior life, and he was quite offended at my making a joke of it. 'I am sure they are,' he said."

"Well now," said Darlington, "after all you have told us, Mr. Merton, you should be a good authority on the question we have just been discussing. Don't you think that, in a general way, a man is more ready to believe in a thing because he wishes it to be so?"

"You mean, I suppose," said Merton, "that men like Kershaw believe Roman vestments to be perfect because they are determined to find everything that is Roman perfect?"

"Well, it seems to me from what you have been saying," said Darlington, "that men of this stamp have made up their minds to find their ideal realised when they enter the Church. They are sick of constant contention and are enamoured of the idea of an authority which they are to reverence as infallible, which is to be decisive, and to set all fruitless disputation at rest. And then they expect her to fulfil more than she ever could fulfil or has promised—to decide on matters which she has neither the power nor the will to decide on; and with this expectation in their minds they see in the customs of Rome—which are merely *private* customs—the decisions of authority."

"They follow Rome in matters in which she acts, so to speak, as a private person, and not officially," said Merton, who was more intent upon the peculiarities of Kershaw than upon the application Darlington was making of them. "They remind me of those who imitate the mannerisms of a great man as though his very imperfections must have a touch of his Divine genius. They are like the actors who imitate Irving's way of walking and articulating, whereas most sensible men know that these are, to say the least, not at all essential to his greatness as an actor."

"I can't help admiring it," said Ashley. "It is

devotion of the intensest sort which loves even the most insignificant thing connected with its object."

"I can't agree," said Darlington. "I think it is ten to one that such a mind is a small one, and loves *only* what is unimportant; that it is incapable of appreciating true greatness. The actor who takes most note of Irving's gait and voice will not be his most intelligent admirer. A greater mind will take no note of them, but will pass to the *soul* of his acting. It is the small mind that observes his peculiarities, and ten to one stops short at *them*, and fails to appreciate anything beyond."

Merton and Brabourne here looked at their watches, and, finding that it was late, wished the others good-night and left the room.

"At any rate," resumed Darlington, "it seems pretty clear that the converts of whom we speak supply us with an illustration of the principle I was supporting. Here are men maintaining in opposition to the arguments of those who have the very best right to speak, that all Rome's ecclesiastical customs are perfection even from an artistic point of view, and are designed as models for the rest of your Church; and all this simply because they have made up their minds beforehand to find Rome all perfect."

"I think," said Ashley, "that both their expectation and their belief arise from a naturally sanguine disposition. That seems to me the solution of the whole difficulty we raised. It is a matter of temperament; a sanguine man is ready, a despondent man slow, to believe what he wishes. Ask Father M'Arton yonder" (pointing to a grave-looking priest who was reading a book and had taken no share in the conversation) "if he believes that Macmillan will publish his translation of the Eclogues. He is very anxious to think that he will, but he is not at all a cheerful man, and I don't think you will find him very *ready* to believe it."

Here Walton, who had for some time been occupied with his own thoughts, interposed. "Temperament has its effect, no doubt; but it is a very imperfect account to give of the matter to say that is *all*. A man may be ever so sanguine, and yet in the case I gave before of his having a large bet on a horse at the Derby, he won't be over ready to believe on slight evidence that he has won. On the other hand, there may be far stronger reasons against the truth of the coxcomb's high opinion of himself, and yet he won't give it up. The coxcomb is not *honest* with himself. He nurses the pleasure of his vanity; and as there is no external test, as he is not forced to verify or disprove the truth of his view, he is able to keep it. The man who has the bet, on the contrary, is forced by the circumstances of the case to be honest with himself. He knows that the truth of his belief will soon be tested. He will soon know whether it is right or wrong, and there is little pleasure in the mere expectation, if after all it proves wrong."

"This seems to me to be a new point," said Darlington, "and I don't quite follow you."

"Well," said Walton, "I have been trying while you were talking to see the essential distinction between the cases that have been cited on both sides. I fancy I can point it out by an example which has occurred to me, which I think you will admit to be true to nature. There are two very different states of mind—anxiety that something should be really true, and the wish to have the pleasure of believing something. Here are two pictures. First take some lazy, comfort-loving, and selfish man. He is walking with a companion on a sea beach. No one is visible near him. Suddenly he hears what, he half suspects, might be the shriek of a drowning man, beyond some rocks at the end of the beach. His companion thinks it is only children at play. The rocks are hard to climb, and at some distance off. The man is readily persuaded that it *is* only children at play, and that there is no call on him to climb the rocks, or assist anybody. There is one attitude of mind—one picture. Now for another. An affectionate mother is placed in exactly the same circumstances as my lazy man. She thinks she recognises in the shriek her son's voice. Her companion says it is only children at play; but this *does not satisfy her*. She entreats him to help her to climb the rocks, and they arrive just in time to rescue her son—for it is her son—from drowning. Now surely you won't deny that the mother would be far more desirous to be convinced that her son was not drowning than the lazy man in the parallel case;[1] yet her wish, far from making her

[1] A friend to whom I showed these pages objects that the illustration is not apposite, as the mother's prompt response to what she takes for her son's cry for help is instinctive, and so affords no guarantee for the action of one who has not the mother's instinct, under similar circumstances. I have,

believe it, only makes her take all the more pains to satisfy herself as to the true state of the case. Genuine conviction that the fact is really as she hoped is what she wants; and wishing for it doesn't help her a bit to get it. Our other friend, on the contrary, was not really and truly anxious to ascertain the *fact*. He wished to banish an unpleasant idea from his mind. I don't think he was truly or deeply convinced that there was no call on him to climb the rocks. He was not anxious to be *convinced* that there was no call: he only cared to *think* that there was none. He did not wish to *adjust his mind to the fact* at all; he only wished to have a comfortable *idea*, and to banish an uncomfortable suspicion. He was not primarily anxious that the *fact* should be as he wished; if he had been he would have used every means to ascertain whether it were so or not. If it is a matter of some thousands to a man that Oxford should have won the boat-race, he is not ready to believe it on slight evidence; on the contrary, he examines into the reports he hears far more carefully than another would."

All listened attentively to Walton's explanation, and most felt that he had thrown light on the subject. There was a pause before Ashley said—

"Don't you think that in the case you have given the fact that there is an immediate prospect of the belief being verified, and again the fact that it is a question of *immediate action*, may affect the frame

however, retained it, as I cannot myself see that the mother's action is, strictly speaking, instinctive. Let those, however, who think that it is so substitute for the mother a very affectionate friend, and judge for themselves whether in that case also Walton's picture is not true to nature.

of mind of the individuals concerned? Of course in religious belief the case is otherwise. One has to wait for verification until the end of one's life."

"The only effect that I can see," said Walton, "is that it ensures a person's being honest with himself. Where there is *no* immediate prospect of verification he can enjoy the luxury of a false belief without danger of discovery. Where there is an immediate prospect he feels it is of no use to think of anything but truth. If you observe, my lazy man, who was *dishonest* with himself and shirked his duty, took care that there should be *no* immediate test of the truth of his thought. Had he expected such a test, I think he would have climbed the rocks and made sure of the facts."

"Then," said Darlington slowly, "as I understand you, you hold that where there is a real anxiety and wish about the *thing*—an honest desire for the truth of the *thing*, and not merely for the pleasure of the *thought*—that desire makes you *less* ready rather than more ready to believe."

"Precisely," said Walton; "a shallow self-deceitful thought, called only by a misnomer 'belief,' may well enough be the result of wishing to believe; but true conviction never. I remember well a lady of my acquaintance who used to think her nephew a perfect paragon of perfection, and far the cleverest man at his college at Oxford. She sucked in eagerly all the civil things that people said in his favour, and systematically disbelieved less flattering reports. Here was one sort of belief. It arose from her wish

—but her wish for what? That her nephew should *really* be the cleverest and most successful man?"

"I suppose so," said Ashley unguardedly.

"Not entirely so, I think," said Walton; "but mainly from her wish for the *satisfaction of thinking* that he was so. The actual fact was of secondary importance to her; but it is of primary importance to him who wants a real and deep conviction. I remember, too, in that very case that the truth of this was evidenced in a most amusing manner when this brilliant nephew was trying for a fellowship which was of some consequence to him. She paid far more attention to and was rendered far more anxious by arguments against the probability of his success, and seemed very doubtful as to the result-quite prepared for his failure; and why? Because *here* it was the *fact* of his success which was of moment, and not the pleasure of her own subjective impression."

"You are getting dreadfully metaphysical," said Darlington, laughing.

"I admit then," continued Walton, "that where the satisfaction of believing a thing is what is desired, and the correspondence of your belief with objective fact is a matter of small anxiety or importance to yourself, the wish is often father to the thought. Belief is readily obtained, although its quality is extremely bad. But where the truth of the *fact* is of the first importance, and an untrue belief is useless,—where *genuine conviction* of the fact in question is desired, the desire will not beget readiness but rather caution in believing. It will make a man less easily convinced than another by the evidence ready to hand. He so much wishes that the thing should be true that he fears to believe it, holding, in the words of the proverb, that it is 'too good to be true.' But, on the other hand, he is more ready than another to give himself every chance of discovering whether what he so much wishes for *be* really true. He is interested in the subject, and his desire will make him search for a road to certainty, instead of waiting until such a road is unmistakably pointed out to him. The wish then, as I have said, may be father to a shallow self-deceitful *idea*, but it renders *true conviction* in a certain sense (as I have explained) slower, although proportionally deeper and surer."

Here, for a time at least, Walton's homily came to a halt; and Darlington, who had been much interested with what he said, though a little bored at the argumentativeness and seriousness of his tone, continued turning over in his mind the whole question, and trying to put into shape his own impressions as to how much of truth there was in his friend's view.

"I don't deny," he said, as he absently stirred his empty teacup with his spoon, "that there is some truth in what you say. But as applied to religion it has a fallacy, and remember that 'a lie which is half a truth is ever the blackest of lies.' You have to take it for granted that religious believers have these *deep convictions* and this *anxiety for truth*, and are not satisfied with prejudice. Of course the very thing I should say is that they are prejudiced and unfair. They view all the evidence partially. They ignore half of it."

"Well, of course," replied Walton, "I can't *prove* to you that they are unprejudiced. All I am saying is that if they are honest and anxious for true conviction—anxious about the fact of religious truth with all its consequences, and not only for its consoling power as a beautiful thought, then their anxiety to believe is no argument against them, but rather in their favour. Of course how far one is honest and convinced is a question which each man must answer from his own personal consciousness. I can't prove to another that I am deeply convinced, though I may be certain of it in my own mind."

"I suppose it comes to this," said Darlington, "that all your party are honest, and sincere, and convinced, and the rest, and all others are prejudiced and insincere. This is, to say the least, a decided and marked division of the human race."

"No, my dear Darlington," replied Walton, "you quite misunderstand me. My position in all that I am saying is purely negative. I am only answering your objection. All that I say is that where one is conscious of real conviction, one need not be afraid that it is the result of a wish to believe; and this because a desire to be convinced of a truth makes one harder and not easier of belief. I am defending our side of the question and not attacking you. There may be prejudiced Christians who arrive at the truth in a wrong way, or others who do not deeply believe.

All I say is, that if I am conscious of conviction, I am sure it has not been caused by my wish to believe."

Darlington was somewhat annoyed at a new element he thought he perceived in the discussion. His friend was not content with differing from him intellectually; he seemed to impugn his honesty and sincerity. His annoyance made him lose the thread of the discussion.

"It comes to this," he said. "You feel convinced, *ergo* you are right. What do you say if I reply, 'I am convinced that certainty on these religious questions is impossible; that they are outside our ken altogether; *ergo* I am right, and it is so.' I have just as much right as you to lay down the law. You make your own mind the measure of all truth."

"You persist in misunderstanding me," said Walton. "I allow as much to you as I do to myself. If you feel really *sure* that religious certainty is unattainable, I think that a strong proof that this belief is not the result of a wish to think it so; and that is all that I say in my own case. You tried to make out that one's wishes, so far as they influenced conviction, did so unreasonably; and in self-defence I tried to show that anxiety for certainty that something is true is an assistance in learning the true state of the case; and that it spurs one on to search for whatever proofs on the subject are attainable; and that, far from making one's views of *existing* proofs sanguine, it has the contrary effect. Lastly, I maintain that where belief is the result of prejudice, there is generally a feeling that it is not firm or deeply rooted. The mind is dimly conscious of its own want of candour, and of not having done justice to the question; although, of course, explicit self-examination on the subject would be contrary to the very nature of an uncandid mind."

As Darlington made no reply, Walton pursued his own train of thought.

"I have always thought," he said, "that the shallowness of false and spurious convictions is excellently shown by Newman in quite a different connection in his *Essay on Assent*. He speaks of the confident opinions many people profess as to St. Paul's meaning in a particular text; and then he supposes that St. Paul were suddenly to appear to answer for himself. How each speaker would modify and explain away what he had just been dogmatically asserting! Yet they had really persuaded themselves that their convictions were genuine, until there was a prospect of their being put to the test. When that prospect came, they were exposed to themselves and to others. As long as truth was not of the first moment to them, they tortured their minds into believing what prejudice or fancy dictated; or at best they professed certainty on most inadequate grounds, and where there was in reality no certainty. Their search had been not for truth, but for arguments to support their pet notions. They did not attempt to conform their minds honestly to the evidence before them, but viewed that evidence through the refracting medium of their own preconceived ideas, and gave all their real *effort* to the search for *arguments* in support of their views. Then suddenly, when truth became everything, and its discovery threatened to render impossible the satisfaction of believing, and of defending their own prejudices, the shallowness and unreality of their previous pretended convictions became unmistakable. It is the realising that truth is everything, and the mere repose of believing what is pleasant (if after all the belief is wrong) *nothing*, that makes a conviction worthy of the name, and ensures its being genuine; and surely, as far as it goes, this state of mind renders it more probable that your belief is *right*. It is not believing a thing that makes it true, but the thing being true is all that gives any value to belief. One should realise this. 'If Christ be not risen again, your faith is vain.' These words always strengthen my faith. They show that the Apostle's absolute belief and intense enthusiasm did not make him forget that they rested, not on themselves, but on objective facts for support, and that if these facts were mistaken all was in vain. His conviction must have had deep root to stand against this thought. He felt that he had staked everything on his belief, and so no one could be more desirous for real certainty of its truth than he. Yet he so clearly realised that it was not the present satisfaction of believing, but the truth of what he believed that was important, that his desire and anxiety to be convinced was a guarantee of the depth of his conviction rather than a reason for suspecting it; and it seems to me that the case is the same with any earnest Christian who has a sense of realities. Of course he is anxious to convince himself; but he knows that a spurious conviction is worthless, and so his anxiety makes him all the more careful in the matter, lest he may be staking his all on an uncertainty."

Walton was evidently full of his subject, but his whole tone was out of sympathy with the bent of Darlington's mind, and the latter began to find it hard to bear an active part in the conversation. His friend was so changed. He spoke with such earnestness—unpleasant earnestness. It seemed a sort of reproach to Darlington for being unable to rise to the same pitch. Then all his language about "depth of conviction" and the "necessity of being in earnest" was so new. Talking to him was a strong contrast to the religious discussions he remembered at Muriel years ago. They had been so delightful. Every one interested in the subject; no one unpleasantly excited or anxious: theory after theory mooted, discussed, and criticised; a real intellectual treat. Even to-night they had had a pleasant talk enough until Walton had absorbed the lion's share of the conversation. He introduced a tone of his own. It was like the change from fencing with foils to a duel with rapiers. He seemed to talk not for pleasure but like one who is defending something personal of great value, which he fears may be taken from him. At Muriel an objection used to be welcomed as fresh food for discussion; but with Walton it seemed to hurt and distress him. His answers were wanting in brightness.

They were painfully elaborate and full. He seemed never content until he had pushed his arguments as far as possible, and answered objections to the very utmost that they admitted. In short his tone and manner had commenced to bore Darlington. Ashley was very quick to observe this, and he feared that the good effect of the conversation on Darlington might be undone if it was prolonged. As he saw that Walton was preparing to continue in the same strain, he said, "I think it is getting too late for so exciting a discussion, and you will not sleep, Father Walton, if you go any deeper into metaphysics and psychology." Walton looked up and saw in Darlington's face the true state of the case.

"I fear I have been too warm," he said, "but that is the natural consequence of the subject we have been discussing. Dr. Johnson says that the reason the early Greeks could argue so good-humouredly about religion was because they did not believe in it."

The conversation passed to indifferent topics, and Darlington was thankful for the relief. Walton was obliged to go some ten minutes later, and his departure was the signal for the retirement of those who had not as yet gone to bed; and as Darlington was tired after his journey, he was not sorry to follow suit and make his way to his room. Ashley saw his friend upstairs and wished him good-night, leaving him hardly in the humour to ask himself candidly how far his own views had been affected by what he had heard. The chief impression left on his mind by the conversation was that it had tired him at the end of a tiring day.

DIALOGUE II

DARLINGTON passed a night of unbroken rest and was awakened at six o'clock on Friday morning by a gong, which seemed to him to resound just outside his room, and then to make its way along the winding passages, echoing more and more faintly in the distance. This he rightly concluded to be the signal for the students to rise; and as he was unwilling to lose any opportunity of observing the customs of the place he got out of bed and dressed himself. He left his room at twenty minutes after six, and as he went downstairs heard the sound of footsteps in the *ambulacrum*—the large corridor where students and professors had been walking and talking before Benediction on the previous evening. No voice was audible, however; and when he reached the foot of the staircase he found some twenty or thirty of the theological students, or "divines" as they were called, walking to and fro in perfect silence. He himself paced slowly up and down, not speaking to any one, as it did not seem customary, but wondering in his own mind what could be the meaning of this silent march. As the clock struck half-past six all turned round with almost military precision and went into church. Darlington followed them, expecting to be pleased and interested by the service, as he had been on the previous evening. He was disappointed, however. All assembled in their places, professors and students — excepting the younger boys — but no service commenced. Some had books open before them, which they seemed to be reading; others were apparently doing nothing, but remained kneeling perfectly still, their faces buried in their hands. Darlington irreverently surmised that they had fallen asleep.

Ten minutes of waiting for something to take place was enough for his patience, and he arose from the seat he had occupied in the ante-chapel, and wandered through the adjoining cloisters, which led, as he found, to several smaller chapels, which were sufficiently ornamented with carving in wood and stone and with pictures of various scriptural and historical subjects, to keep him occupied with their inspection until the sound of footsteps in the main chapel warned him, twenty minutes later, that some change was taking place in the monotonous proceedings therein. He hastened back, and found the younger boys all pouring in. Once in their places, they recited morning prayers, one of the divines reading the main portion, and all joining in the answers. Then came mass, a service familiar to Darlington in the course of his travels on the Continent. Each of the Professors said his own mass in one of the chapels which Darlington had just been exploring. He followed Ashley, and listened to him for a time, and then quitted the church. He knew the mass, and did not care to see it through. He made his way to the Professors' parlour, where Dr. Russell, the President, and Ashley found him, reading a book, when they came in to breakfast. Darlington had been curious as to the meaning of the silence in church, and took the first opportunity of asking.

"It was the meditation," said Dr. Russell.

"I understand," replied Darlington, "a mystic contemplation and *reverie*, I suppose, such as Comte was in the habit of indulging in every morning."

"No," said Dr. Russell, rather sharply; "it is not mystical, but very practical. It is a preparation for the duties of the day, and ends with a series of practical resolutions."

Darlington did not press Dr. Russell further, but took occasion, when the President was talking to some one else, to ask Ashley for a fuller explanation. Then he learnt that meditation had been customary in the Church from earliest times, that it had been systematised by St. Ignatius Loyola, that it consisted in reflection on a scene in our Lord's life, or on sin, or death, or any other important truth—an attempt to make it vivid in the mind, so as to have a real effect on conduct, including practical resolutions, and prayer for strength to carry them out. This was, he gathered, an ordinary type of meditation, though there were many technical modifications of it.

"You see," added Ashley to his explanation, "we

believe that we are living in the midst of supernatural influences, and that our actions will affect, for good or ill, our fate for all eternity; but these facts are easily forgotten *practically*. Meditation is intended to ensure what we speculatively believe having the effect on us which it ought to have. We think of these truths just as a father places before his spendthrift son the consequences of his folly and extravagance, which he already knows, but does not reflect on."

All this was very interesting to Darlington, and seemed to him logical and reasonable from Ashley's point of view. He then questioned him about the silence before they entered the chapel, and learnt that the students were supposed, in order to make sure of the thoughts in question taking root in their minds, to read the meditation the night before, and to think as little as possible of anything else until mass time next morning. To help them in this, strict silence was enjoined.

"From your account," Darlington said, "it seems to be a sort of retreat, such as I have known Catholics make abroad."

"Precisely," Ashley replied; "a miniature retreat."

He then explained that the tension on the mind was considerable, and that the younger boys were not thought capable of it; but that at special times they also had similar exercises allotted to them—that is to say, during the regular formal retreats which took place twice in the year. Ashley watched with pleasure the interest which Darlington showed in hearing the particulars of the spiritual training of the students, and took the earliest opportunity he could find to sound him as to the effect of the previous night's conversation, now that he had had ten hours for it to sink into his mind.

"Well," Ashley began, as he and Darlington walked out of the breakfast-room together, "have you thought over our last night's talk at all? Are you ready to acquit us of being unreasonable fanatics who believe, or profess to believe, merely because religion suits our taste?"

Darlington hesitated. "I thought," he said, "that we had an interesting talk, and that there was a good deal in what Walton said. I thought that we got at the truth as far as we went, but I can't see that he really proved his case against me."

"Where did he fail then—what is your difficulty?" asked Ashley.

"I think," said Darlington, "that he analysed correctly the two sorts of wish with respect to a belief—one being the wish to manufacture or to nurse it as the case may be, the other the wish that it should be true. The one is readily father to the thought, the other makes one fear that what is wished for is too good to be true. One begets a belief like Bentley's theory of an imaginary editor of *Paradise Lost*, the importance of which to him was not its truth, but its utility in affording him an hypothesis to rest upon which would warrant his continuing work which interested him. The other is the wish of Penelope for the return of Ulysses, which was so strong that she could not for a long time convince herself that it had come to pass. All this I see; and I think that in the sense which he explained the first class of belief has no great depth of root, while the other, from the caution and anxiety it implies, requires fully sufficient reasons and does take deep root."

"That is precisely what Walton was contending for," said Ashley.

"Wait a moment," Darlington continued. "Now for my point of divergence from him. He seemed to think it clear that the wish of religious believers is of the latter type, whereas it seems to me that facts point to an opposite conclusion. Theirs is no case of breathless expectation of news—tidings of unspeakable happiness, which prevents them from daring to believe with confidence for fear of the shock of disappointment. On the contrary, the belief will not be verified for a long time to come, or at least a time which most people picture as indefinitely distant—the time of death. It is rather the continuance of habits and trains of thought endeared by constant association, just as Bentley wished to pursue the line of study which interested him; or in the case of converts, it is the attraction which religion has for them either by force of reaction, or from a natural interest in and taste for religious thoughts and ceremonies. There is no near prospect of a rough awakening from the dream, and so it is indulged."

"You certainly don't give us credit for much sincerity in our professions," said Ashley.

"You mistake me," replied Darlington; "I don't for a moment think you are insincere. But I say that your principal motive—or one of your principal motives—for belief is a wish, hardly acknowledged perhaps in the case of those who have always believed, to cling to what is dear to you. This is not insincerity any more than a doctor is dishonest who has not probed far enough, and says there is no bullet in a wound when there really is. He thinks honestly that there is none. I am not sure that Bentley was insincere, though, of course, his is an extreme case. He did not care about the truth of his belief sufficiently to test its depth, to probe the bullet-wound thoroughly."

"I don't know that you would find it an easy matter to prove that to many of us religion would be so pleasant if we had not a really deep belief in its truth," said Ashley thoughtfully. "If you examined the details of the life of a Trappist monk (to take a strong case), I think you would find your account of the thing somewhat reversed. He does not believe in religion because he loves it, but he loves what is almost intolerable to flesh and blood because he has a deep belief that it is commanded by God. As to probing and testing the depth of his belief, it cannot surely be more effectually done than by his performance of a series of acts which are worse than worthless if his belief is not true. Surely that should suffice, if anything could, to make him attend seriously to the soundness and truth of his religion."

There was a pause of a few moments. Darlington was conscious that from the very nature of his attack he must be in constant danger of wounding the susceptibilities of a religious man; and the point he was now insisting upon was a peculiarly delicate one, as it seemed to border on a charge of insincerity. He had, therefore, two difficulties instead of one in replying. The first was to find a reply, and the second to express it without giving offence. Ashley, too, had an instinct that the conversation would run more freely if he could rid it of application to actual facts and charges against individuals; and, as his friend was silent, he resumed:—

"However, it is not of much use to appeal to the facts of the case. We have no measure which will positively ascertain the depth of belief in particular instances. Of course, you and I both judge according to our respective opportunities for observation. I may perhaps claim to have seen more of the details of the lives of religious people, while you, no doubt, on your side will charge me with being biassed and unfair. Walton's argument, as I understood it, was rather an assistance in judging how far and under what circumstances one's wishes led one to fallacious belief on the one hand and to reasonable certainty on the other, than a proof that no professing Christians are led unreasonably by their wishes. You brought a charge against us which implied that religious enthusiasm was a sign that belief was unreasonable, and that the wish to believe leads to precipitancy in accepting dogmas; and he showed on the other hand that neither of these were unequivocal signs of fallacy,—that enthusiasm need not be fanaticism, and that there is a species of longing for belief which breeds caution rather than precipitancy. He answered the *primâ facie* objection which you made, and which prevented your looking much further into the question. He said, practically, this: 'Before you dismiss religion as unreasonable because all religious men have the wish to believe, make sure what is the nature of the wish. True enough, there is a wish that begets fallacious belief, but there is another kind of wish which helps and steadies the reason instead of impeding it. Be sure, before you class all professors of religion together as fanatics, that the eagerness they show in the matter is of the former kind and not of the latter.' And in answering so far your objection he answered a doubt which might arise in his own breast or in mine as to whether we may not have been led astray by our wishes. The matter must be always to a great extent one of personal observation, and one cannot hope to record fully or satisfactorily the results of one's observations. Each individual must observe for himself. But Walton's principle is a guide to us. It showed that where we see reason to believe that much depends or is staked on the *truth* of a belief, the eagerness and zeal of a believer are far from being signs that he has been hasty in believing, but rather indicate a state of mind which would require a deep and real assurance; and thus it enables us to ascertain whether or no we have reason to fear that the particular fallacy in question has ensnared those with whom we are acquainted, and with still greater certainty whether it has biassed our own minds,—so far resolving religious belief in our own case into a part of moral probation where candour and conscientiousness are all-important."

They walked the length of the corridor in silence before Darlington resumed. "Look here," he said suddenly, as if he had just found something, "here is my view of what you have been saying, in a nutshell. There is one kind of wish, you say, which makes a man prejudiced, another which makes him reasonable; one which leads him to dreamland, another which makes him confine himself strictly to realities. Now to keep my argument within reasonable limits, take the case of the evidences of Christianity—not to go back to still more fundamental questions. I find that among thinking men, all my acquaintance without exception who hold that they are, in the face of modern criticism, satisfactory and sufficient, are men who have a naturally religious bent of mind, a wish to believe. They are enthusiasts, and do not pretend to be impartial in the matter. Those who, being quite equally capable of understanding them, have no bias either way, say, at most, that they leave the question undecided. The only men who regard the matter as settled on the affirmative side are, as I say, men with religious cravings. Then I ask, which kind of wish can I attribute to them. Can I attribute the wish that makes one *cautious* and *slow* when they are *less* cautious and *less* slow in believing than those who are indifferent?" He paused. "Can I?" he repeated.

Ashley looked puzzled. "I think," he said, "that they may be on a different footing. Those who are indifferent may take less pains in the matter and dismiss it in comparative carelessness."

"No," persisted Darlington. "I speak of people who have read all the standard books on evidences, and who take really a great interest in the whole matter—though, as I have said, quite without any party feeling."

"It is so difficult," said Ashley, "to answer a vague statement like yours. If I knew the people to whom you refer, perhaps I should have more to say in explanation;" and then he added after a pause, "I remember that you quoted yesterday the cases of Hume and Johnson. Well, there I should say that there was at least as much of the wish not to believe about Hume as of the wish to believe in Johnson."

Ashley did not feel satisfied with the completeness of his own answer, and was somewhat relieved at seeing Walton's portly form making its way towards them.

"Good morning, Darlington," he said as he approached. "I want you to walk over with me to Greystone and see my mission and church. You have found out already the difference between the new man and the old, and now I want you to see something of his new mode of living, and of the haunts and habits of the animal."

"I will go with pleasure," said Darlington. "Would you believe it? we are already at this early hour plunging into the very thick of theological argument, and you are just in time to help us."

"Come then—and you come too, Ashley," said Walton. "We can talk as we walk."

Ashley excused himself. "I have a lecture to give," he said; "but we shall meet again later."

The other two started without more ado, and Darlington lost no time in propounding his theory to Walton in its new shape.

"How can I suppose that the wish of these people is of the kind which makes belief slow and difficult," he repeated, "when I find that they believe sooner and more confidently than those who have no wish in the matter? And the only alternative I have left me—on your own principles mark, Walton—is to suppose that their wish is for the gratifications attendant on belief, and not a deep desire—as you explained it—for reasonable assurance of its truth."

"No doubt," said Walton musingly, "one who is very anxious in the whole subject will see more in the evidences than one who cares less about the matter."

"That is the very thing I say," said Darlington. "He puts something into the evidence for his pet doctrines which is not there. This is plainly unreasonable. Evidence is evidence, and must, if conclusive, convince any reasonable man.[1] If I find that an impartial man is far from convinced, while one who is notoriously a partisan professes himself satisfied, it is plain common sense in me to ascribe it to prejudice."

"I don't know," replied Walton. "I think that is a very insufficient account of the matter. Impartiality is, true enough, a remedy for one intellectual vice. But there are others which may be quite as fatal. But first let us see what right you have to take it for granted that one who sees more in an argument than another does so through prejudice."

"Don't distort my statement," interrupted Darlington. "What I say is that where I find one estimate placed on arguments by all impartial critics, and another only by those who are notoriously and confessedly interested in one side of the question, it seems a plain conclusion that these last add the weight of their own bias to arguments which in themselves are insufficient. If dispassionate thinkers of my acquaintance state clearly the arguments on both sides, can even show keen appreciation of the Christian and Catholic position, but finally declare the case 'not proven,' it seems plain to me that those who profess not only to see a probability but to possess absolute certainty on the believing side,

[1] It may be as well to observe at the outset, for the benefit of Catholic readers, that Walton's argument concerns exclusively what theologians call the *judicium credibilitatis*, or act of the intellect, whereby the evidences for revelation are judged to be convincing. He would, no doubt, consider any further question of technical theology out of place, as being unintelligible to one in Darlington's position.

being, as I have said, men of strong religious emotions, have been influenced by those emotions to believe what reason quite fails to establish. This is the plainest of conclusions, drawn on the principles of induction. It is an instance of one of Mill's canons. Here are phenomena agreeing in many respects, differing in two. On the one side there is the judicial temperament and suspense of judgment. or rather a decision that certainty is unattainable; on the other, strong religious cravings and a profession that certainty is attained. Reasoning power and evidence are the same in both cases, therefore the inevitable conclusion is that bias is at the root of this professed certainty."

Walton reflected a few moments before he spoke. He was trying to see at what point exactly the issue between them lay.

"It comes to this," he said at last. "If you have two men equally endowed with logical acuteness, the one without any bias, the other anxious for religious belief, and if the former considers, after reading the recognised works on the subject, that the evidence is insufficient, while the latter is convinced, you think it plain that the latter is unreasonably biassed by his wish—that those conditions which have determined his mind to belief as distinguished from suspense of judgment, are not reasonable motives, but prejudice."

"How can they be reasonable motives," said Darlington, "when I am supposing that all the reasons are equally known to the other? We had better keep to our assumption of exactly similar intellectual power, though of course there is something rather grotesque in abstract principles and typical cases."

"Now I should say," said Walton, slowly and deliberately, "that granting every one of your conditions, which as you say are of course never accurately realised in fact, granting equal ability, the same evidence before both, impartiality and indifference on the one side, and great anxiety to believe, if possible, on the other, if the latter man does believe, it is, as you say, owing—at least, indirectly—to his craving and anxiety; but that his belief is, or may very well be, eminently reasonable:" and he looked at Darlington, conscious that he was propounding what was at first sight a paradox.

"My dear Walton, how can a craving or wish which *hastens* belief do so reasonably? That is contrary to your own principles, and it is absurd. His wish can't put more into the evidence than there is in it."

"No," said Walton; "but it may make him *find* more than the other finds. I know what you are going to say," he said, as Darlington tried to interrupt him; "you are going to say that in our typical case the *same* evidence is before both. Granted. And they are both equally able to apprehend its logical force. Granted too. But the religious-minded man may get beyond its logical statement; he will *feel* its force——"

"Exactly," interrupted Darlington. "He will

feel more than reason warrants. That is what I say. Such men let feeling do duty for reason."

"No," persisted Walton; "he does not substitute feeling; rather his feeling and his interest in the matter stir his reason to activity. There is a perception which one whose mind constantly dwells on a subject and who loves it acquires, which is beyond expression in words, and which is outside the sphere of verbal evidence; such a man acquires a special power in his estimate of evidence relating to the subject in question. Look at the musician who is devoted to a special composer. He can decide whether such a piece is or is not by him, merely by means of comparing it with the norm which his familiarity with the style of his favourite and his store of memories enable him to establish. He could not fully express the evidence on paper, but it is none the less evidence to him and *reasonably* apprehended. quite untinged with bias."

"That is not a fair comparison," rejoined Darlington; "a musical ear is a special gift. We are speaking of plain, straightforward evidence of historical facts. This appeals to that reasoning power which all mankind possess, and not to any special sense."

"The parallel is not exact," replied Walton, "but it will help me to explain what I mean. Let us take another typical case—this one shall be mine and not yours. To make my case more apposite, I suppose two men of equally good musical ear. One has studied Mendelssohn carefully, the other far less so. A fragment of MS. music is found: there is considerable circumstantial evidence to show that it is by Mendelssohn. The man who is less closely acquainted with Mendelssohn's style, pronounces the case unproven; the other confidently asserts that it is not by Mendelssohn. The evidence is before both. Both are equally talented. One is devoted to Mendelssohn, the other has not made his works a special study. What is it which enables one to decide confidently and rightly while the other is in doubt? It is a certain personal perception acquired by the close attention which he has been led to give to the subject by his interest in Mendelssohn's works. One of the items of evidence on paper would be, 'There are passages which render it difficult to suppose that it is by Mendelssohn:' this is to be weighed against strong circumstantial evidence that it is by Mendelssohn. The MS. is in his handwriting, it is found among other fragments undoubtedly genuine. Now, though both critics hear the array of arguments, the particular one from internal evidence assumes gigantic proportions in the mind of one of them. He manipulates it, so to speak, with a master's skill, gets out of it all that is to be got, and it decides the whole question. Why is this? Does not the other understand this particular item of evidence? Yes; but he has not acquired that personal power which enables him to *weigh it truly*—his appreciation of it is vague and (as he himself feels) uncertain. Thus though the evidence might be similarly *stated* by both—I mean that each might give a similar list of arguments *pro* and *con*—the relative weight attached by them to this particular item would differ *toto cœlo.* One grasps the full force of what the other only half understands."

"Of course," said Darlington, rather impatiently. "All this is true enough of music. It is true of any art; and for this reason, that all that is really important in it is beyond the sphere of plain evidence and appeals to a special sense. If that sense has been cultivated in a particular direction, no doubt it is more acute in that direction."

"Yes, but mark," put in Walton, "the direct perception only affected a portion of the evidence."

"Oh! that was a mere trick of yours," said Darlington. "You put that in for the sake of making the case seem at first sight parallel to religious evidence. It is plain that the real essence of your example is in the special musical perception of one man, which is not shared by the other. The rest of the evidence was mere pretence. You might as well suppose two men—one blind and the other not—judging of the evidence for the presence of a third party in a room. You might give a list of signs which both could perceive—a step heard unlike that of either, the sound of a cough unlike the accustomed cough of either—I won't say of a voice, as that would be unmistakable even by the blind man; the rustling of a newspaper proceeding apparently from a direction different from the position of either, and so forth. The blind man is not, you will say, certain; but the other clinches the argument by special personal perception, namely, the sight of his eyes. I think it would be shorter to say that one man sees a third party in the room, and the other hasn't eyes, so he can't see. Unless you take the Christian evidences out of the category of reasoning altogether, and suppose one man to have a sort of spiritual sense which the other has not got, your parallel falls altogether. If you maintain, as you profess to, that they are a matter of reasoning, just as a fact is which has to be proved in the law courts, this personal element of which you speak finds no place at all. It is either another term for a special sense, as in the case of art, or it must mean prejudice. Fancy a juror who refused to convict Lefroy on the ground that there was a personal element in his appreciation of the evidence which made him believe the prisoner to be not guilty! I think that if it were afterwards discovered that he was a friend of Lefroy's, people would not be slow in suspecting what the nature of the personal element was."

"Well, I will meet you on your own ground," said Walton, a little nettled at Darlington's confident tone, and at the apparent common sense of his answer. "You have not treated my example fairly, but I do not care to insist upon it at present. I will take a case of ordinary circumstantial evidence. I maintain, in spite of all you say, that there may be circumstances in which one man may, from his knowledge of character or from his acquaintance with particular persons, or his intimate familiarity with the details of some science, take a different and a far truer view of evidence before a law court than the average educated juryman who has not this assistance. And his view may be purely personal in the sense that he is in possession of no further evidence on the subject; but facts in the existing evidence may be to him, on account of his antecedents, of different significance; and this will not indicate a prejudiced mind but rather special clearness of sight. Take for instance a charge of fraud against some one of whose integrity you are absolutely sure. My case will not be strong enough unless you think of some individual. There are many whom you *think* incapable of such a thing, but some whom you *know* to be so. I should imagine that one who knew Dr. Johnson or Dr. Arnold most intimately would have had the absolute assurance of which I speak in their regard."

"Oh! I quite agree," said Darlington, not thinking for the moment of the connection of his admission with the argument; "there are persons whose character is completely formed and fixed in uprightness, for whom a downright dishonourable act would be a moral impossibility. I could mention persons of whom I should say this from my own knowledge of them."

"Well then," resumed Walton, "suppose the strongest evidence of a circumstantial kind were brought against such a man, a juror, to whom this evidence is quite intelligible and convincing, would decide against him in spite of his previous good character. Your assurance that he is incapable of the act may have *some* weight, but little in comparison with the overwhelming evidence against him. You cannot convey to the juror the *personal knowledge* which is in your own mind, and the only indication you can give of it is to him vague and unreliable. He cannot be sure that you are not biassed, though you yourself may be conscious that you are not. He cannot distinguish the interested partisanship of a friend, from the clear serene feeling of certainty, begotten of intimate knowledge, which is in many cases its own guarantee that it corresponds with truth. Thus your own certainty of the man's innocence is, as I have said, personal and yet reasonable. Your judgment differs from that of the juror, though you have the same evidence before you. The juror judges as nine-tenths of those who see the evidence would judge. But you, through your close acquaintance with the ground of one particular portion of the case for the defence—that portion which relates to the criminal's previous good character—have acquired a sense of its force which makes you able reasonably and confidently to differ from others in your estimate of the whole matter. And I would add a fact which seems to me important, that your judgment would carry with it a sense of *power* and *knowledge* as distinguished from a feeling of impotence to take another view, or inability to enter into it. The juryman would not have a feeling similar to yours. Your state of mind would be, 'I am perfectly sure'; his would be, 'the circumstances of the case are such and so significant that I see no room for doubt.' "

He looked at Darlington, but saw from his face that he was not following his remarks further, but was turning over the example in his mind.

"Well, Darlington," he continued, "will you allow some reason to a personal view of evidence in the case I have given?"

"You have yet to apply it to the real question at issue," said Darlington; "and I cannot see where you will find in Paley or Butler anything at all parallel to the intimate knowledge we may have of a friend's character. But anyhow your instance seems to me unreal. Overwhelming evidence against a man of unblemished character is not a common thing, and practically the difference of view would be much less than you describe. The friend would be shocked at the evidence, and the juror would be slow to convict, even on strong evidence, if the prisoner were held by his friends to be a Dr. Arnold in integrity."

"Of course I stated an extreme case to point my moral," said Walton; "that I take to be the whole *rationale* of an illustration, to show the working of a principle in an instance where it is unmistakable, in order that one may be ready to admit it in what is more complex and obscure. But I do not admit that my instance is unreal or improbable. The history of Lesurques and Dubosc was exactly a case in point. The story will be familiar to you from the English plays founded upon it. I remember Charles Kean in the *Courier of Lyons*, and you no doubt have seen

Mr. Irving's last version of the same story in the *Lyons Mail*. It was a case of mistaken identity, and took place in France in the last century. Lesurques was a man of good position and spotless integrity, and had been singularly fortunate and prosperous in his career. At least so he is represented in the play. He considers himself 'the happiest man that ever lived,' and the story of his death is consequently all the more tragic. The robbery of the Lyons mail took place at a posting-house kept by his father, and on the very night on which the crime was committed Lesurques himself was on the spot intent, as he said, on some act of kindness to his father. When the mail was robbed he was actually, it appeared, seen by several witnesses, among them his father, taking part in the crime and in the murders which accompanied it. The evidence against him was overwhelming, and on the strength of it he was guillotined; and too late it was discovered that the real criminal was a man, called in the play Dubosc, resembling him exactly in features and general appearance.[1] Surely this is as strong a case as any imaginary one I could invent! The evidence was direct and apparently conclusive. Mistaken identity was his only possible plea, and he was quite unaware at the time of the existence of this villain who was his exact counterpart; and when challenged to prove an *alibi* was unable to do so. His guilt seemed proved; and those few friends who knew him and trusted him in spite of all, must have

[1] This discovery is, in the play, previous to the time appointed for his execution; and he consequently escapes.

appeared to the world at large utterly beyond the reach of sensible argument. They were trusting to a vague, undefinable feeling, and going in the very teeth of evidence as conclusive as circumstantial evidence could be; and yet if Lesurques were such a man as I have supposed, and said to his friend, looking him full in the face, 'I declare before God I am innocent,' the conviction produced, and reasonably produced, in that friend would be absolute and incapable of being shaken."

"Certainly that is a strong case," said Darlington; "but I should say that in reality the friend and the outside world were not viewing the *same* evidence. The friend had a past knowledge of Lesurques, which the jury and others had not. Here was a separate item in the considerations before his mind."

"No doubt," replied Walton, "you may look at it so; but that does not affect what I say. Whether you call this personal element fresh evidence, or consider the evidence to be the verbal statement, and the knowledge which colours it as imparting a perception to the mind in its estimate of it, it comes to the same. It is a mere question of words. What I want to show is that this element most frequently exists, and carries the mind to truth instead of prejudicing it."

"I think again," said Darlington, after a few minutes' reflection, "that knowledge of the character of a friend is very unique, and will hardly be found to help you if you are giving principles for the estimation of *historical* evidence. You can have no friendship with the dead, and a past fact is not proved by anything resembling personal acquaintance."

"Have patience," continued Walton. "I have given the case of knowledge of character first, because it seems to me to be a particularly strong instance of personal perceptions as affecting one's view of verbal evidence. It is not the only instance, though I believe that something very similar to it bears an important part in the impression produced on each man by the study of Christianity. What I wish to show is that in all evidence there are items which appeal more or less to personal perceptions, and that in many cases those perceptions will differ in individuals, without implying a want of candour in those holding either view, but simply a lesser or greater power of judging in the particular subject-matter."

"Oh! you are going through all the cases given in Newman's *Essay on Assent*, I suppose," said Darlington. "I quite allow that a good general is a good judge of military position, a good scholar of Tacitus' style, a man with a turn for politics of a political situation, and the rest. These are all questions of what is called 'implicit reasoning.' I should have something to say on this subject, but it is not the same as that of which we now speak. I am purposely confining myself to the recognised explicit arguments in favour of Christ's divine mission and miraculous history. Paley's *Evidences*, Liddon's *Bampton Lectures*, Butler's *Analogy*—it is of such works I speak. I am not supposing an intellect which travels under ground, as it were, and emerges, with no knowledge of the road it has traversed, in a state of Christian belief—declaring that, though it cannot give reasons for its conclusion, that is no sign that they do not exist, but only that they are implicit. That is a special puzzle which I am not at present trying to find out. Let us keep to plain, explicit evidence. There are many who profess that the recognised explicit evidences suffice for them, and it is enough for the present to consider them."

"What you say only helps to bring me to the central point of my argument," said Walton. "What I particularly want to show is that, even where arguments are stated most explicitly, there is a personal element in their full apprehension. I can understand your considering the knowledge of character of which I spoke as a conclusion gained by implicit reason and *added* to the evidence. That is not the account I myself should give, simply because the mind is so constantly affected in its judgment by its store of impressions formed by past experiences, that to isolate one seems to me unscientific. However, let us now take the plainest and most clearly stated evidence we can think of. Some murderer has, as Lefroy, the Brighton murderer, did, escaped from the police, and it is their business to trace him. He has been clearly traced to Stoke-on-Trent. They find that a man answering to his description was seen at Stoke-on-Trent station on the day after the murder a short time before the 10.15 train started for London. Again at Stone one of the porters noticed a similar man in the same train in a first-class carriage; and when the ticket-collector took the tickets at Willesden, he, too, noticed the man, who, it so happened, was unable for some time to find his ticket. Further inquiry results in a similar declaration on the part of five other porters. Now here is a very simple chain of evidence. Any reasonable mind on considering it would come to the conclusion that the man who was seen at Stoke had in all probability gone to London. Here you will say that there is no personal element in appreciating the evidence at all. Credible witnesses see him at different places on the line, on close examination they give an exactly similar account of his personal appearance and dress, and the conclusion is a mere matter of common sense. Now I quite agree that all reasonable men will conclude alike here; but I wish to point out that in each case there is an exercise of personal judgment, though, for reasons I shall give, the result is for each the same. There are certain suppositions which would invalidate the conclusion. The witnesses *may* have committed perjury, in spite of the good character they previously bore. There may have been a man exactly similar to the man seen at Stoke, and dressed in the same way; and this second man may have been the loser of his ticket, while the original man may have been walking on the platform to pass away his time, and left it unperceived without entering the train. Now, as I have said, any reasonable man will dismiss these suppositions—and why? Is there any clear logical statement which will disprove them? Take one of them only—the first. How can you logically prove that eight men of unimpeachable character have not every one of them committed perjury (supposing that to be the only possible flaw in the evidence), and that merely for the fun of the thing and without any further motive? You can't *prove* it, but it is wildly improbable. And why do you judge it improbable? Because our knowledge of human nature tells us that men do not do such things. This is surely a decision on personal grounds. No doubt these grounds are shared by all men; but they are personal to each. The fact that all men have sufficient personal experience of human nature to make their decision in such a case the same, makes one forget, until it is pointed out, that the decision is arrived at, not by logical rule, but by a process similar to that by which Lesurques' intimate friend was convinced of his innocence, with this entirely accidental difference—that in one case all have the experience requisite for a true decision, in the other case only a few."

"Oh! of course there is always judgment to be exercised in weighing evidence," said Darlington. "Perhaps it would not have occurred to me in the case you gave, as it is so simple that one would hardly be at the pains to analyse it—just as one may never have reflected—any more than M. Jourdain did, until it was pointed out to him—that he had been talking prose all his life. But I don't see what you gain by the long explanation you have just given. It seems to me much ado about nothing. Because an exercise of common sense is justified in the case you have given, that is no proof that the view of an excited enthusiast is warranted by reason. I should rather say that your instance heightens the contrast I gave, and tells in my favour. It shows that sober-minded men judge alike in matters of evidence, and that their judgment is reliable."

"I am afraid that I shall have to be somewhat tedious in my explanation," returned Walton, "and shall only be able to draw out my meaning by a dull train of examples, extorting admissions out of you the full meaning of which you will not see—in true Socratic style. But I will try to be as brief as possible. The only point which I insist upon in my example is what you have granted;—that even in the simplest evidence there is an exercise of personal judgment amenable to no law, but ratified by the mind's own positive declaration."

"Clearly," said Darlington, rather impatiently, "it is not all a logical train like Euclid."

"Now one step further," said Walton. "In the example I have given the logical part of the argument attracts most attention, because the other part is plain, and is hardly expressed in words. One would express the thing, 'He was seen at such a place and at such another place, and therefore it is plain that he has gone to London.' One might even imagine a case where this aspect would be more strongly exhibited."

"I see what you mean," said Darlington; "you need not enlarge upon it."

"Let us now take a case," pursued Walton, "where these proportions are reversed. To avoid being more tedious than is absolutely necessary, I will plunge *in medias res* at once. Let us take one of the very books you have named—Liddon's *Bampton Lectures on the Divinity of Christ.* Perhaps the third lecture will suit our purpose as well as any. It is on the work of our Lord in the world as a witness to His divine mission. He draws attention to the unique history of the Jews, to the unpromising nature of Christ's scheme, and its audacity; and yet to the calm confidence with which He proposes it, its novelty, its realisation by powers and forces unparalleled in the past history of the world, and so forth. Now the mere logic of his argument is of the simplest. It amounts to this: the phenomena of which I speak are such as to render impossible the supposition that they are due to anything short of special divine interposition; therefore divine interposition must have taken place. The whole force of the argument lies in the judgment of the mind as to how far the antecedent proposition is warranted by the facts of the case."

"You speak truly, O Socrates!" said Darlington, laughing.

"That is to say," said Walton, waxing more earnest, "the just and right estimate of the argument depends principally, not on clearness of head, not on logical consecutiveness, but on the accurate gauging of, on the one hand, the marvellous facts of Jewish and Christian history, and on the other the powers and capabilities of unassisted human nature."

Darlington nodded assent.

"In other words, on this very personal element of which we have spoken. You read Liddon's lecture to a friend. You say at the end, 'Do you see Liddon's argument?' He replies at once, 'Oh yes! he states it most lucidly; I understand it thoroughly.' You press him: 'Do you think it powerful?' If he is a sensible man he replies, 'I will think it well over, and then I will tell you how it impresses me.' And it is this thinking it well over, this mental digestion, this personal apprehension of the considerations, which is the important and critical part of the matter."

Darlington did not say anything; but his face, when Walton looked at it, did not betoken agreement, but rather dissatisfaction at being unable at the moment to find words for his difference of opinion.

"Let us add to this argument in question," continued Walton, "that of Liddon's fourth lecture, in which he insists upon the unique personal character of Christ, on its moral beauty, its superhuman consistency, its possession of qualities incapable of co-existence in mere man, the lowliest humility together with the most absolute self-assertion, the contrast of His conscious greatness with the self-abasement of the prophets, His enthusiasm, and at the same time His 'sweet reasonableness' and entire freedom from fanaticism. Here is another argument calling, not for logical power, but for personal appreciation and just judgment."

Darlington had by this time shaped his difficulty. "You really are not touching my position in all you are saying," he insisted. "No doubt the particular arguments you are speaking of call rather for calm and true judgment than for a power of following a train of syllogisms. But, in the first place, they are only a tithe of the arguments available on the whole subject; and in the second place—even if we confine ourselves to them, as you are doing—my original objection holds good. It is plain that an unbiassed man will judge more truly than one who has strong religious emotions and a desire for belief. It is all very well for you to say that there is a personal element in the view that each man takes of the evidence. No doubt that is true in a sense; and it makes it impossible to put your finger on a fallacy as you can in mere logic. But the personal element, as you call it, is merely the exercise of the power of judging, which is far more likely to be correctly exercised by one who is perfectly unbiassed one way or the other, than by one whose reason is disturbed and prejudiced by a wish to come to one conclusion rather than another."

"Now we are really getting at what I want," said Walton. "I maintain that in estimating considerations such as I have mentioned, an active interest and sense of the importance of the conclusion to which they point, and a certain amount of emotional sympathy with them, are absolutely necessary. A man who does not apply his emotional and imaginative faculties cannot feel them, cannot get beyond the mere logic of them—that hard rind of truth (for it is true as far as it goes) which George Eliot lays down as the limit of the knowledge of the unimaginative and unsympathetic. The calm, lawyer-like man who studies the matter as though it were an illustration of some interesting legal principle, and not of deep practical importance to himself, stands no chance of knowing their full force. No doubt such a man runs no risk of overrating it, but he runs the greatest risk of underrating it."

"My dear Walton," interrupted Darlington, "what should we do if we accepted this strange theory of yours? We should have our law courts supplied by enthusiastic jurymen, or intimate friends of the prisoner or of the witnesses for the prosecution."

"No; the cases are not parallel," said Walton, a little puzzled. "The law courts go on the principle that it is better to acquit a guilty man than to hang one who is innocent. They dare not risk the influence of bias either way. The outside world cannot be sure what is partisanship and what intimate knowledge. Personal certainty of which I speak is safeguarded, as we shall see, by a sense of personal responsibility. The certainty is your own, and if you conclude wrongly it affects yourself and no one else. The case is different with the juror, who is deciding what affects another, and fears no evil result to himself from a wrong decision. But we shall see this better later on. Let me first show more clearly what I mean in reference to the arguments from our Lord's work and personal character. It is a very different thing to know a fact and believe it on the one hand, and on the other realise fully its significance. This of course is taken for granted in our whole ascetical and spiritual system. The monk commences his day by an hour of meditation in order that that world of whose existence he has no doubt may be to him a reality as well as a truth. The sinner makes no question that hell exists; but if its existence were vividly before him—were, as I have termed it, realised by him—it would be so strong a motive as infallibly to deter him from sin. And the same principle holds good with regard not only to the effect of belief on our acts, but also to the weight of one belief as an argument for another. Cardinal Newman says in one of his sermons that it is a very easy thing for a man to sit in his study leading a student's life and to work out theological problems about hell without feeling the slightest difficulty in believing in its existence. But if he comes to mix with his kind, and it stands before him as a reality that hell must be at all events for some human beings, for A or B or C or D, he then finds it very hard to think it possible that even the worst of those with whom he has been in contact could be deserving of so awful a doom. Here is an instance of an argument so commonly urged *against* Catholic belief not being done justice to or felt in its full force, because it is not realised. I don't of course believe the argument to be conclusive; but I give it as an instance which, so far, will tell for your view of one of our dogmas, and which at the same time illustrates the principle on which I am insisting. Now just as a man may apprehend the idea of eternal punishment, and may understand the difficulty raised against its justice from the absence of all proportion between the sin of a finite being and a penalty which shall have no end, and yet may not feel the real force of the objection because he realises neither of the considerations which it involves, so may a man apprehend the meaning of Liddon's argument from Christ's unique personal character, and yet quite fail to be duly affected by it. He may hold with Mill that Christ's character is indubitably historical, and with Rousseau that the invention of such a career and personality is a more incredible hypothesis than their existence. And yet he may wholly fail to realise the argument to be derived from it either for His divine mission or for His actual divinity."

"It is rather a vague argument," said Darlington; "I should be sorry to stake much on it. I think that Mill's own conclusion with respect to it—that Christ's life was a perfect translation of the rule of right from the abstract to the concrete, and that He had *possibly* some special mission to mankind—is quite as much as you can hope to draw from it."

"Its statement is vague, certainly," replied Walton; "but I think it has far greater significance than you suppose to one who has studied it reverently. But let us keep to the point. What I insist on is that the strength of the argument, such as it is, does not depend on the considerations involved in it being known, but on their being realised. I do not say that it is by itself conclusive. But it has considerable force, and that force is only perceived where Liddon's statements are felt as realities as well as believed in as truths. I want you to mark this contrast between knowing a fact and realising it. Enoch Arden thought he could bear to see his wife after she had become another's, thinking him dead. But he had judged wrongly. Miriam had told him all, and he knew what he had to expect. But he had not fully realised it. It was as yet a sort of dream. When he saw the reality and felt vividly all that was involved in what had happened, he broke down. Do you remember the lines :—

> Now when the dead man come to life beheld
> His wife his wife no more, and saw the babe
> Hers, yet not his, upon the father's knee,
> And all the warmth, the peace, the happiness . . .

And so forth—

> Then he, *tho' Miriam Lane had told him all,*
> *Because things seen are mightier than things heard,*
> Stagger'd and shook, holding the branch, and fear'd
> To send abroad a shrill and terrible cry !

Grignon, in that amusing play of Scribe's, *La Bataille des Dames,* can face all dangers in imagination, but when they come in reality he is an arrant coward. And though the contrast between his attitude towards imaginary dangers and real ones is of course exaggerated for the sake of amusing the audience, it is sufficiently true to nature to illustrate what I say. In the pictures he forms the dangers are not, to him, realities, and he believes that he can face them. The spirit of his heroic mother possesses him, and he promises himself all possible soldierly achievement. But in the field of battle or in time of real danger the caution of his prudent father prevails, and it is only when he cannot fail to realise his danger that he gauges accurately his own powers. Here, then, is another aspect of the personal element in the estimate of arguments. The individual effort to transform a dead fact into a living reality is absolutely essential in such arguments. And if I am to be philosophical over it, I should describe it, in the case of historical facts, as consisting, at least partly, in the endeavour to clothe that which is apprehended in the first instance by the intellect only—involving of course some faint picture of the imagination—with the emotion and imagination which it would naturally have excited in the actual witnesses:—not as though one were to take the feelings of an excited mob, and the exaggerated conclusions which they might draw in their excitement, as infallible guides, but rather endeavouring so vividly to picture historical scenes and characters by means of those elements of emotion and imagination which constitute the actor's power of sympathy, that they, in turn, affect us as they would have affected us had we ourselves been among the mob."

"What you are speaking of," said Darlington, "seems to resemble the gift of an historian like Gibbon, who could make past facts stand out with wonderful vividness. I don't know," he added, smiling, "whether he will help you as an instance of its religious effects."

Walton was pursuing his own line of thought, and unconsciously suggested the answer to Darlington's question.

"I have just said," he continued, "that the actor's power of sympathy constitutes an element in what I have called realising a scene or an historical character. But I think that there is something beyond this mere emotional aspect of it. There is a deep sense that it is a fact, with practical consequences and effects on the world around, and possibly on yourself."

"I don't quite see your meaning," said Darlington. "It seems to me that the emotional appreciation which you described involves that, and that which you speak of now is nothing additional."

"No," pursued Walton; "I think that there is something over and above emotion—deeper than emotion. Grignon may have had a very vivid emotional picture of his dangers in the battle-field, and yet have remained as brave as a lion; but when danger was actually present, and he steadily felt that it concerned him, and might lead to practical results of a serious nature in connection with his own comfort, his courage evaporated. I think it was Charles Kemble who used to relate how he felt Mrs. Siddons' tears streaming down over his own face when he played Arthur. Yet human grief which concerns facts has something far deeper than the actor's sympathy with it. Mrs. Siddons could have wept had she lost a child in the play; but the aching sense of reality, with all its consequences, which the death of her own child would have aroused, could never have found place on the stage. There is one side of belief which is closely allied with emotion and imagination; another with facts, consequences, and action. Bain, I think, had this latter element in his mind when he spoke of belief as being 'readiness to act.'"

Walton paused, feeling that he had not fully

expressed his meaning, and yet not at the moment seeing his way further.

"I am afraid," he continued, "that I am rather fragmentary and scrappy. But I think some of the most important psychological truths are hard to express quite clearly. They are recondite in proportion to their intimate connection with ourselves. Newman says of certain motives for religious belief that we cannot see them, just as we cannot see ourselves: and in defence of my own imperfect account I can only cite George Eliot's expression. Do you remember how she speaks somewhere of 'that complex, fragmentary, doubt-provoking knowledge which we call truth?'"

"I think I see your meaning, though, all the same," said Darlington, reflectively.

"Anyhow," continued Walton, "be the analysis what it may, this realising facts as distinct from merely knowing them is a very important factor in giving just weight to many an argument. Do you remember, in the second act of Meyerbeer's *Etoile du Nord*, the scene in which Pietro, who has had too much to drink, condemns Caterina to be shot, not fully realising who she is? I remember that Faure's rendering of the play of feeling and mind used to bring very vividly before me the contrast of which I speak. He made it evident that he had recognised her, long before he had sufficiently recovered his mental balance to realise (I can find no other word) the effects of what he had done, and the necessity for immediate action. At length it comes upon him in full force. What had been a sort of dream, with no facts for consequences, and no necessity for personal effort, suddenly appears to him as it really is, bound up with his own responsibility and with the very life of her who is dearest to him. He makes a tremendous effort, throws off the effects of the wine in a moment, and sends in an agony of mind to countermand the sentence—though he fears it may already be too late."

"I remember the scene well," said Darlington. "Caterina is disguised as a soldier and strikes Gritzenko, the corporal, who has just reprimanded her for looking into Pietro's tent."

"Well, now," continued Walton, "let me try and show more clearly, by an example, how this element of realising may affect the conclusions one draws from a certain class of arguments. Some one says in 1780: 'The awful misery and oppression which the common people are undergoing in France, must lead before long to a terrible revolution;' and he mentions fact after fact. This is at the dinner table of M. le Marquis de R——, who is entertaining guests at his *château*. He is sipping his claret and listens with much interest. Some days afterwards other guests are dining with him, and he repeats with great gusto, as giving a zest to the entertainment, the sensational facts which he has heard. 'F—— thinks,' he adds, that it must ere long lead to a general revolution.' Neither the facts nor the revolution are realities to him. He could not draw the conclusion, though he can repeat it. He does not *see* it, because it is the vivid apprehension of the facts which leads to it, and that apprehension he has not got. But M. le Comte de V——, who is at his table, takes in every word with hungry avidity. After each of the details he is visibly shocked, and the whole company remarks how moody he becomes. He leaves early. 'Do you know, M. le Marquis," asks one of the guests, 'what makes our friend so much out of sorts?' M. le Marquis does not know. 'I think the facts you mentioned came home to him rather unpleasantly. He has been something of an absentee from his property, and his agent appears to have ill-treated his tenants past all bearing. They make little distinction between servant and chief, and one of them attempted to stab him the other day. I fancy that your account of the oppression which goes on, often unknown to the landlord, made him feel what reason there might be to apprehend another attempt of the same kind.' But in truth M. le Comte has been made very serious by the details in question. The facts which were forced on his attention in connection with the attempt on his own life, have given him a keen sense of the possibilities of serious results, and the whole question—both the oppression and the consequent danger to himself and to the State—is very real in his mind. You see at once my meaning—the danger was a conclusion from the reality of the facts. The Count realised the facts, and so could infer the danger. The Marquis could not see the reality of the danger, because excellent claret and the dinner party were much more real to him than anything else."

"The Count might easily be carried too far by his fears," Darlington remarked.

"As usual," said Walton, laughing, "you always want me to answer everything at once. Hear me out first. All I say at present is that there was a *just* conclusion to be drawn, and no one could draw it by logic, but only by realising the facts and their significance. I think, then," he continued after a pause, "that this element of realising the considerations involved in some of the Christian evidences, throws considerable light on your original question. The man who is intensely in earnest and anxious for knowledge, if it is really attainable, will take far more pains than another to do this. If he is anxious in the way I described for a belief, if it is only knowable as true, his anxiety tells both ways; it guards him, as we saw yesterday, against over-estimating the force of arguments, and yet at the same time it stimulates him to use his utmost endeavour to appreciate fully all that may help him to find or hold what he is so anxious for. 'Where there's a will there's a way,' says the proverb. A man who is bent on passing an examination, finds his faculties stimulated and works with a concentrated energy and success, which he cannot command in the absence of such an incitement. And in the same way, if a man feels keenly that religious belief, if attainable, is all-important to him, his whole nature becomes intensified in the search for it. He will marshal the evidences which are offered to lead him to it with an activity of mind, and will ponder them with an earnestness, which one who views the whole matter as an interesting problem only can never possess; and so he is convinced sooner, not through bias, but because the arguments, instead of remaining logical *formulæ* outside him, have taken full possession of his soul, and are felt not as vague ideas, but as facts vividly realised in all their connection with each other and with himself. To draw, then, for the moment, only a partial conclusion, is it not at least a possible hypothesis, that when Gibbon gave five causes which he thought would account for the spread of Christianity by merely natural forces, he had failed, through want of earnestness, both to gauge correctly the powers of human nature, and to realise the significance of the phenomena with which he dealt? And when Locke, on the other hand, said that he found in Scripture alone sufficient proof of the divinity of Christianity, or, to take a more satisfactory instance, when Newman finds in the very phenomena which Gibbon explains away the strongest confirmation of his belief, is it not, on the principles we have allowed, at least possible that he may have intensely realised and felt the true force of what would have been but partially understood by one who was less in earnest?"

"Well," said Darlington, slowly. "one could not prove that it had not been so."

"I don't know whether you see," continued Walton, smiling, "that you have already considerably moved from your original position. You commenced by saying that if one who was anxious for religious conviction was satisfied by evidence which, to one who was indifferent, seemed insufficient, it was plain that he had been biassed ; and now you grant that it is at least possible that his anxiety may have made him see what the other failed to see."

Darlington did not answer at once. "I will hear you out," he said, after a few moments. "I have a good deal to say, but I want thoroughly to understand you first."

"There is another very important element in Christianity," Walton continued, "which depends in the last resort on personal effort for its due appreciation. We have already spoken of remarkable traits in the character of Christ, which should stand before the mind as real facts in order that their true significance may be felt. But I think it possible to get beyond the mere knowledge of admirable qualities. We have seen this in the case of a personal friend. There is sometimes a knowledge of him so intimate as to give a sort of electric sympathy with what goes on in his mind, and enable us to predict within certain limits what would be his action in this or that case—and still more confidently what it would *not* be. The process whereby this takes place is worth noting. It may be, and often is, in some such way as the following :—First we see him perform isolated acts of generosity, public spirit, tenderness of sympathy, and so forth. Gradually these instances are multiplied. We see by dint of constant association with him that they are no products of a changeable spirit, which may give an alms through physical pity one day and have a dependant turned out into the street to starve through ill-temper or dyspepsia the next. Thus in time the acts assume a harmony, and are regarded as qualities. Not only has he done this or that act of kindness or high-mindedness, but we see that he *is* kind and *is* high-minded. But we may know this of many a man—know very many of his good qualities and frailties too—without feeling, as we should express it, that we thoroughly understand him. There is an additional blending into harmony which we do not yet perceive—and that is the proportion and interconnection of his various qualities which form his *character*. Once we know the forces at work in the motion of the heavenly bodies, we can calculate the position of a planet which has not been directly observed. The discovery of Neptune was, as you know, made in this way. We have the key both to phenomena we have observed and to those we have not. We have found it by a careful study of those we can observe. The character is the key to a man's qualities; and there is a perception of *character*, as distinct from a mere knowledge of various qualities, which close and constant study will give, and which enables us to predict, with greater or less certainty, what a man would do under circumstances in which we have not seen him. It cannot be exactly expressed, but it consists in a feeling that, as I have put it, we *understand* the man in question; just as an actor must understand the character he depicts, being unable, if he is intelligent, to represent a mere series of abstract virtues and vices. Now surely a very close and constant study of Scripture gives this sort of knowledge of Christ—not perhaps quite in the same degree as actual knowledge of a living man could do, but still in a very remarkable degree. It is clear that the subtle perception shown in Dr. Liddon's lecture of the significance of the juxtaposition in Christ of certain qualities is, to a great extent,[1] the result of close familiarity with, and contemplation of, Christ's character in the Gospels; and I say that this same process may make one's perception keener and keener until at last His personality stands out clearly, and is seen in its full harmony. I do not pretend to draw out fully the results of this; but I have seen the fact strikingly illustrated in many holy men I know, whose minds dwell constantly on sacred history. The Christian spirit is a phrase commonly used, and really implies as its foundation much the same thing. When a man feels that his knowledge of our Lord is so intimate that he knows almost on each occasion of his own probation what He would have done in similar circumstances, he acquires a trust in Him which renders it inconceivable that He should have professed to be what He was not in reality. And, again, he feels the unsatisfactory nature, the inconsistency and discord, of any view other than the Christian. M. Renan's Christ, with His "tenderness of a vague poetry" towards women, His mixture of belief in Himself with hypocrisy, and the rest—which have to be explained

[1] I say "to a great extent," because he may have been aided by the remarks of other commentators.

as being Oriental, that is to say, outside the experience of ordinary readers—is to him an impossible personage. His subtle perception of the harmonious interrelation of qualities in the Scriptural Christ makes him feel that you cannot destroy as much as M. Renan does without destroying more. His reason revolts against the theory that the raising of Lazarus was a pious fraud quietly acquiesced in by Christ for the sake of gaining influence. The 'frightful accesses of enthusiasm' which Renan speaks of jar unspeakably with the calm and divine dignity which he has come to know and worship. He has a keen insight into the links between one quality and another, and draws, not from a broad half-stated argument, but by finest and subtlest perception, the old conclusion 'Christus si non Deus non bonus.' M. Renan is, he sees, a bad character-artist. He has the dull perceptions of one who ornaments a Gothic church in the Italian style.[1] A real artist would destroy more, or destroy nothing."

"All this seems to me very hazy and unreliable," said Darlington.

"No doubt," replied Walton; "the very remark which you would have made to the friend of Lesurques who was true to him, and believed him innocent in the face of the strongest evidence. He would have said, 'I know him too well to think him capable of this crime, or to believe that he could assure me of his innocence, being all the while guilty; such ideas are

[1] The hideous Renascence altar in Amiens Cathedral is an instance of the effect of such a combination.

out of harmony with his whole character;' and you would have laughed at him for trusting this vague, unreliable impression rather than the strong, definite, tangible evidence on the other side. It is of the essence of this kind of personal experience that its record should appear to another unsatisfactory, vague; —that is the very strength of my argument. There is something beyond the verbal record, which that record cannot convey."

"But, after all," said Darlington, "Scripture *is* but the verbal record."

"Don't let us split straws," replied Walton. "You see plainly what I mean. Boswell's *Johnson* gives to the careful student a knowledge of Johnson far more accurate than can be analysed verbally, and surely one is not paradoxical if one attributes the same power to the scriptural sketch of our Lord. The record in Scripture or in Boswell's Life is not an *analysis*, but a sketch, which has to be carefully studied to be appreciated. Here, then, is another instance in which it is not the logical apprehension of the verbal statement, but the individual effort to penetrate behind the words, which enables one to understand the force of the argument in question; and I would ask, Who is the man who is most likely to do such arguments ample justice? I should say, to put it on the lowest ground, that in this, as in all else, the instinct of self-preservation holds good. If a man is (as religious-minded men are) filled with the thought that knowledge of the highest kind possible and greatest personal importance is offered to him, which if not attained, by his own fault, may result in the greatest unhappiness to himself, it is plain that he will do his best to attain to it, and devour all considerations placed before him as the necessary conditions, with hungry avidity. And if at the same time he is conscious that his whole life must be based on that knowledge, if attained, he will be unable to stake his all on an uncertainty, and will be thus protected from any unduly sanguine view in the matter. In other words, the greater the effort he makes to realise the gravity of the whole issue and its practical bearing on himself, the more likely is he, as a consequence, to enter fully and justly into all that tends to throw light on what he feels to be so important."

"I see that he should be anxious for truth in the abstract," said Darlington; "but it seems to me unjust and dangerous that he should be anxious to join the believing side any more than the Agnostic side in any discussion. Both parties stand in the same position with reference to an ordinary inquirer, and he should do equal justice to both—striving, as you say, to enter fully into and make real and vivid in his mind the considerations on the Christian side, but testing their validity by criticism, and not forgetting to study and do justice to the objections which the sceptic has to urge, or which arise in his own mind. One side has no greater claim on him than the other; to give greater attention to one seems to me prejudiced and unphilosophical in attitude. Both are candidates for approval on the same footing."

"No—thrice no!" said Walton; "they are *not*

on the same footing. The Christian Church offers you not an alternative view of life but a prize, the greatest of prizes—certain knowledge about the highest interest of life. The Agnostic offers a blank—ignorance. Do your best to obtain the prize, and if indeed you find it to be unattainable, then, and not till then, rest contented with the blank."

Darlington looked puzzled, but said nothing.

"This then seems," Walton continued, "to be the reasonable attitude towards the credentials of Christ and His Church—anxiety to gain the knowledge they offer, and not a simple wish for abstract truth; or rather a keen desire to know the truth on that particular subject, as distinguished from the rather apathetic and uninterested impartiality which seems to me involved in a mere vague wish for truth in the abstract. It is plain that the more effort you make to see the truth of Christianity, the more evident it will become, if you fail to do so, that it is incapable of being proved; so that whichever view is the true one, the greater the effort the surer the knowledge. Then, again, the anxiety and interest must be, as we have seen, for this knowledge as felt to concern ourselves practically, and not for a problem interesting as intellectual food only. 'Seek, and ye shall find.' This has a wide application even intellectually. If you seek for interesting arguments you will find them, and in them is your reward. And if you seek to know that which affects your highest interests, you will find that, too, if it is to be found. If you feel it all-important that revelation, if divine, should be known to you as such, your efforts to enter into and understand its credentials will be all the more intense and successful. 'La vérité,' says Lacordaire, 'est une œuvre de silence et de la reflexion.' You will ponder deeply the considerations pointing to its divine origin. They will be to you realities; subtle and significant connections in them will unfold themselves in the course of your reverent meditation, which would escape one who studied them with a different aim and spirit."

"I must study all sides of the question," said Darlington; "that is only common sense."

"Master one thing at a time," replied Walton. "If you are constantly touching on every point of view you will be Jack of all trades—or views—and master of none. Study that which professes to be the one solution of the awful enigma of existence, make sure that you have felt deeply and truly its harmony and the significance of its proofs, conscious that true personal appreciation differs widely from the external view which the average mind takes at first sight. At least do not wash out one picture and replace it by another until you are sure that you have done all in your power to appreciate the first."

Darlington persisted, "You must study the other side."

"I will talk that out some other time," said Walton; "it would lead us too far now. If our arguments are convincing, that is no more necessary in such a case than it is to hear all the sophistical objections which might be made to one of Euclid's conclusions. At present all I contend for is that you should *first* give yourself every chance of appreciating the true significance of Christian evidence, and for this purpose you must, at least for the time, concentrate your endeavours."

"Anyhow," Darlington said, "these principles of yours apply only to a very narrow portion of Christian evidences. Christ's character, the growth of the Church, and destruction of Jerusalem are of course remarkable facts, but they are only a tithe of the evidences. There is the whole question as to the alleged miracles—most of all, the Resurrection. Then, again, a critical inquiry is necessary as to how far we are justified in believing many of the marvellous facts alleged. Much of the Scripture is disputed as to its authenticity. These and kindred matters call for dry historical research in which all your personal effort, and reflection, and realising, and the rest have no place. They only affect a small portion of the argument."

"I think their effect is far wider than you suppose," said Walton. "I cannot pretend in a moment to show how wide, but I may suggest one or two ways in which they act. No doubt their province is in the first place what we have been considering. But look at their indirect influence. Consider, for one thing, the practical effect upon a mind which is engaged, even over the purely critical portion of the argument, of a keen sense of the uniqueness of the history and character of Christ and His Church. One who goes to work without this feels, nowadays, that he is defending a losing cause when he attempts to state the Christian side. All the presumption is against a breach of nature's uniformity. His own constant experience has worked deep into his mind a sense of the improbability of what is unlike the general course of phenomena. Then, again, he is cowed by the ridicule of a host of scientific writers who laugh at his superstition and lack of 'exact thought.' Surely he is in danger of under-estimating the arguments, as feeling it highly improbable, before he looks at them, that they can be conclusive. Whereas, if he has truly realised that Christ's character is—to use the language of one whose whole education and belief were opposed to Christianity—unlike that of all other men, whether predecessors or successors, that the story of the Jewish people and of the Christian Church is quite unparalleled in history, and so forth, then, even apart from the actual and direct proof to be found in these considerations, he has in his mind that which will give him heart and hope in his study of what remains. His mind, instead of being filled and biassed, as most minds are, by a sense of the improbability of what is unfamiliar, is impregnated with the thought of a great marvel. If one marvel is true, why should not other marvels follow in its train? Then, again, the probabilities of the case are affected at every turn. The realising of what Christians have done gives an idea of human nature and its powers quite different from that which naturally and habitually exists in the average lounger of this civilised age. And as we have seen, our estimate of human powers and qualities affects constantly the weight which we attach to circumstantial evidence. It affects the *à priori* probabilities of the case, and may give an entirely different view of the credibility of witnesses. If we realise the conduct of the Apostles after the Resurrection, we see how deep must have been their assurance of its truth. Such an hypothesis as a pious fraud in the matter becomes at once absurd. If you reflect you will see that a similar effect is produced upon the weight of evidence at every turn. I do not say that those considerations which depend *entirely* on the personal effort, and qualities I have mentioned, for their just appreciation,—the internal evidences of credibility, as Catholic theologians call them—are in themselves conclusive; but I do say, and I can at least speak for my own case, that a mind may be perplexed and depressed by the intricacy and subtlety of critical questions, and that considerations similar to those of which I speak, if vividly present to the mind, may, by their own direct weight combined with the indirect assistance and courage they give in appreciating more complicated arguments, raise such a mind to a clear and serene sense of certainty in the whole matter, not necessarily solving every difficulty, but giving ample assurance that it has found the truth."

"Yes; it is all a *feeling*, and an *assurance*, and the like," said Darlington. "I cannot trust such things; they are too vague."

"Vague to you," returned Walton, "as the criteria of good art to one who is no artist, or—I say it again—the account which Lesurques' friend would give from his intimate knowledge of him to one who had not that knowledge. It is the account that is vague; the perception itself you can't judge of because you haven't got it. How often am I to say this?"

But Darlington was growing tired, and hardly listened. "No sensible man," he insisted, "could trust to such uncertain shadows. He might have an impression that he saw further than another, but no real confidence."

"Well; there, at least, plain facts are against you," said Walton. "It would be absurd in me to attempt to enumerate a tithe of the great thinkers who have based their whole lives on a view of religious evidence which was so far personal and outside its logic as to differ from the view which they themselves originally took. Lacordaire's conversion is as good an instance as I can remember of a change of this kind. I think it is in one of his 'letters to young men' that he says that when he looks back and tries to find the logical causes of his conversion, he can see nothing beyond the Christian evidences, which had always been familiar to him, although they had failed to *impress themselves on him* as long as he was surrounded by the atmosphere of sceptical discussion which he breathed in at the University; but which convinced him after quiet, earnest reflection. In other words, while his interest in them was purely speculative, they were insufficient; but when he meditated reverently upon them, not confusing his mind with every theory and objection under the sun, but allowing these particular considerations to assert themselves and sink deep into him, he realised their importance and significance, and felt their conclusiveness. His appreciation of them became more complete, and raised his mind from scepticism to a clear vision of the truth."

Darlington shook his head and looked incredulous.

"Well," said Walton, "I don't want to insist further upon the degree of confidence which may be reasonable, as that is going beyond my original point, and raises many other questions. I should say, even apart from any supernatural element, that there is much more in the mind than we have contemplated in our discussion to account for its certainty in such a matter. All that I here maintain is a view exactly opposite to the one you enunciated as a sort of truism at starting. You said that of two men equally able to understand the logic of a series of arguments in favour of the divine origin of Christ's mission and revelation, the cool-headed and impartial man is plainly he who will judge them at their true worth rather than the religious-minded man. I think I have gone far towards showing that, on the contrary, the logical apprehension being an extremely minor point, the mind which passively receives their logic with impartial indifference is the worst possible judge of their true worth; and perhaps all the more so for this reason, that he is so completely satisfied with his ready grasp and neat presentment of the verbal shell, that he never dreams that the whole strength of the argument lies beyond it."

"You will find it hard to reverse my ideas so

much," said Darlington, "as to make me believe that impartiality is not essential to a correct estimate of all evidence. Other things may be needed as well, but that most of all."

Walton looked annoyed. "You either cannot or will not see my meaning," he said. "Of course no one denies that partiality in the sense of bias is to be avoided. What I have been pointing out is that indifference is fatal, and earnestness for knowledge essential. What would you say if Newton had professed himself indifferent as to whether he succeeded in making fresh astronomical discoveries, or failed? Should you say that that showed the needful attitude of impartiality which ensured the evidence being valued correctly, and that without it he would run the risk of rash conclusions, and would believe on an insufficient induction? or should you not rather say that if he cared so little about it he would probably not succeed if discovery were at all difficult? I say again that we must secure ourselves from being biassed by our wishes, not as the juryman does, by indifference as to results, but as the physical explorer does, by a longing for true knowledge."

This seemed to strike Darlington. "True," he said, "that is a new aspect of what you insisted on last night. It brings before me better than anything you have said its connection with our present subject."

"There is Greystone," said Walton, pointing to a small church two or three hundred yards in front, with a house adjoining it; "let me try and sum up what I have said before we reach it. I have endeavoured to point out how different the value of a certain class of arguments may appear according as our personal appreciation of them is complete or incomplete; and that this difference is not such as can be expressed in the statement of them, but must be felt by the individual mind, because their force does not lie in the logic of them, but in the reality, significance, and connection of the facts they bind together. We have seen that familiarity with a subject, acquaintance with a personality, the effort to realise truths in all their bearing, are therefore of such assistance to our apprehension that they may show an argument to be very strong and definite which would without their assistance appear very weak and vague. This may account for the fact that persons deeply interested in the truth of a particular allegation find arguments in its favour conclusive which to others are not so, without any supposition of bias or prejudice. Then again, so far as the true personal estimate of arguments implies effort and pains taken, it is more likely to be attained to by him who is anxious to be certain of the truth these arguments profess to establish, as feeling it of the greatest practical importance to himself to have correct knowledge on the subject, than by him whose interest in the matter is speculative and purely intellectual—the instinct of self-preservation being, as I have said, the strongest of stimulants in such a case. And a similar instinct is, as I explained yesterday, our best safeguard against being hurried prematurely into belief by bias. Then we saw that a considerable portion of the Christian evidences are of such a nature as to depend for their force almost entirely upon the personal appreciation of the individual, and so to come under the principles I have mentioned; and that these evidences play, indirectly, a very important part in the whole argument. This being so, I have said that the attitude which you supposed to be truly philosophical is, in their regard, unphilosophical. A state of mind which implies equal readiness to be satisfied with Christian belief on the one side and Agnosticism on the other affords no guarantee that the necessary effort will be made to realise and appreciate the force of the considerations whereby the truth of Christianity is established. An active speculative interest in all views is no sign that the patient reflection and reverent consideration which are necessary if the Christian arguments are really to touch us, will be given. Indifference as to results shows that there is no sense of the danger of ignorance and the blessedness of knowledge. And the mind which fails to realise such truths as these may well fail to realise much more. Absence of passion suggests apathy. A judicial frame of mind will not seem the most hopeful to one who remembers that 'the kingdom of heaven suffereth violence, and the violent carry it away.' No doubt these qualities are admirable in a court of law for the very same reason that they are out of place here. The very fact that twelve jurymen are to agree upon their verdict implies that the evidence is to be of such a kind as to *exclude* special personal appreciation, such as knowledge of an individual character. The outside world cannot be sure whether such professed knowledge is in a particular case genuine or the result of bias, therefore it is eliminated. Then again, so far as personal effort is required, one may say that its necessity is to some extent precluded by the work of counsel. The facts of the case and their connection and significance are depicted by them in glowing terms, so that all that is required on the part of the jurymen is to be receptive and impartial. In religious inquiry, on the contrary, the really philosophical and reasonable frame of mind is one involving earnestness, effort, and sense of the gravity of the issues, and of the blessedness of knowledge. A passion for knowledge is as indispensable to the religious as to the scientific inquirer. And if knowledge be attained, who can doubt that what is so beautiful will beget enthusiasm—nay, that an enthusiastic love for its beauty will help in the perception of its truth—just as a love for the goodness of my father may make me delight more and more in his society, and so become more intimately acquainted with his character?"

They had reached Greystone and entered by the wicker gate of the presbytery garden. "You have not proved to me," Darlington said, "that religious believers fulfil the necessary conditions even if I grant what you have been saying."

"No," replied Walton, "and I do not suppose it is certain that all who profess belief do. Of course the same faults which prevent others from feeling the force of the evidences would, naturally speaking, prevent them too. And it is quite impossible to judge with certainty how far those faults do or do not exist in others, although with regard to ourselves we can be more certain; in the same way as a master cannot know with certainty whether a boy's assertion that he has found his lesson too difficult is genuine or a mere pretext for idleness; though the boy will know in his heart of hearts whether his efforts have been honest and ungrudging. I think, though, that I have shown certain qualities to be *essential* to a right estimate of the question, which qualities are associated with one's idea of an earnest and religious mind. I do not wish to sit in judgment on professing believers. I only show that the religious bent of mind which you spoke of as making you suspect bias and unfairness may well indicate the presence, not of unreasonable partisanship, but of a sense of the reality of religious problems which lights up with reality all that bears on them—just as our friend the Count, who felt the reality of his danger, saw the significance of each reason for fresh apprehension. This leads to a further sense of the blessedness of knowledge, of the wretchedness of ignorance, of the wickedness of apathy in such a matter, of possible personal danger in culpable ignorance, and consequently to a passion for knowledge. And this sort of wish to believe, so born and so bred, this longing for certain knowledge concerning the highest and noblest interests of life, may well be not only no obstacle, but an indispensable assistance to what is in the highest sense a reasonable view of the matter."

"You seem to me to place the whole thing now on a footing which makes it impossible for many to value your creed correctly," said Darlington. "What am I to do if my mind is not religious but sceptical?"

"I don't want you to drive me to personalities," returned Walton; "but of course the question goes further back. One must ask how far a man may not be responsible for the fact that he is not awake to a real danger, or has lost the highest instincts of his nature by neglect."

"Well, it is useless arguing the matter on this footing," said Darlington. "If I have lost my eyes, arguing won't make me see."

"No," said Walton, "but if you give a fallacious *simile*, I will answer you by one nearer the mark. One who has not skated for thirty years may not at once be able to keep on his legs, but after he has been on the ice half an hour, trying hard, the old habit returns. Anyhow," he added, "to put it on the lowest grounds of common sense, that passion for religious knowledge which arises from a sense of possible personal danger and responsibility, seems to me the only reasonable attitude for one who is awake and in use of his senses. We won't discuss this further now," he said, as Darlington attempted to speak, "or we shall never see anything of the church or presbytery. I merely end by saying that you may have my full mind, that for one who professes ignorance, and hears many able men, whose mode of life is based on the belief they profess, declare that knowledge is capable of being attained by one who is thoroughly in earnest, and that if by one's own fault it is not attained the most terrible punishment will ensue, the reasonable attitude must involve such a sense of possible personal danger as will beget a desire for more knowledge. Then again, the apathy of a Hume or a Gibbon on the bed of death is from any point of view *unreasonable* even more so, if possible, for an Agnostic than for a believer, as the former has no clear knowledge of a merciful Providence, which is a certain guarantee of just treatment. A sense of the insecurity of ignorance, and the consequent longing for knowledge, is as much the only reasonable attitude in such a man as in one who is told seriously by some, who profess to have good reasons for knowing, that there are dangerous precipices here and there among the hills where he is rambling on a pitch-dark night."

"I reserve my defence," said Darlington, as they entered the presbytery grounds; "we shall, as you say, do no justice to your architecture and vestments if we go on talking." But he could not help adding: "To me, though, it seems that stirring oneself up to a frenzy of fear about things outside our ken, which we cannot control, is folly. I do not constantly think of railway accidents when I am in a train, because it would do me no good. Fear is meant as a protection, and should not be indulged in where it is of no practical use."

"And that is where we join issue," said Walton. "I say that it *is* a protection in religious inquiry, and that it *does* lead to knowledge and the consequent aversion of danger. You have never tried the experiment, and I have, *experto crede*."

And they walked into the house without another word, and were greeted by Walton's housekeeper, who asked if she should have luncheon ready for them after they had seen the church.

Greystone Church was a very simply constructed Gothic edifice of stone, and its chief interest to Darlington lay in the fact that it was the scene of the work to which Walton was devoting his life and energies. The house adjoining it was meagrely furnished, and Walton's study seemed little better fitted up than a monk's cell. The only article in it which attracted attention was a large wooden crucifix with a beautiful ivory figure, carved, evidently, with the greatest care and skill. This stood on the table at which Walton was accustomed to sit.

"It is very handsome," assented Walton to his friend's comment on it; and, in answer to his further questions as to the reason for placing it in front of his desk, he explained: "It is a very common custom with us. Out of sight, out of mind, you know. It helps one to keep the true object of life before one. It is another recognition of the principle we have been talking of—the necessity of keeping constantly before the mind the thoughts on which belief rests that they may support both our faith and our hope."

In the church Darlington observed the "Stations of the Cross," and Walton gave him the information he required with respect to them also. "They are, as you see," he said, "pictures representing the different scenes of the Passion. The people walk in procession every Friday, stopping at each while I read an account of the scene it represents, and praying for strength and forgiveness at every station before going on to the next. It makes them think: it makes them realise all that our Lord has done for them. 'With desolation is all the world made desolate, because no man thinketh in his heart.'"

They walked back to Sandown in comparative silence. Darlington could not help having a certain feeling of moral inferiority after he had heard some of the details of Walton's self-denying life. "Still," he argued to himself, "such a feeling is quite unreasonable. Walton's self-denial and devotion are based upon a belief which to me is unreal and superstitious. No doubt, if I were called upon to work for a great cause which really appealed to me, I should not be found wanting. All I lack is opportunity and motive." Possibly, however, even after he had said this to himself, he had a lingering doubt as to whether he were not partly responsible for his lack of opportunity. But such a frame of mind was unusual with him and unpleasant, and he cast it off before they reached home. No attempt was made by either to resume serious conversation. Both felt that they had had quite enough of it, and neither saw much chance of producing any marked impression on the other. Darlington's frame of mind was one with which Walton was well acquainted. The latter had been subjected to the very same influences at Muriel in years gone by, and had worked his way through almost every argument and consideration by which his friend was still influenced. The apparent absence of any impression produced upon Darlington during the conversation set Walton thinking. How was it that two minds so similar to each other in their very choice of arguments should come to such opposite conclusions? And then he remembered that there had been a time when religious scepticism had enjoyed a short reign in his own mind. He had faced the very considerations which he had endeavoured —he was conscious with what imperfect success —to place before his friend, and he had been for some time unconvinced by them. An event had then happened,—a misfortune, which had for a time embittered his life and thrown him back in great seriousness upon religion, and the very same train of thought which in his previous state of active and irresponsible speculation he had dismissed as an insufficient basis for belief, broke upon him with a new force and cogency when he was thus brought face to face with the realities of life. And, remembering this, he moralised, and came once more to the very conclusion which he had endeavoured to impress upon Darlington, that it is a very different thing to state a fact and to realise it; to express an argument and to feel its force: and that it is only a recognition on the part of the Church of a very plain and obvious law of the human reason which induces her to recommend a system of spiritual training which gives the reasons for belief every chance of "biting," if I may use the term—of being felt in their full weight and significance, as well as heard and known as facts.

DIALOGUE III

THE great Orme's Head at Llandudno, with the pleasant sea breezes and sea views it offers to those who walk round it on a bright spring day, was the theatre of another discussion between Walton and Darlington on the wish for religious belief. A year and a half had gone by since Darlington had visited Sandown, and their meeting at the same hotel at Llandudno was purely accidental. Walton was to leave the place on the afternoon following the day of Darlington's arrival, and anxious—partly from a feeling of duty and partly from his interest in Darlington—to have some conversation with him as to his present frame of mind on matters of religion, he proposed a walk, *tête-à-tête*, for the following morning. Not that Walton was in a general way over-ready for such discussions, or anxious to force them on others; but he thought that he had discerned something in Darlington's mind, when they had met at Sandown, which led him to hope that real good might be done by talking to him. There was in him real candour and a complete absence of that tendency to object for the sake of objecting or argue for the sake of arguing, which is a sure and plain sign that discussion will come to no good. Walton felt that if two men were on the whole looking for the same thing—truth,—they might at all events approach nearer to understanding one another, and that this circumstance which he thought he had perceived at Sandown with reference to Darlington and himself, removed their discussions widely from such debates as are often carried on between men of opposite convictions. Disputants are too often really occupied in finding and elaborating arguments, each in favour of his own foregone conclusion, rather than in weighing conscientiously what is urged on both sides, modifying their own statements, where they are seen, in the light of others, to be exaggerated, and adopting what seems true, irrespective of its apparent conflict with their own views.

A bright April morning promised to give the great Orme every chance of offering them his very best of breezes and scenes; but long before they had reached him light conversation had given place to serious, and the beautiful blue water of the Llandudno bay appealed to them in vain for admiration, and passed unnoticed and without effect on them, absorbed as they were in their discussion, except, perhaps, that it may have helped to stimulate their minds, and conspired with the sea breezes and cloudless sky in giving freshness and interest to a subject which might else have grown tedious now and again.

"I suppose," Walton said, "that you have forgotten all about our 'wish to believe' conversations at Sandown when you came down there last year with Ashley?"

"No, indeed, I haven't," said Darlington; "they set me thinking a good deal. I have often gone over the whole question in my own mind since I left you."

"Well, and with what result?"

Darlington smiled and did not answer at once. "I'm afraid," he said, "if you talked to me now you would find me a more confirmed sceptic than ever."

Walton made no reply, as he saw that Darlington was preparing to explain himself further.

"I must say," the latter went on, "that I thought the whole line you took was a very ingenious mixture of truth and falsehood. You stated clearly and cleverly certain truths which one must assent to, and then by a sort of logical sleight-of-hand you juggled in a falsehood to suit your book, and presented the argument anew, falsehood and all, as though I had accepted it without reserve. In our first talk you contended, rightly, that great anxiety to find something which is of great importance to be true, tends to make one slow of belief,—that the man who has a couple of thousand on a boat-race does not lightly believe he has won; and then, when this much was established, you assumed that it was equally agreed that a religious enthusiast had this sort of caution-breeding wish. When we walked to Greystone, again, you went through a long list of examples to show that a thirst for true knowledge might quicken the mind in acquiring it, and then proceeded to talk as though the 'wish to believe' and the 'thirst for knowledge' were convertible terms."

"Come," interrupted Walton, "you will hardly question that in these days the very title you accept —Agnostic—is a confession that this is so. You can hardly deny that if religious knowledge is attainable it must take the form of religious belief. The wish, then, for definite belief is the same, on religious matters, as the wish for knowledge."

"No," said Darlington, in a tone indicating a somewhat contradictious vein, "I don't admit that at all. Socrates said of old, that in this one respect was he wiser than other men, that they, whereas they knew nothing, thought they knew something; while he, on the contrary, was conscious that he knew nothing. If one is ignorant, the highest knowledge is to be aware of one's ignorance."

Walton was too much taken aback by this view to say anything at the moment, but Darlington soon went on—

"I quite demur to your assumption that your belief is a high state to aim at. Nothing that is false can be high, and it gives you an unfair advantage in your argument—or rather in the rhetoric of your argument—to assume that positive religious belief is a thing which an exalted mind must necessarily aim at, as constituting the only *knowledge* conceivable on the subject. The knowledge of the limit of one's own faculties is the really high knowledge. Suppose a man comes to me and says he dreamed last night that he saw the man in the moon. He saw him vividly, and is convinced that he exists. He had had a strong cup of green tea before going to bed, and in consequence had had many visions, and among them that. He asks me to try green tea to-night, and to see if it won't lead to my seeing the man in the moon. I tell him I don't care to try the experiment, and he reproaches me with my want of earnestness in the matter. 'The only knowledge offered,' he says, 'on that subject is a belief in the man in the moon. Are you mean-minded enough to rest content with blank ignorance? You should wish to believe, for the wish to believe is clearly here the wish for knowledge.' I reply that on such a subject the highest knowledge is a knowledge of the limits of my reasoning and knowing power; that I am sure no such vision of the man in the moon can be real evidence of his existence; that the impressions of a dream are not trustworthy means to knowledge, and so I quite deny that the wish to believe is a wish for knowledge."

"Now I aver," said Walton, "that it is you who are juggling and slipping into your parallel something completely unlike the circumstances of the case we are dealing with. You allowed at all events in our last talk that there *is* much more to be got out of religious argument by one who has a keen sense of the personal importance of the matter to himself, than by one who views it without this stimulus to his mind. You have no right to parallel specially keen insight in reasoning to what one sees in a dream."

"Oh! of course," said Darlington, "that is overstated by me. But I do think that in essence it holds good. I think that the attempt to extract certain knowledge out of the stock religious arguments is almost as wild as the profession that a nightmare tells you the truth."

"You have never had the stimulus of an earnest wish to believe," said Walton, "and so you cannot tell what it will do in the matter. Until you have given your mind to the whole question with the dispositions I have spoken to you of, you can have no right to pronounce certainty unattainable. You can only say that you have not attained to it."

"I have the impartial wish for truth," said Darlington. "I consider that this is all the *stimulus* which you really showed as being necessary—nay, not apathetic," he continued, reading Walton's objection in his eye, "impartial in the highest sense, a keenness that truth may prevail, in whatever direction it may lie. You can want no more than this. Such a wish makes one feel the necessity of doing one's best in the matter, and of doing ample justice to the whole case."

"It does not give the power," Walton said. "A man can't labour without hoping for success. If the process of religious conviction, in one who is in search of truth, involves, as we have seen, sustained personal effort, the impartial hope that truth may prevail will not light up his mind in its journey along the path pointed out as leading to belief. If the path be rugged, as the path of hopeless effort must be, he will abandon it. He must have the hope that the considerations he is pondering will lead to something;

and that is, in the sense I have explained, the wish to believe if it be possible to do so reasonably. The belief held out is at least and at lowest parallel to the glimpse of a possible new discovery which the astronomer may get, and you will scarcely maintain that he is prompted in following it up by a mere *abstract* love of truth. He trusts that this *particular* thing will prove true. Suppose there are signs of the existence of a hitherto undiscovered planet. He at once follows up the clue, not with a mere wish to know the truth in the abstract, but with a very strong wish to find more clues, and ultimately to find convincing reasons for believing that the planet exists. His love of truth is directed to a hope for discovery in this particular matter. This it is which stimulates his efforts. And this is, as I say, the wish to believe if reasonable belief is possible—a wish for conviction that what seems probable is true. The only reason why the wish to believe has ever been opposed to the wish for truth is because it is so frequently an insincere wish—a wish to maintain or hold a thing, and not the wish to know it to be true—that we are unaccustomed to think of it in this latter aspect. It is in reality the concrete form which the abstract wish for truth constantly takes."

But this seemed too strange a conclusion for Darlington to accept it. "You cannot," he said, "identify things so different. According to you, the partisan is a philosopher."

Walton reflected as to how he could convey his meaning better.

"I amend my phrase," he soon said. "I will not call the wish to believe the wish for truth, but, as I did at first, the wish for knowledge. Not but that these two may be explained as being the same, but because I think it will show where your fallacy lies. The wish for truth is often taken to mean merely the wish to avoid error in reasoning—the wish not to draw any conclusion beyond what is warranted by one's premises. In this sense an indifferent man who merely states that he does not know whether the soul is immortal or not, or whether natural or revealed religion be true or not, may have a wish for truth which cannot be identified with a wish to believe. But it is at the point where some one comes to him and says, 'If you bestir yourself there is more to be known,' that he has to show whether he has this merely negative wish for truth, or, in addition, the positive wish for all attainable truth,—the wish for knowledge. And it is only this last wish that, in all active investigation of the different lines in which knowledge is proposed, must take the form of the wish to believe."

Darlington, however, could not get rid of the feeling that this was all paradoxical, and ran counter to received expressions and acknowledged axioms.

"Let me try," Walton continued, "to put what I am saying in a fresh light. The wish to believe which I have advocated is, as you will remember, intimately bound up with the sense of the importance to oneself, often to one's own safety, of true knowledge on the subject in question. This it is which raises it to a passion, and it is on its being a passion that its effect in intensifying one's whole nature depends. Now one cannot have a passion for an abstraction. The wish for knowledge in the abstract, if very intense, must fix itself, must direct itself, must spend its energy in some definite work. It casts about it for some concrete means of satisfaction. A man struggling in the water in fear of drowning has a wish for abstract safety. But this expresses itself in his adoption of the most promising means of attaining to safety. He catches hold of some floating wood, tries to construct a raft, lashing it together by means of ropes he has found. Here we see his wish for safety in the abstract converting itself into the hope that he may succeed in these definite endeavours to find safety. Similarly, the man wishing for abstract religious knowledge casts about him for a clue. In what direction is he to seek it? Mark, again, it is *knowledge* he wants, and not merely truth negatively, which is content with indolent ignorance, under the plea that such a state includes no false convictions, as including no convictions at all on the subject-matter. I say, then, he casts about for a clue, and when he sees something which appeals to him as being possibly the knowledge he is in search of, his wish for truth—or as I prefer to call it, for *knowledge—becomes* the wish to believe. Here is what he has been looking for. Here is the definite direction in which he is to look for truth. I am looking for the will of John Jones of Birmingham at Somerset House, as I have reason to believe that it contains information which is of some importance to me. I only know within twenty years the date of his death, and there are many John Joneses. Each one I find I hope to be John Jones of Birmingham. I look at his will carefully. My wish for the abstract true John Jones of Birmingham becomes a wish that this concrete John Jones may be the one I want. And I reason thus. If this be indeed the true John Jones, I have found what I wanted and my labour is over; and so that is my first wish. And then there is this additional consideration: if he be not the true John Jones, I have at all events, by doing my best to ascertain whether he *be* the true John Jones, clearly proved that he is *not*, and so have narrowed the channel of my search. I check him off in my note-book as a false John Jones, and so when I come to search again I shall know at all events that the will bearing the date in question is not the one I want, and so shall have one will the less to look through. Again, if I find other things besides the name which lead me to suspect that it may be the right Jones, I pay my shilling and read the will through, having a further motive for so doing. Though he *may* not be the John Jones I want, these may be signs that he is a relation—a father or an uncle—and some of the information I require may be in this will. And so, I say, the man who is looking for religious truth takes what is promising and beautiful. Can this be the knowledge I am seeking for? he asks. It is so noble, so elevating, so consoling, so practically helpful to him, that he trusts it may. His wish for religious truth becomes the wish to believe—the hope that this may prove to be the truth,—and at the same time he feels that the only way to find truth is courageously to attempt to find it in every direction which promises well. His first hope is, then, that it may prove true —the wish to believe, if belief be reasonable; his second thought is 'anyhow let me do my best to see *whether* or not it be true;' and he reflects at the same time that it is highly improbable that what commends itself so much to his own highest instincts and to the moral nature of very many, has not at least some admixture of truth in it; and the keen search which the beautiful prospect stimulates him to make will at all events have this good result, that he will with quick eye note and appropriate whatever grains of new knowledge there may be mixed up with superstition and inaccurate theory."

Both walked on for some little time without any further remark. Darlington was the first to break the silence. "Suppose," he said, "that a frightful religion presented itself—an immoral religion with immoral deities—revengeful, unjust, untruthful—a worse edition of the impure paganism of classical Greece. Would you advocate a 'wish to believe' in it as the best way of investigating it? Should you say that the abstract wish for knowledge as to what exists behind the veil, and what we are to look for after death, must take the shape of a wish to believe in such a theory if it were propounded?"

Walton reflected. "Wait a moment," he said. "Let us see how far this would be really, and not verbally only, the legitimate issue of what I have been saying. I have said that the longing for true knowledge as to our ultimate destiny, and as to the invisible powers controlling the universe, as to the import of the voice of conscience and of our moral nature, as to the meaning of life, and as to the end to be achieved, takes the shape, when a promising clue is found, of a wish that it may prove a clue to real knowledge—a wish to believe. But, remember, the knowledge we seek and hope for is a knowledge *satisfying* our moral nature, and giving a definite meaning to those very aspirations which make us long for knowledge. We want an object of reverence which shall be real, and which shall at the same time explain and satisfy those instincts; an aim which can be definitely seen, towards which we may direct the moral action of our lives. But a wish to discover that impure and immoral deities are all that exist behind the veil, that there is no sanction to morality, and no basis in the aim and meaning of life for the moral impulses, would be the very opposite of this. It would be more like a wish to disbelieve. It would amount to a wish to disbelieve in anything great or noble, and a resigning of all hope for religious knowledge properly so called."

"And yet," said Darlington, "if knowledge is your one object, it seems to me that you should wish to know the best or the worst, whichever may be true."

"Yes," said Walton, "I grant it. But I should *hope to find the best true.* And I contend still that your supposition would not be knowledge in the sense of ampler knowledge. Suppose it to be true, I should not blink its truth; but it would be by the keen sense of its horror and the intense wish to find it false that I should learn its truth."

"You must change your principles then," Darlington insisted. "If the wish for knowledge is supposed to make a man jump at every fresh theory that is started, and turn into a wish to believe in it, you have no right to make an exception where the particular knowledge proposed is different from that which you were prepared for."

"I must explain my principles more fully, not change them," said Walton. "You are giving me an opportunity of defining their limits and full nature for myself and for you. In the first place, you will remember that one of my conditions was that there should be a promising clue to knowledge—a clue sufficient to stimulate the mind with a hope for success. Now I should deny that any religion not satisfying in some degree our moral aspirations, *could* offer itself as a promising clue to knowledge. The very ground on which we believe that knowledge is attainable on the subject is that those aspirations point upwards to something above us. A religion, then, destitute of claim on our reverence, has not even that condition of promising well which is essential to our being physically able to hope that it may turn out to be knowable as true. It is only from the union of the internal evidence of the spiritual nature with the external credentials of the religion in question that certain knowledge is to be looked for; and a so-called religion which is not only unsupported but directly contradicted by the former, has in it no promising element. The highest ground it can assume is that of a possible truth, one of many possible truths, on the hypothesis that no truth in the matter is knowable by us. It is only the glimmer from above detected by conscience which can light up the soul with hope and give the wish to believe. Look at it again in this light. Compare the matter, as we have done, with strictly physical discovery. Suppose, *per impossibile*, that a theory were suddenly proposed which purported to show that the great laws governing the movements of the heavenly bodies on the Copernican hypothesis —laws giving harmony and form and meaning to observed facts—have been rashly generalised, and do not square with fresh observations; that in reality the planets move at random and without any one fixed law for all, and that the fixed law had been assumed from some curious twist in our observing faculties, which had given an apparent regularity to their motions, just as one who looked at objects through a succession of glasses of various colour might rashly infer, if he did not observe the glasses, that the objects in question in passing along the road acquired these various hues in regular sequence. Now I say that the passion for knowledge in such a case as this would not assume the shape of a wish to believe. If this were true, there would be no *gain* of knowledge, no fresh unity in our conception of things, no further reduction of the chaos of facts to the order of principles, but, on the contrary, the destruction of much that had been supposed to be knowledge. Thus to assume that each fresh hypothesis must be examined, if the principles I have advocated be correct, with a wish to believe in *it*, is not to carry out but to contradict those principles. There will be in such a case a wish to believe, but to believe what is *highest*, not what is lowest; in good news, and not in bad; in what, if true, is ampler knowledge, and not what, if true, is evidence that what had been fondly reckoned ample knowledge is in reality a delusion. And on exactly the same principles a religion proposed, which gives as a full explanation of the basis of life, of creation, of the aim to be lived for, of the ruling powers over the universe, an account which, if true, would show that those very phenomena which we had looked upon as clues to knowledge were not so, would arouse a wish not to believe but to disbelieve. A suggestion which, if true, would disprove the most promising and credible explanation of our moral nature and of life as a whole—an explanation which likewise gives coherence to human knowledge and an aim for human action; a suggestion in which it is involved that what we had thought to be a light from heaven is but an *ignis fatuus*, that

> 'He is only a cloud and a smoke who was once a pillar of fire,
> The guess of a worm in the dust and the shadow of its desire;'

such a suggestion, I say, when looked at by one who has the passion for religious knowledge, arouses at once a wish, not to believe it true, but to believe it false. I conclude, then, by saying that it is no exception to my principles, but only their legitimate outcome, to say that the wish to believe, which I have explained as the reasonable and indispensable stimulus and assistance in the discovery of truths in the matter, is the wish to believe in something nobler, giving wider knowledge, giving also a knowledge which completes the half-arguments which had suggested our search, which elevates us in the sphere of being, and not knowledge which would show that all our aspirations were meaningless, and which would only be a knowledge of the hopeless darkness which is our lot. And I have, I think, said enough on former occasions to show that if indeed the hypothesis that there is no elevating knowledge to be gained were true, the wish to believe it untrue, if this wish were the offspring of the passion for true knowledge in what is all-important, would not blind us to the fact, but, on the contrary, would give a keen and painful sensitiveness to the misery of our fate."

Darlington, without exactly dissenting, felt still puzzled. The religion of immoral divinities seemed to him still to be knowledge proposed, he said,—unpleasant tidings undoubtedly, but still, if true, it must be knowledge. It proposed to give an account of what was really existing behind the veil. This must be proposing fresh knowledge. No doubt if this involved exposing the falsehood of what had formerly been reckoned knowledge, it did not give fresh unity to our conceptions; but a fresh truth, which involved the overthrow of the most cherished idols, seemed to be still in a real sense fresh knowledge. Walton thought for a moment, and said—

"That is merely an ambiguity in the word knowledge. I expose it thus. The passion to know all truth, which is the radical passion, in what concerns one intimately, pleads 'let me know the best or the worst, whichever is true; the best being knowledge enlarging and ennobling, the worst the fact (if so be) that such knowledge is unattainable.' Thus the passion for enlarging and ennobling knowledge is the first hope implied in the radical wish for all truth. It is a wish that the truth may prove to be what is best. And this last passion becomes, as we have seen, a wish to believe in a definite system or professed revelation which promises well and offers a clue to the enlarging and ennobling knowledge which is longed for."

They walked on again in silence. And if the reader observes that Darlington made no reply, and that Walton was again the first to speak, and is tempted to exclaim, "Dialogue indeed! it would be better called monologue; Walton is prosing all the time;" I would ask him to bear in mind a few facts in human nature as bearing upon persons with the mental history of Darlington and Walton, and upon the stage which the discussion had reached. Walton had, as we have seen, passed through a mental phase very similar to Darlington's, and consequently his thought was, whether for good or for ill, ahead of Darlington's. He had digested, sorted, and arranged much that was somewhat chaotic in his friend's mind, a process which, whether rightly or wrongly performed, whether leading to the lawful repose of certainty or to the fool's paradise of prejudice, was necessary before his mind could rest in a *decision* of any kind. Darlington's silent and listening attitude came then from the feeling that he was having a good deal of useful mental work done for him, and that much that had been vague in his own mind was being arranged and classified,—a process which could not fail to help him to clear his thoughts, whether or no the arrangement was such as ultimately to satisfy him. His silence meant then that he felt he was learning, though not, as the too sanguine controversialist would hope, that he was accepting the ultimate conclusions towards which Walton's principles professed to converge. Again his difficulties lay less in the fact that he saw flaws in his friend's reasoning, and more in the novelty and paradox of much that he said; and such difficulties do not suggest a mode of answering back or joining in the discussion, but rather a feeling of wonder and a wish for further explanation, until the paradox seems so intolerable as to prompt exclamation rather than argument, and appears to the listener to refute itself by its very strangeness. And as this point had not yet arrived Darlington remained silent, half listening and half musing. Walton, after a minute or so of silence, continued—

"I believe, though, that we have been speaking of an impossible state of things. The moral instincts of humanity do not allow of the existence of an utterly immoral religion. All religions have contained a germ of truth—an element of true knowledge; and I still say that where there is an element of fresh knowledge in a religion, satisfying the cravings of our moral nature, where such a religion is on the whole a step upwards from our present state; if it be proposed as a whole the wish to believe is the reasonable attitude, though if it be the honest and conscientious wish I have spoken of, it will gradually cast off the superstitious beliefs, the ritual absurdities, and impure ceremonies which accompanied some forms of paganism, and will prepare the mind for fuller and more complete knowledge. This is undoubtedly the principle on which St. Paul went when he made use of the religion of the Corinthians, mixed up though it was with superstition, to lead them to the truth. Their religion had in it a ray of light from heaven, though refracted so often and through such varied *media* of prejudice, immoral habit, false legends, and corrupt teaching, that the direction whence it came was scarcely discernible. St. Paul's work was to point out the refracting *media*, to show that they dimmed the light and deceived those to whom it came as to its true direction; and by teaching them and making them understand more clearly the laws of the light, to lead them to distinguish between the appearance of it as it reached them and what it was in itself. And when they had learnt to do this, and longed to see the light with the naked eye, in its true brightness, coming straight from the throne of God, once they recognised and admitted that there were *media* which dimmed and perverted it, he gave them power to remove the *media;* and the light flooded their hearts and took possession of them. And they recognised that this true light which enlighteneth every man who cometh into the world was, when seen aright, the word of God which is taught in the Christian Gospel."

Darlington found his mind filled by this time with a new set of ideas, which did not readily take their place side by side with the principles which habitually dwelt there. There seemed to be an element of truth in all that Walton had been saying, and he was far too candid not to admit and to feel this. But on the other hand, it seemed at variance with much which he had been accustomed to regard as axiomatic. That one interested in coming to one conclusion rather than another should, under any circumstances, be a better judge and view the state of the case more truly than one with no prepossession, seemed to contradict canons of reasoning so generally acknowledged that they must be substantially sound and correct. Then again, that an enthusiastic man should have in any sense a quicker eye for the truth than one whose reason worked in the normal way, undisturbed by passion, was a conception which took the edge off the familiar contrast between the visionary and the man of common sense, the fanatic and the sober-minded man. And although Walton had, both on the present occasion and in former conversations, gone some way towards explaining the limits of his theory, and that it differed from received expressions rather than received opinions, that it contradicted an exaggeration of a recognised truth and not the truth itself, still these explanations had not become sufficiently fixed in Darlington's mind to dispel his feeling of mistrust and repugnance. The qualifications which Walton had been introducing into his explanation were too minute and subtle to stay clearly in his mind on their first introduction; and much in the same way as a beautiful landscape seen but once dwells in the memory rather in its broad outlines, and in the emotional effect it wrought at first sight, than in all the qualifying details which give to it its true character and its full interest in the eye of an artist, so it was the broad aspect of Walton's theory which was uppermost in Darlington's mind, and the effect which had been produced on him at first hearing this strange canonisation of prejudice, emotion, and fanaticism, and the still stranger disparagement (as it seemed) of reasoning as it is carried on by an able and impartial man. "Where is all this to end?" he thought to himself. "We may have enthusiasts for Catholicism, enthusiasts for Protestantism, enthusiasts for atheism. Each will claim to be right, and will appeal to his own enthusiasm as a witness to the truth of his creed. The only way in which we have been accustomed to look for a common measure of minds, and a truth which reasonable men shall recognise, has been by the elimination of these elements of excitement and passion, by the calming of the disturbed mind, and the appeal to reason stripped of passion. Here is a theory which is not content with tolerating passion, but encourages it." He had not, as I have said, got full hold of the root principle which Walton was advocating, and which alone could explain and limit properly his half-expressed conclusions. He had not mastered the fact that it was passionate reasoning and not passionate feeling, an enthusiasm for ampler and higher knowledge, the essence of whose beauty is its truth, and not for a beautiful idea as such, which Walton advocated, and that a very deep sense of the all-importance of truth and the fatal consequences of error or ignorance may enable one to gain assistance from the weapons of passion and enthusiasm without any danger of their misleading. He did not fully see that a weight which is sure to overbalance the reason if not counterbalanced by another weight, might make it steadier and firmer if so counterbalanced. Impassioned reasoning, guided by what Newman calls the heart and the eye for truth, leads to truth. But an equal amount of passion, without the sense of responsibility and of the importance of truth, carries the mind to any prejudice which it is set on defending, much as wine may enliven and render more intelligent the discourse of a serious man, while it gets the better of another and stops his speech altogether. These elements in Walton's theory he had understood, but had not digested or assimilated. How could they be a sufficient explanation of the matter, he reasoned, viewing the matter externally and without following them closely or endeavouring to see their full bearing, when a contrary set of ideas are embodied in the received first principles for judging of all evidence?

This was the form in which he put his difficulties when he next spoke to Walton.

"How can you account," he said, "for the fact that impartiality is always looked upon so much as a first essential in the estimate of evidence that once it is admitted that a man is not impartial but interested especially in one side, enough has been said, and it is assumed without further argument that he is not a fair judge, that he will lean to the side he favours? This is an admitted first principle in weighing historical evidence as much as any other, and the proofs of Christianity *are*, of course, mainly historical. There must be a great truth at the root of so acknowledged an axiom; and even though I did not entirely see my way through the very different view you seem to take, I should be slow to abandon an intellectual rudder which has been reckoned serviceable and fitted for its work by all men in all ages."

"No doubt," said Walton, "there is a great truth at the root of it, and, properly explained and limited, I should never dream of denying it. Let us consider the matter a little closely. It will really be only the application of the very principles on which I have been insisting, and which you suppose to clash with it."

He paused, as though trying to get the issues clearly defined in his own mind.

"You ask me," he went on, "what right I have to advocate one set of principles for the true estimate of historical evidence, and another for judging of religious evidence; and again how it comes about, if my principles are the true ones for religious inquiry, that so different a set of principles have passed into the very grammar of rules for weighing evidence. I think I can best answer your whole difficulty by showing why and in what class of cases the current principles are sound, and by pointing out how different individual religious inquiry is from such cases."

And he seemed again uncertain how to begin, and how to express his meaning at fullest advantage.

"I would first ask you to bear two things in mind," he said. "Firstly, to take the Christian evidences alone. A man who looks at them for purposes of religious inquiry must necessarily feel their strength to be supplemented by those very considerations in his own mind which prompted the inquiry. The need he has for a religion, the completeness of the satisfaction which Christianity affords to that need, the powerful appeal of Christ's character to his moral nature, here are specimens of the supplementary personal evidences which an individual inquirer has over and above the historical evidences viewed on their own merits. The *testimonium animæ naturaliter Christianæ*, however unscientific it may be as a proof, is now, as it ever has been, a very strong motive in the individual mind for belief. And the same remark applies to the testimony of the conscience to the truth of natural religion. I remember developing some of this more in full to you some time ago. The second thing I would have you bear in mind is that the evidences and proofs of natural and revealed religion, as looked at by the individual inquirer, are proofs of a matter on which knowledge is all-important to him, and on which the truth, whatever it may be, is fraught with momentous consequences in respect of his own destiny and bearing on his own immediate conduct."

"Yes, but that does not alter the character of the proofs," Darlington said. "The evidence in a case of a disputed will is fraught with great consequences to the plaintiff, and slight to the judge; but yet the proofs are there, not more or less visible to one than to the other, and must be judged by both according to the recognised rules."

"It does not alter the character of the proof," said Walton slowly. "No, but it changes the principles I should instil into each as essential to his judgment as to its true value being sound. Let me try and show my meaning. Just outside the town of Basingstoke there are the ruins of an ancient chapel—the chapel of the Holy Ghost, which was for many years the chapel of the guild of the Holy Ghost,—a teaching guild of early origin. The chapel stands in the middle of a very old burial ground, and antiquaries have ascertained that there are good reasons for supposing that there were graves there as early as the reign of King John. A theory has been started, resting upon a certain amount of circumstantial evidence, that while England was under an interdict in John's reign, this place was first used as a burial ground, burial in consecrated ground being denied by the Church's ban. I do not care to go very closely into the exact amount of evidence which there is for this theory. There is the *à priori* ground that it was not unfrequently the custom in time of interdict to bury the dead outside the city walls, and to consecrate the ground as soon as the interdict was removed. We will suppose that there is some additional evidence. Now the antiquary who judges of the evidence asks, we may suppose, what is his most reasonable frame of mind—how can he best secure himself, in judging of the evidence, against a wrong conclusion. He is told that he should look at the evidence with absolute freedom from bias of any kind; that he should have no wish to come to one conclusion rather than another, but should be equally ready to see the insufficiency or the sufficiency of the evidence. This is no doubt sound advice. But on what ground is it given? what are the reasons which would make a wish to come to one particular conclusion a dangerous element perverting his judgment? Be it observed that the fact is bye-gone both in itself and in its effects. The fact of his decision being true or false neither has nor will have any effect on him. His interest in the matter is purely speculative, although doubtless lively enough. The facts concerning him practically, and most vividly before his mind, are the present ruin and the associations which his researches enable him to weave around it and the stock of his discoveries which he is constantly adding to. If he can decide that this account is true, here is an additional element of interest added to it, a fresh link in the chain of his discoveries, an additional completeness given to his history of the place. The danger, then, against which he is to guard is that of drawing a conclusion, insufficiently proved as true but never provable as untrue, for the sake of the harmony and completeness it gives to his work. The intellectual error feared is not his wishing that one conclusion rather than another should be known as true, but that it should be accepted and adopted without sufficient reference to its truth. There is no element in the discovery of a matter the truth in which has no effect on the inquirer, which can ensure the interest in one side remaining identical with the interest in the *truth* of one side. Consequently the warning to be given is 'lean to neither side,' simply because in such a case leaning would imply a readiness to conclude without deep conviction. But take a case—a strong case—of a matter intimately affecting one's own personal safety, and you will find, I think, that the same principles do not apply. Documentary and verbal evidence is brought before the Czar of Russia tending to prove a plot for his assassination on the morrow; on the other hand, some one comes to him, in whose opinion he has much confidence, and says he can prove that the evidence is a scare. Would any one say to the Czar that in looking at the whole case he was to have no interest in finding one side true rather than the other? Surely not. If one conclusion means personal danger, and the other safety, it would be of little use to give him such advice."

"Of little use, perhaps," said Darlington, "because he could not follow it. But it might nevertheless be the best advice that he should, if possible, remain calm and clear-headed."

"You do not take me yet," said Walton, rather distressed that he could not convey what seemed to him so clear; "I should say that such an attitude would give him probably a less rather than a greater clearness of head. But let me finish my explanation. I say that in such a case indifference is impossible; and also it would be not only unnecessary as a safeguard, because his sense of the importance of true knowledge secures him from bias, but would be absolutely an impediment. It would lessen the activity of his mind and the quickness of his perception. It is his sense of danger that prompts him eagerly and carefully to examine all the evidence. Take this away, let him be indifferent, and his motive is gone."

"Oh, of course," Darlington said, "I do not say that he should be indifferent in the sense that he should not realise the importance of the matter; but only that he should still, if possible, examine the evidence impartially, with equal readiness to conclude in favour of either side."

"But what I would have you note," Walton said, "is this: that *very fact*, which makes it all-important to him to *know the truth*, is a fact which makes it impossible for him to do otherwise than wish, and intensely wish, that *one side should prove true rather than the other.* You cannot have the keen personal importance felt without the wish that one side should prove true. The condition, nay, the very reason of that keen personal interest in knowledge of the truth which spurs his mind to active and truth-seeking inquiry, is, in this case, the personal danger involved; and you *cannot* have a keen sense of personal danger without the wish for safety."

"I do not quite see," Darlington said, "that you can bring religious inquiry under these principles. The pressure of immediate personal danger, no doubt, has a great effect in leading the mind to cast aside all prejudice; as the bare possibility of making a mistake is felt to be so far more serious a consideration than anything else, that there is no temptation to look at anything but truth. But in religious inquiry there is no such pressure. The verification is far off and not under your own control, and a man who is attached to some form of belief may readily prefer the indulgence of his hobby to looking straight at the truth."

Walton began to feel as though it were hopeless to make his friend keep clearly in mind the real point of his remarks.

"Why are we still at cross purposes?" he said, with something of irritation. "I am labouring to bring home to you that one who has a sense that a matter concerns him vitally, that one conclusion means safety, the opposite one danger, one happiness, the other unhappiness, cannot be indifferent as to which conclusion the evidence points to, but has, nevertheless, in his anxiety to know the truth, an absolute guarantee that he will be fair-minded; and you reply that men may not have the sense that the truth of their religion does concern them vitally. I do not say that all have. What I do say is that in proportion as they have it, in the same proportion will they be sensitive to the happiness of finding a religion which they love to be true, or to the unhappiness of finding religious knowledge, which is so much to them, incapable of attainment. That very keenness with which they perceive the matter to be all-important involves a sense as to *why* it is all-important. It is all-important because it is bound up with their happiness. And the more keenly this is felt, the more as a necessary consequence is the conclusion desired which is for their happiness. I conclude, then, that *this sort* of wish to believe is only a sign of that keen interest in the real state of the facts which will lead to truth, and you reply that a wish to believe where there is no such keen interest may lead to error. I state that, where the whole desire is that good news should be true, it gives an eye for truth; and you reply that the wish to indulge a hobby may lead you astray. We are really going back to the very beginning of all our conversations on the subject."

Darlington's face did not express precisely agreement or disagreement, but rather some bewilderment in his mind, which might have been the result of his gradually progressing assimilation of the ideas which Walton had been setting before him. Walton at all events interpreted his expression in this sense and was encouraged to proceed.

"No doubt," he went on, "where the importance of the matter is very immediate, and where it takes the form of pressing personal danger, my principle is more apparent; and for this reason, among others, that the importance of knowing the truth and the bearing of the facts on oneself *must* be felt. A man cannot fail to realise them. But what I say is just as true in cases where the importance is not so immediate, provided one takes the trouble to realise it. There is, I remember, in Arnold's *History of Rome* an account of the attitude of the Roman people when the news of Hasdrubal's defeat and death at the Metaurus reached Rome, which will perhaps illustrate what I have been saying better than so immediate an instance of personal danger as that of the Czar. It was, as you remember, an eventful victory, and involved the destruction of one of the Carthaginian armies. Still it did not decide the war. Hannibal's army remained untouched, and still threatened the Romans. Again bear in mind that Rome was not directly threatened, so that the personal danger was not so pressing or so irresistibly forced on the mind as in the other example I gave. Still the matter concerned the present and future interests of the Romans sufficiently to make the news of victory very good news and the news of defeat very bad. They were so eager, Arnold tells us, to know the true state of the case that the senate sat from sunrise to sunset, and the forum was crowded from morning to evening, as each hour might bring the news, and no one could bear to run the chance of missing it. Then when the first report of the victory got abroad, far from readily accepting the evidence, they scrutinised it most closely. 'Men dared not lightly believe,' he says, 'what they so much wished to be true.' It was said that two horsemen of Narnia had ridden home with the news. But this did not seem sufficient. They wanted more unexceptionable proof. The truth of the report seemed liable to objections. 'How,' they asked, 'could a battle fought in the extremity of Umbria be heard of two days afterwards at Rome?' But then came stronger evidence. A letter was read from Acidinus himself, who was in command at Narnia, and had heard the news from the lips of the two horsemen themselves. But many still cavilled at *this* evidence. The men *might* have been fugitives who trumped up a tale to hide their own shame. Soon, however, came the news that officers of highest rank were on their way from the victorious army and were bringing a despatch from Livius and Nero the consuls. This seemed more promising, and in their intense anxiety to learn the true state of the case the Romans could not quietly await their arrival. 'The whole city poured out to meet them,' says Arnold. And when at last the despatch had been read in the senate-house and the forum, and the facts were conclusively established, they were welcomed with enthusiasm. A ringing cheer spread through the ranks of the people, and they sped to the temples to offer their thanks to the gods. Now here you have, as it seems to me, an excellent instance of every point I have urged on you in these discussions. There is the intense eagerness to know the truth in so important a matter, which led the senators to remain all day in the senate-house and the people in the forum, and which made them too restless to wait for the consuls' despatch. Then you have the keenly critical examination of the evidence, the readiness to see its weak points, the wish to have it supplemented and confirmed: and throughout the whole story you have as strong a case as can be well imagined of the point on which I have been most recently insisting. Was the attitude of the people in their careful balancing and sifting of the evidence one of judicial impartiality? one of indifference as to whether the evidence proved sufficient or insufficient. On the contrary, the intense sense of the all-importance of the matter which made their investigation so careful and so accurate, contained in it as a part of its essence an intense wish to believe the good news true. Take away this intense wish to believe, and the whole motive power to active inquiry and critical inquiry goes with it. A man who was capable of saying, 'I will look at the evidence with an equal readiness to find the news true or false,' would thereby show that he had none of that sense of the immense importance of the matter which riveted the senators to their seats and crowded the forum, lest one half-hour of absence should lessen their chance of knowing all that was to be known."

Darlington, although now accepting far more nearly than before what Walton had been saying, seemed here again to see a theory, plausible and seemingly true, but which conflicted with acknowledged facts.

"Surely," he said, "you can't and won't deny that, theorise as you may, numbers of men *are* biassed in religious matters by their wishes. Even if you shut your eyes to it in the case of your own co-religionists, you must see it in others. Many a Salvation Army convert, many a Swedenborgian, many a Methodist Ranter, adopts his creed from purely emotional motives. He is hurried on by his wishes. You deal with ideas and not with facts in all that you say."

"I do not deny it," Walton answered. "Even in the case of Catholics I suppose that, naturally speaking, this may happen. All I say is, that to preach indifference as to the result of one's inquiry is to advocate the wrong remedy. The cure for superstition is not indifference but earnestness and seriousness. If I had found, supposing I had been in Rome at the time we have been speaking of, some man so wrapped up in his own private studies and theories, and so little realising the importance of the matter, that he could, in judging of the evidence, incline easily towards the pleasanter side; that he at once said, before there was really sufficient evidence, 'Oh yes, I was sure that Nero would defeat Hasdrubal,' I should not preach indifference and impartiality as the best remedy for his unreasonableness. I should say, 'Rouse yourself up and realise the importance of the matter; the good effects of victory, the evil effects of defeat.' I should appeal to his own interest to make him sensible of the reality of the events that were going on. 'You are in want of money. While the Carthaginian panic lasts no one will lend it to you. If this news of victory be true, you can get it. Your son wants to sell his land, but no one will buy it while they fear that it may be taken from them any day by the invader. If they advance upon Rome, he has no chance of selling it.' I should not be satisfied that he was in a state to do the fullest justice to the matter until I had in this way aroused in him a strong wish to believe the report true, but a wish based on the thought of facts and consequences, differing entirely in its character from his previous wish. If I told him to look at the evidence without bias merely, true enough, he might no longer draw a rash conclusion. But his interest would be dead. He would not have the motive to seek to know all the proofs available. He would not go to the forum and hear Acidinus' letter, or go to meet the messengers of the consul. If, on the contrary, I make him realise the importance of the matter, he not only weighs scrupulously what he has of evidence, but his intense wish to believe in the good news leads him to go where he is likely to learn all that is to be learnt on the subject. And so I say, that to ask a superstitious man, who has been, as you say, unduly biassed by his wishes, to look at religious argument with indifference as to what conclusion may be true, is to preach the wrong remedy. No doubt mere impartiality may make him unlearn a false conclusion, but it cannot bring him to a true one. I should say to him, on the contrary, 'Realise the gravity of the issue, and that all the aim of your life depends for its value on the truth of your creed.' I should endeavour to make him change one sort of wish to believe for another,—a light one for a serious one. Then if the creed he has lightly adopted be true, his sense of the importance of truth will lead him to examine it more closely and to see its truth more clearly; and if it be false, this same sense will make him sensitive to the weakness and unsatisfactory nature of his grounds for belief. It is this realising of the importance of knowing the truth that prompts the search for truth and gives the eye for truth. I should not pull a man's eye out because he saw crooked. I should endeavour to make him see straight. The blind man does not see crooked because he does not see at all. And so the indifferent man avoids any admixture of superstition in his insight into the spiritual world because he has no insight at all."

"Well then," Darlington said after a pause, "as I understand you, you would say, applying your principles to such a case as my own, that if I look upon the Christian revelation as very good news if true, and very helpful to me, and very important, as bearing on my practical life and future expectations, that state of mind is, if I realise the gravity of the issue, my best security for finding out its truth or its falsehood as the case may be; but that a judicial attitude of mind is no guarantee that I shall know the full strength of the case. It may lead me to see the weak points and not the strong, whereas the other makes me alive to both. It will secure me against believing without reasons, but will not necessarily lead me to find all the reasons. It will cure superstition, but will not build up religion."

"Yes," said Walton with some hesitation, "that substantially represents what I should say. But you must always keep in mind that it is the sense of the bearing of the facts on yourself which is your great safeguard. I think I may sum the matter up thus:—The rules for judging of evidence on a matter where the *truth* can have no important effect upon oneself one way or another are one class of rules. The mind is viewed in such a case by the philosopher as its physician, and he examines it to see what disease is most likely to creep into it. Take historical evidence, for example. He notes that it is the *decision* on a particular matter, with its links binding it to the various views and historical theories of the inquirer which is in such a case uppermost in this inquirer's mind; and he warns him to 'take care not to be filled with the neatness of theories and the symmetry of subjective views. If you want truth, you must view the evidence with no previous bias in favour of this or that theory or view. Such things will sway the mind and tend to make it a little dishonest. The pleasure of consistency, which is tangible and verifiable, is a snare which may entice you from that sobriety of judgment which will land you in unverifiable truth.' But, on the contrary, in a matter of great personal importance, this particular disease cannot attack the mind if that importance is realised. Here it is not the decision, but the *truth* of the decision which is important. No man will indulge a hobby or bask in pretty theories if his doing so will cost him his life, or, more truly, no *serious* man will do so. The only danger in such a case is that a man should not be serious. Therefore the philosopher-doctor will say to a man in such circumstances, not 'Be indifferent as to your conclusion,' for he knows that where one conclusion means life and the other death this would be absurd; but, 'Realise the danger, and the importance of knowing the truth, as you have to act on it.' To take a concrete case: suppose it to be a report, with some grounds assigned, that your house is to be broken into by thieves to-night. He will not say, 'Examine the evidence, without a wish to come to one conclusion rather than another,' as this would be absurd and also useless. It would be absurd, because a man by nature prefers safety to danger; and useless, because fairness of judgment is already ensured by the vast importance of knowing the truth. If it is true, you must take all precautions, send for the police at once, and so forth. He will say rather, suppose he finds you placid and undisturbed, talking of it quietly and giving a list of the reasons for believing and the reasons for disbelieving, 'You do not realise your danger nor the necessity of finding out the truth. If it be true, there is no time to be lost. You must warn the police at once.' The fact that you were indifferent which conclusion the evidence pointed to would be an infallible sign, not of a reasonable frame of mind, but of an eminently unreasonable frame of mind. Realise the possible danger, and you at once wish to believe that it is not really existent. The absence of a wish to believe in such a case is an *infallible* sign that you have not the strongest motive power to the discovery of truth. The keen sense of the personal importance of a matter *must* involve a keen wish. If knowledge is all that is important, there is the wish for knowledge. If, as is the case with most inquiries, one state of facts is looked upon as good news, another as bad, the more the importance of the matter is felt the greater the wish to believe in the good news. And in such a case it is plain that if the keenest sense of its importance is the best guarantee of thorough inquiry, the strongest wish to believe will be its necessary accompaniment. The more the importance of the Metaurus victory was realised, the more carefully was its evidence scrutinised and the more intense was the wish to believe it true.

" Now to apply this in detail, though it is hardly necessary to do so very fully, to the attitude of the mind in weighing and investigating the Christian evidences. If they are viewed merely as the proofs of a past fact, with no personal and present effect on ourselves, then I might allow that, so far as the historical evidences go, indifference as to the conclusion to be drawn would be the best security for their being fairly viewed, not because it is a supremely good assistant in the search for truth, but because it is the best one available under the circumstances. The mind cannot trust itself to resist the temptation of building up a theory, neat and satisfying, in harmony with its own preconceptions and prejudices, which may involve a slight deflection from just judgment; as the fact of the judgment being absolutely just or no can never be known by any effect which its true nature will have on ourselves. The inquirer must therefore constantly ask himself, Am I viewing the matter impartially, or am I interested—not, be it observed, in *finding* one particular conclusion to be certainly true, but in deciding for one conclusion before its truth is ascertained, because it squares with my theory and so forth? But viewing the evidences as consisting both of internal and external evidences, of the personal examination of one's spiritual nature as well as of history, of *à priori* presumptions, of the necessity for a religion, of the meaninglessness of life without one, of the improbability that God, whom we have learnt to know, would leave us in hopeless darkness, of the nature of the Christian law and Christ's character—both felt by meditation and study to be unearthly—of these and the like motives for belief, added to the historical evidences, and all felt to converge upon the truth and knowableness of a fact of supreme present importance to be known, and calling, if true, for immediate and constant resulting action, we have quite a different set of principles to apply. It is both absurd and useless to ask any one who is led to love Christianity and to see reasons for thinking it not improbable that it may be true, to be indifferent as to the result of his further study: absurd, because if it offers knowledge satisfying his whole nature, he *must* hope that he shall find it true; useless, because if he realises in the supreme importance to himself of a true conclusion, he has a security for impartiality far higher than that afforded by indifference."

And now the reader has had a very full account of Walton's view—indeed Walton has taken good care that he should know it, and has expressed it very fully. Much to the detriment of the even balance of the dialogue, and of the regular alternation of twelve or fifteen lines apiece which a dialogue with any pretensions to naturalness is supposed to have, Walton has, unluckily, committed an unpardonable breach of such recognised rules. Darlington hadn't his twelve lines ready, and Walton, whose mind was full of a subject which had cost him much labour in the thinking of it out, had scores of lines, all prepared and waiting to be poured forth. Darlington had been so much occupied with taking in the full import of what his friend said, and with the internal confusion in his own mind which had not yet subsided, that he had not even had a sufficient sense of propriety to say at the right intervals, and in default of something better, "You speak truly, O Walton," or, where he did not follow him, "Explain to me, O Walton, what is this you are saying." His mind had, however, been far from inactive, and although at the time he would have been unable to give any account of the effect of the conversation upon him, it *had* an effect which became manifest to him by degrees. Although it is doubtless true that the set convictions of a thoughtful mind are not readily touched by argument, still argument felt to be sound will at least have a considerable effect on the explanation given of the ground of conviction. And when Darlington had probed the degree to which Walton's remarks had influenced him, he found that some such change had taken place in himself. He was inclined to admit that he had been inaccurate and too general in supposing that an interest in the truth of a particular conclusion necessarily implied unreasonable partisanship; he admitted that such a result was not to be feared where everything depended on the conclusion drawn being true: further, he was disposed to allow that, in following up what appeared a very hopeful clue to knowledge, an intense desire for knowledge bred a hopefulness that the clue in question would prove to be a clue to true knowledge. I do not think that he would have made an exception to this rule for any kind of knowledge. He was disposed so far to think that his own abstract principles had been inaccurate, and that there was a species of "wish to believe" which was inseparably bound up with serious reasoning in a matter where one conclusion involves happiness and another unhappiness. Surely then, we are inclined to say, his *convictions* must have been modified. If he allowed that his own attitude in the matter had been unreasonable, and Walton's reasonable, this must have considerably shaken his previous views and theories. And yet the truth is that there was no radical change in his convictions, and this from no halting in his reasoning, but from the fact that in the very act of accepting Walton's analysis he detected a further consideration in his own mind, a further element in his own basis of unbelief, which from the nature of the case Walton was unable to touch. To put it as shortly as possible, he saw that a "wish to believe" of the kind fully explained by Walton was the reasonable attitude where a really promising clue to knowledge was found. This seemed plainly true in physical discovery, and he saw no reason to limit it to this one branch. He also, though not so readily, admitted to himself that religious knowledge must, if attainable, be a process of individual investigation and discovery, as appealing to much which a man must study in his own heart for himself. But the insertion of one little phrase into his admission will show how so promising a change of view collapsed completely so far as immediate change of convictions went. Darlington would have inserted between "if" and "attainable" the words *per impossibile.* That is to say, his original conclusion dwelt so strong within him as to take away from his mind the force necessary for actively applying Walton's principles. A promising clue which lighted up the mind with the hope of discovery should indeed give birth to the "wish to believe," but such a clue he had not found. Truths about another world and the Author of our Being were to him too hopelessly beyond the reach of the human mind to give him any zest in the inquiry. From several remarks which his friend made to him in the course of the afternoon, before he left Llandudno, Walton suspected his state of feeling, even before Darlington had expressly acknowledged it to himself. And he saw that here was a radical defect, quite outside the reach of all argument. "I shall pray," he said, "that you may acquire enough seriousness and a sufficient sense of the need of religious knowledge and of the import of that part of your nature which should tell you that your search for it would not be vain, to make you work at the matter in earnest. At present you are stagnant. If your study of everything else were handicapped by such a state of mind you would learn nothing. You have no real wish for knowledge in the matter."

Did Walton think that his conversations with his friend had been useless? No. He was not a sanguine man as to the immediate result of such conversations. And he knew well that the initial stage of conversion depends on that grace which is given as a reward for earnestness, and which intensifies natural earnestness in its effect. But he did hold that, once that initial stage was reached, it was important that a man of active mind should not be hampered by any feeling that he might be surrendering to a wholly irrational impulse; and so he was, surprising as it may seem, not only not disappointed, but pleased beyond all expectation with the degree of acquiescence which Darlington had ultimately given to his principles. He looked upon this acquiescence as the removal of that very serious obstacle to the working both of natural reason and of grace which would have been presented, in case Darlington should ever be led to look at the matter in a more hopeful spirit, by the idea that a longing for belief was unmistakably a snare and a source of fallacy, and that a state of calm impartiality was the only safe attitude to be assumed in such matters. He considered it very important that the sentimental, irrational, fanatical enthusiasm which may lead to the wildest superstition should be clearly separated in his mind from all those deeper religious feelings which give the yearning for true religious knowledge and the power to gain it; and that Darlington should clearly see, in case he felt himself influenced by the latter, that the unreason attaching to the former was not to be found *there*. In order to fix this practical issue in Darlington's mind, his friend wrote him a letter some weeks after they had parted company. The following is an extract from it:

We have, then, three attitudes of mind in religious inquiry. We have first the credulous attitude, which implies flippancy in belief, readiness in its adoption, equal readiness in changing it; so slight a depth of conviction that belief can hardly be distinguished from imagination; an easy surrender to ideas begotten of hope or of fear. Such an attitude is absolutely unreasonable, and in its most direct relation to the theme of our discussions it may lead a man to adopt Christianity from a momentary excitement which its beauty produces in him, his belief having no root, and being unaccompanied by any deep sense of the importance of a true decision. Such an attitude might lead as readily to the grossest superstition as to truth, and it does not seem unreasonable to say that a belief so skin-deep and so lightly assumed could not stand the test of constant action, depending for its worth upon the truth of the creed adopted. We have next the *law-court* attitude of mind, excellent for investigating matters in which the evidence is all expressed in words, and which arouse in us mainly a speculative interest—in which the true state of the case has no bearing on our own personal welfare. Such an attitude demands absolute impartiality and indifference as to what conclusion the evidence may point to. It is suspicious of any excitement, as experience has shown that excitement in such cases disturbs the reasoning power. It goes on the principle, perfectly sound in such matters, that passion is an opposite force to the love of truth, because passion generally acts in self-interest, and self-interest in such things generally involves prejudice; and so the only way to go safely towards truth is to eliminate passion. This attitude will undoubtedly lead to scepticism, as implying the absence both of fanaticism and of the passion for all knowledge attainable on matters of religion. It will overthrow a false religion, but will fail to find a true. And there is lastly the *religious* attitude of mind properly so called. And this is the attitude for viewing all proofs connected with knowledge which is of vital importance to one's own self. The first essential of this attitude is a deep sense of the importance of the knowledge and of the bearing of the fact to be known upon oneself. This immediately issues in the passion for true knowledge based on this sense, and thus passion is enlisted on the side of reason. And here we must make a distinction. If but two alternatives are before the mind—the sufficiency or insufficiency of a proof explicitly before us, in most cases the fact that the matter is of vital importance will presuppose that one decision is considered to be supremely good news, the other supremely bad. This is in most cases the very ground of the all-importance of the matter; and in such cases the intense longing for knowledge is inseparably bound up with the intense wish to believe in the happier alternative—a wish making you as keenly sensitive of its falsehood (if so be) as of its truth. But viewing religious inquiry as a whole, not merely as the scrutiny of recognised verbal evidence, but also as the active search for all those minute signs of God and of a revelation, not fully expressible in words, which may be found in the human soul and in the world, the importance of the genuine wish to believe is shown far more clearly. In this aspect the wish to believe in any higher and more ennobling form of religion, which manifests itself and gives good promise of being true, is the concrete activity of the abstract wish for religious knowledge. The wish for knowledge gives keen sensitiveness to every clue, and the wish to believe is the motive force that follows up the most hopeful clue. Thus I should say that it would be the abstract wish for knowledge which would make a mind sensitive to the *primâ facie* notes of the Church; which would prevent any unconsciously dishonest blinking of facts telling for her; which would note with quick eye her works, her system, her actions, her wisdom, the sanctity of her heroes, until this general sensitiveness had taken in enough to give a sense that she offered indeed the most promising clue to knowledge; and then the definite wish to believe would come in. A man who had concluded thus much would proceed then to investigate her more fully, with an earnest desire that what he had been led to look on as a promising source of widest spiritual knowledge, should prove to be such in reality. And I may add that this last aspect of it, viewing, as it does, the wish for knowledge on religious matters as a wish which causes the mind to be keenly sensitive to all clues, and takes the form of the wish to believe when a promising clue is found, seems a far more complete view of the whole question than any which could be gained by confining our attention to the scrutinising of a particular line of evidence—as, for instance, Paley's proof of the resurrection. Such scrutiny is at best but a part of the process of religious inquiry. The co-ordination of different lines of evidence, the realisation of their combined effect, the search for such as may be within our own reach although perhaps not accessible to all, these are essential to our knowing all that is to be known.

And these presuppose the earnest and active personal wish for knowledge on the subject. There are many rival theories, and of none of them can it be said that the logical apprehension of their *primâ facie* evidence is convincing. Consequently the mode of procedure must be to choose what appears the best, and then to throw oneself into it, and with the hearty wish to find it true and effort to master it; to study its credentials, not by apprehending their logic only, but by the personal appreciation and full realisation of the facts which the logic combines, and of facts which may be too inadequately however unmistakably seen for logic to combine them at all,—facts of human nature, facts of history, phenomena in the working of the religion, which can only be taken in by one whose whole heart is in the matter, and which must ultimately, so far as reason goes, turn the balance which was left undecided by the *primâ facie* aspect of verbal evidence as it existed patent to all alike.

THE END

www.ingramcontent.com/pod-product-compliance
Lightning Source LLC
Chambersburg PA
CBHW021119270326
41929CB00009B/951

* 9 7 8 3 7 4 4 6 6 0 5 4 9 *